# 宿州市博物馆
# 铜镜集萃

Collection of Bronze Mirrors in Suzhou Museum

宿州市博物馆　编

文物出版社

图书在版编目（CIP）数据

宿州市博物馆铜镜集萃 / 宿州市博物馆编 . —— 北京：
文物出版社 , 2024.9
ISBN 978-7-5010-8405-0

Ⅰ . ①宿… Ⅱ . ①宿… Ⅲ . ①古镜—铜器（考古）—宿
州—图集 Ⅳ . ① K875.22

中国国家版本馆 CIP 数据核字 (2024) 第 073024 号

# 宿州市博物馆铜镜集萃

编　　者：宿州市博物馆
执　　笔：傅　静

责任编辑：智　朴
责任印制：王　芳

出版发行：文物出版社
社　　址：北京市东城区东直门内北小街2号楼
邮　　编：100007
网　　址：http://www.wenwu.com
邮　　箱：wenwu1957@126.com
经　　销：新华书店
印　　刷：北京荣宝艺品印刷有限公司
开　　本：889mm×1194mm　1/16
印　　张：18.5
版　　次：2024年9月第1版
印　　次：2024年9月第1次印刷
书　　号：ISBN 978-7-5010-8405-0
定　　价：360.00元

# 编 委 会
## Editorial Board

# 目 录
## Contents

# 概　述

## 一、宿州历史沿革

宿州市位于安徽省东北部，处黄淮腹地，是苏、鲁、豫、皖四省交界之地。现辖砀山县、萧县、灵璧县、泗县、埇桥区，总面积 9939 平方公里。

宿州历史可追溯到距今 8000 年前的新石器文化时期，史前文化遗存丰富，偏早阶段的以小山口遗址和古台寺遗址为代表，大汶口文化时期遗址、龙山文化时期遗址分布较多，同时，还有几处岳石文化遗存。

商周时期，宿州属夷的势力范围，淮夷、徐夷等部落在这里繁衍生息。西周时期至春秋时期，宿州多为宋国属地。周庄王十四年（公元前 683 年），宋国将位于山东东平境内的宿国迁入域内作为附庸。这是作为地名的"宿"字第一次进入宿州的历史。

战国后期宿州属于楚。楚本为江淮大国，经过与秦国的长期战争，政治中心逐渐被迫自西向东转移，两淮之间便成为其最重要的根据地，因此战国时期的宿州受楚文化影响颇深。秦统一中国后，广置郡县，今宿州市各县区大部分属于泗水郡，西北的砀山属于砀郡。

西汉时期，宿州各县区分别隶属于徐州刺史部的临淮郡、楚国，兖州刺史部的梁国，豫州刺史部的沛郡。东汉时期，宿州属豫州沛国、梁国，徐州彭城国、下邳国。

隋朝统一全国，本地建置有彭城郡所领符离县、蕲县、萧县；下邳郡所领夏丘县（治所在今泗县城）；梁郡所领砀山县。随着汴河的兴盛，唐宪宗元和四年（809 年），为了保护汴河的漕运，始建宿州，领符离县、蕲县、虹县，宿州也迎来了历史上的发展高峰。

五代十国期间，宿州地区再度陷入南北分裂割据的局面。北宋时期宿州分属于京东西路与淮南东路。宋哲宗元祐元年（1086 年），把虹县所属零壁镇析出建置为县，至宋徽宗政和七年（1117 年），将零壁县改为灵璧县。此时，宿州属淮南东路，下辖符离、蕲县、灵璧、临涣四县，其余萧县、砀山分别属于京东西路的徐州与单州。宋高宗绍兴十一年（1141 年），宋金议和，宿州成为金国南部疆土。

元朝时期宿州分属河南江北行省的归德府与淮安路及中书省济宁路，其中宿州、灵璧、萧县属归德府，虹县属淮安路的泗州，砀山属济宁路。明朝时期，宿州属南京直隶区的管辖范围，其中宿州、灵璧、虹县均属凤阳府，砀山、萧县均属徐州。康熙六年（1667 年），撤销江南省，分为江苏、安徽两省，宿州属安徽凤阳府。乾隆四十二年（1777 年），移州治于虹县，后又撤销虹县建置并入泗州。砀山、萧县属江苏省徐州府管辖。

宿州历史悠久，文化遗存丰富，近年来宿州的考古事业也在日新月异地蓬勃发展，考古成果颇丰。

## 二、宿州地区铜镜发现与研究

在宿州经济飞速发展的进程中，为配合大型工程建设，安徽省文物考古研究所、宿州市及所辖县区文物保护部门先后抢救性发掘了一批汉墓，发现并出土了大量精美铜镜，如：

1985 年龙城镇在萧县县城西 1.5 公里虎山脚下建窑场烧砖取土时发现一批古墓葬，引起县政府和当地文物主管部门的高度重视，并及时组织业务人员对该墓葬采取了抢救性清理发掘，共计发掘三座西汉石棺墓，出土器物 61 件，其中铜镜 5 件。❶

1999 年 1 月至 4 月，安徽省文物考古研究所在萧县白土镇张村北面的山坡上的西汉墓地进行了抢救性发掘，共计发掘墓葬 22 座，出土文物 170 余件，含铜镜 7 件。其中 9 号墓出土的铜镜，镜周围发现有近方形漆皮和朽木痕迹，此痕迹外还有一种痕迹，一头椭圆，一头收缩成捆扎状，似为袋类，应属装镜之物。18 号墓出土的一面铜镜位于头部附近，同时铜镜旁边置有一铁剑。❷

1999 年至 2001 年，为配合连霍高速公路安徽省萧县段工程建设，安徽省文物考古研究所会同宿州市及其下辖县区文物部门联合对位于萧县县城东南老山口（属白土镇）至萧县县城西南瓦子口（属丁里镇）一线高速公路工程建设中所涉及取土场工地发现的汉代墓葬进行考古发掘，其中包括萧县白土镇冯楼、张村汉墓，丁里镇王山窝汉墓，杜楼镇车牛返汉墓以及孙圩子乡破格汉墓五个地点。此次共发掘汉代墓葬 151 座，其中有 40 座汉墓随葬有铜镜，出土铜镜共计 46 件。❸

骑路堌堆是一处新石器时代遗址，位于宿州市西寺坡涉故台西 200 米处。为配合铁路建设，安徽省文物考古研究所于 2000 年 6 月至 7 月间对该遗址进行了考古发掘工作，发掘汉墓 3 座，其中有 2 座汉墓随葬铜镜，共计出土铜镜 2 件。❹

萧县陈沟墓地（西区）位于萧县龙城镇陈沟行政村西南部明山脚下，东邻 311 国道。2010 年 8 月至 10 月，为配合安徽省柏星房产置业建设工程，安徽省文物考古研究所对建设用地范围内古墓葬进行了抢救性发掘，清理墓葬 63 座，出土各类珍贵文物 203 件，其中铜镜 2 件。❺

萧县陈沟墓群（东区）位于安徽省萧县龙城镇陈沟行政村南部，地处东部山脚坡地，西邻 311 国道，东南距萧县县城 3 公里。为配合萧县蓝石房地产开发建设工程，2010 年 11 月至 2011 年 1 月，安徽省文物考古研究所等单位对建设占地范围内古墓葬进行了抢救性考古发掘，共清理墓葬 61 座，其中汉代墓葬 56 座。发掘出土珍贵文物 206 件，其中铜镜 2 件。❻

下面就以 1999 年至 2001 年为配合连霍高速公路安徽省萧县段工程建设而发掘的萧县汉墓为例❼，对宿州出土铜镜做简要分析（表 2）。

此次发掘的 40 座汉墓中，其中 1 座汉墓随葬铜镜 3 件，有 4 座汉墓随葬铜镜 2 件，其余 35 座汉墓都随葬铜镜 1 件，共计出土 46 件铜镜（表 1；图 1~3）。

通过对考古材料的整理分析，发现铜镜在墓葬中的摆放位置相对比较固定，大部分随棺入葬或位于头部附近，少数置于胸部，也有与铁剑、环首刀等随葬品同出的情况，还有一些墓葬因被扰而铜镜位置出现挪动的现象。46 件铜镜中有 37 件保存较好，3 件虽残损，大部分尚存，6 件残损锈蚀严重，无法辨别其形制。铜镜绝大多数制作工艺精巧，颜色纯正，且无论繁简都装饰有纹饰图案或铭文，部分在出土时还附着有朽木和绢布等织物细绢纹痕迹（表 3）。

## 表 1 萧县汉墓出土铜镜数量对比表

| 同一个墓内出土铜镜情况 | 出土铜镜 1 件 | 出土铜镜 2 件 | 出土铜镜 3 件 |
| --- | --- | --- | --- |
| 墓葬数量（座） | 35 | 4 | 1 |

## 表 2　萧县汉墓铜镜出土情况统计表

| 序号 | 墓葬编号 | 出土铜镜数量（件） | 铜镜编号 | 铜镜纹饰 | 出土时是否有附着物 | 铜镜出土时置放位置 | 备注 |
|---|---|---|---|---|---|---|---|
| 1 | XZM7 | 1 | XZM7：4 | 四乳八禽镜 | | | 墓道被扰乱，位置有挪动 |
| 2 | XZM8 | 1 | XZM8：3 | 蟠螭纹博局镜 | | 随棺入葬 | |
| 3 | XZM9 | 1 | XZM9：15 | 四乳双龙镜 | 铜镜外有漆皮痕迹 | 随棺入葬 | |
| 4 | XZM11 | 1 | XZM11：3 | 简化蟠螭纹镜 | 出土时装于方形漆盒内，盒已朽，难以提取 | 与随葬陶器置于墓底北端 | |
| 5 | XZM14 | 1 | XZM14：23 | 星云纹镜 | | 随棺入葬，头部附近 | |
| 6 | XZM16 | 1 | XZM16：1 | 昭明镜 | | 随棺入葬 | |
| 7 | XZM18 | 1 | XZM18：1 | 四神博局镜 | | 随棺入葬，头部附近 | |
| 8 | XFM38 | 1 | XFM38：5 | 铜镜 | | 墓室东部 | 残成碎片 |
| 9 | XFM58 | 1 | XFM58：3 | 日光镜 | | 墓底南端，头部附近 | |
| 10 | XFM65 | 1 | XFM65：5 | 四神博局镜 | | 墓底南部，头部附近 | |
| 11 | XFM85 | 1 | XFM85:1 | 昭明镜 | | 墓室南端 | |
| 12 | XWM39 | 3 | XWM39：4 | 四神博局镜 | | 墓室南端 | |
| | | | XWM39：6 | 连弧纹镜 | | 墓室南部 | 与铁刀在一起 |
| | | | XWM39：13 | 连弧纹镜 | | 墓室南部 | 与铁刀在一起 |
| 13 | XPM65 | 1 | XPM65：5 | 铜镜 | | 墓室北部 | 残成碎片 |
| 14 | XPM66 | 1 | XPM66：3 | 昭明镜 | | 随棺入葬，头部附近 | |
| 15 | XPM72 | 1 | XPM72：1 | 日光镜 | | 随棺入葬，头部附近 | |
| 16 | XPM73 | 1 | XPM73：2 | 连弧纹日光镜 | | 墓室北部 | |
| 17 | XPM75 | 1 | XPM75：2 | 四乳八禽镜 | | 头部附近 | |
| 18 | XPM87 | 1 | XPM87：1 | 连弧纹日光镜 | | 墓底东北部 | |
| 19 | XPM93 | 1 | XPM93：1 | 四乳四螭镜 | | 墓室北部 | |
| 20 | XPM94 | 1 | XPM94：1 | 四乳四螭镜 | | 墓室中部 | |
| 21 | XPM108 | 2 | XPM108：1 | 草叶纹镜 | | 墓室北部，头部附近 | |
| | | | XPM108：2 | 云雷纹地蟠螭镜 | | 墓室北部，头部附近 | 旁边有一铁剑 |
| 22 | XPM111 | 1 | XPM111：7 | 云雷纹地蟠螭镜 | | 墓底南部 | |
| 23 | XPM112 | 1 | XPM112：6 | 铜镜 | | 墓底南侧 | 锈蚀成数块，不可复原 |
| 24 | XPM121 | 1 | XPM121：3 | 铜镜 | | 墓底南侧 | 锈蚀成数块，不可复原 |
| 25 | XPM128 | 1 | XPM128：1 | 四乳四螭镜 | | 棺外，墓室北部 | |
| 26 | XPM145 | 1 | XPM145：2 | 草叶纹镜 | | 随棺入葬 | |
| 27 | XPM150 | 1 | XPM150：1 | 云纹博局镜 | | 头部附近 | |
| 28 | XPM158 | 2 | XPM158：10 | 连弧纹日光镜 | | 棺内，头部附近 | |
| | | | XPM158：1 | 连弧纹昭明镜 | | 棺内，头部附近 | |
| 29 | XPM163 | 1 | XPM163：13 | 连弧纹日光镜 | | 墓底西南侧 | |
| 30 | XPM164 | 1 | XPM164：1 | 四叶蟠螭纹镜 | | 墓底东侧 | |
| 31 | XPM166 | 1 | XPM166：2 | 四乳双龙镜 | | 墓底东侧 | |

| 序号 | 墓葬编号 | 出土铜镜数量（件） | 铜镜编号 | 铜镜纹饰 | 出土时是否有附着物 | 铜镜出土时置放位置 | 备注 |
|---|---|---|---|---|---|---|---|
| 32 | XPM170 | 2 | XPM170：1 | 星云纹镜 | | 随棺入葬，头部附近 | |
| | | | XPM170：2 | 铜镜 | | 随棺入葬，头部附近 | 残碎，形制不明 |
| 33 | XPM171 | 1 | XPM171：1 | 简化博局镜 | | 墓室北部 | 位置被扰乱 |
| 34 | XPM173 | 2 | XPM173：1 | "长宜子孙"连弧纹镜 | | 墓底西侧 | 位置被扰乱 |
| | | | XPM173：2 | 四乳四禽镜 | | 墓底西侧 | 位置被扰乱 |
| 35 | XCM3 | 1 | XCM3：2 | 四神博局镜 | | 头部附近 | 旁有铁书刀 |
| 36 | XCM4 | 1 | XCM4：10 | 昭明镜 | | 头部附近 | |
| 37 | XCM7 | 1 | XCM7：2 | 简化博局镜 | | 墓室西侧 | 与铁削同出 |
| 38 | XCM11 | 1 | XCM11：1 | 昭明镜 | | 头部附近 | 旁有铜刷 |
| 39 | XCM20 | 1 | XCM20：4 | 四乳四螭镜 | | 墓室西部 | |
| 40 | XCM41 | 1 | XCM41：9 | 铜镜 | | 墓室东部 | 锈蚀严重，形制不详 |
| 合计 | | 墓葬 40 座，铜镜 46 件 | | | | | |

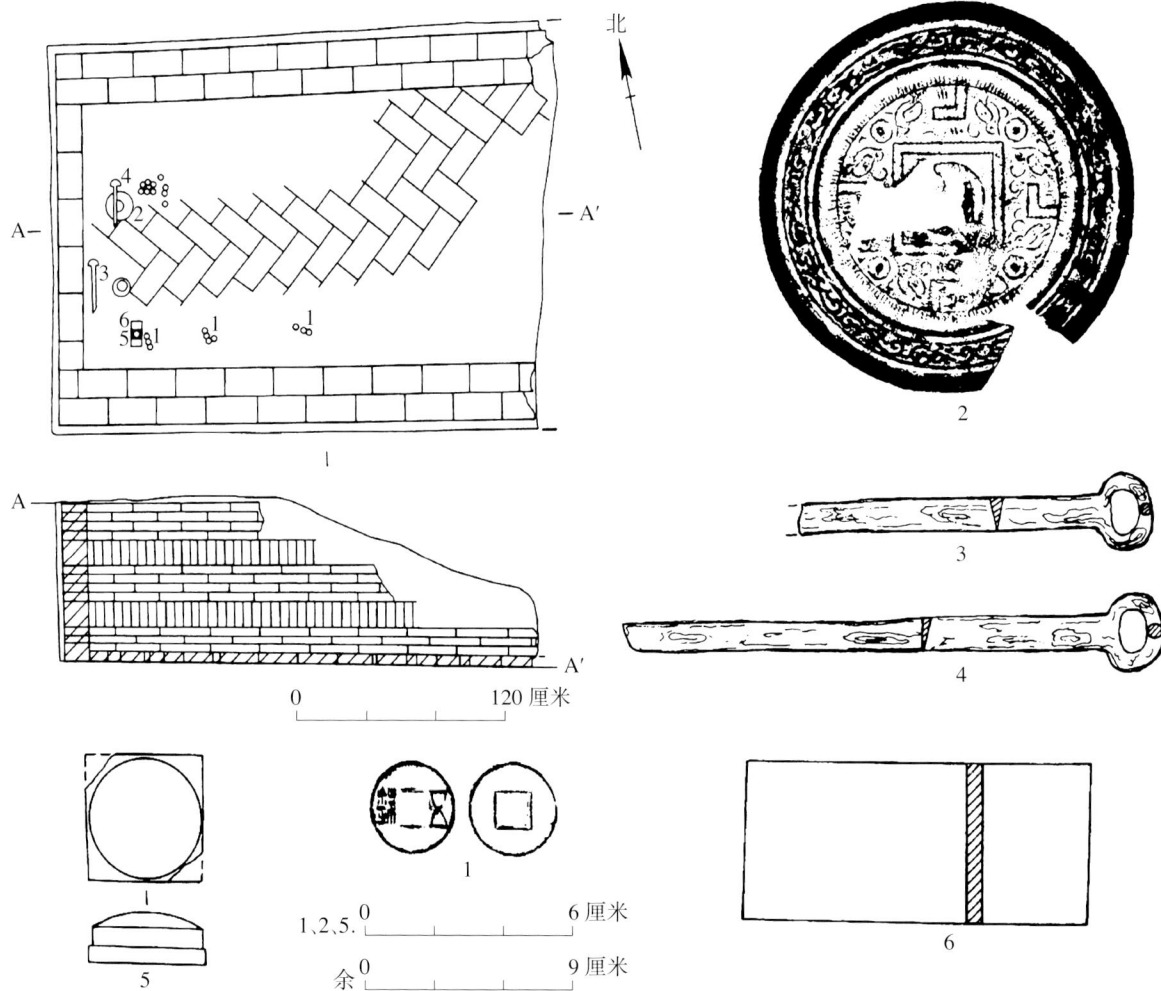

图 1　XCM7 随葬品分布图 [8]

安徽省萧县县城西南杜楼镇车牛返自然村东山坡车牛返墓葬发掘区西南部（2000 年 9 月～2001 年 4 月发掘）

1.铜钱　2.铜镜　3、4.铁削　5.研子　6.石砚

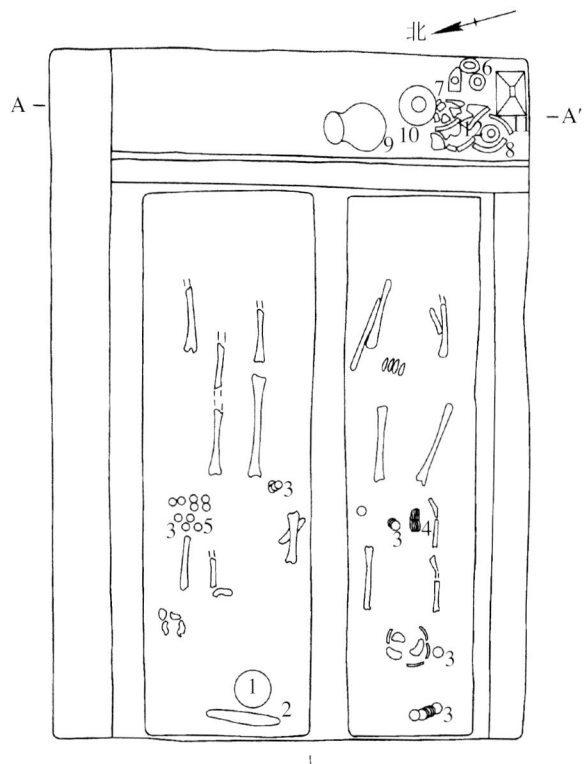

**图 2 XZM18 随葬品分布图** [9]

萧县县城东南部白土镇张村村北山坡上张村墓葬发掘区北部

（1999 年 1 月～4 月发掘）

1.铜镜 2.铁刀 3.铜钱 4.珠饰 5.石塞 6.陶圈

7.陶灶 8.陶仓 9、10.陶壶 11.陶钫盖 12.陶磨

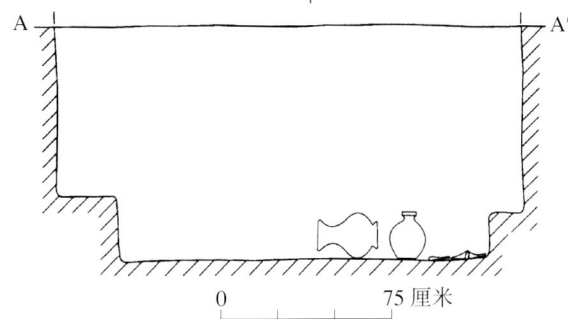

**图 3 XPM75 随葬品分布图** [10]

萧县县城西南部孙圩子乡破阁村东南山坡上破阁墓葬发掘区中部

（1999 年 12 月～2000 年 4 月）

1.铁镇 2.铜镜 3.铜钱 4.铁剑 5.铜带钩 6.铁书刀

7、9.陶甑 8.铜剑镡 10.陶器盖 11.陶圈 12.陶仓盖

13.陶壶 14.陶瓮 15.陶鼎 16.小陶盆 17.陶杯

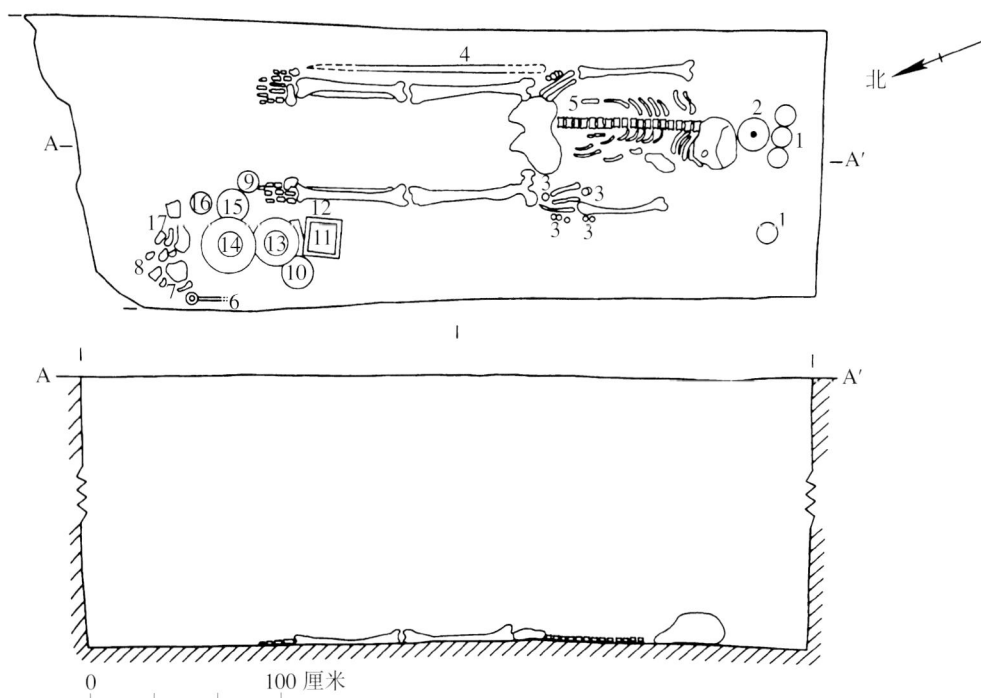

表 3　萧县汉墓出土铜镜纹饰类别统计表

| 序号 | 纹饰类别 | 铜镜数量（件） | 备注 |
|---|---|---|---|
| 1 | 蟠螭纹镜 | 5 | 云雷纹地蟠螭镜 2 件，四叶蟠螭纹镜 1 件，蟠螭纹博局镜 1 件，简化蟠螭纹镜 1 件 |
| 2 | 草叶纹镜 | 2 | |
| 3 | 四乳双龙镜 | 2 | |
| 4 | 星云纹镜 | 2 | |
| 5 | 日光镜 | 6 | |
| 6 | 昭明镜 | 6 | |
| 7 | 四乳禽兽纹镜 | 7 | 四乳四螭镜 4 件，四乳四禽镜 1 件，四乳八禽镜 2 件 |
| 8 | 博局镜 | 7 | 四神博局镜 4 件，云纹博局镜 1 件，简化博局镜 2 件 |
| 9 | 连弧纹镜 | 3 | 连弧纹镜 2 件，"长宜子孙"连弧纹镜 1 件 |
| 10 | 铜镜（样式不详） | 6 | 锈蚀严重，形制不详 |
| | 合 计 | 46 | |

铜镜纹饰主要分为 9 类，都是当时在汉代比较流行的纹饰。

铜镜的随葬方式也间接反映了当时社会的丧葬文化及宗教信仰。目前铜镜研究大部分都是针对铜镜纹饰、形制及铸造工艺等内容，而对铜镜出土状态研究较少。王锋钧先生曾发表了《铜镜出土状态研究》一文，结合考古发掘与文献资料，通过对各时期铜镜出土状态进行多方面、多角度的研究，总结了古人置放铜镜的方式以及铜镜随葬方式所反映的观念、信仰与风俗。在铜镜置放位置及方式上，他指出不同时期墓葬中铜镜的出土状态呈现出不同特点，经研究发现，历代随葬铜镜多数出自棺内，棺外的相对较少。棺内铜镜，主要分布在头部、胸部、腹部、胯部、腰部、手、足、面罩、棺壁等位置，其中在研究资料中约占一半的铜镜都是出自墓主头部，在西周至唐代墓葬中也可见到铜镜置放于墓主腰侧、足后的情况。江苏地区汉墓中可见死者手中握镜或镶镜于面罩板中。唐代墓葬和明代墓葬中可见铜镜置放于墓主腰后或腰坑处。棺外铜镜的置放位置也具有时代及区域特征，比如战国时期楚墓中的铜镜多置于头箱，少数置放于边箱；秦人墓多见置于头龛正中。汉以后，大中型墓中棺外的铜镜多与其他随葬品同置墓室或侧室，部分置甬道或天井下。铜镜悬于墓顶或挂于墓壁的情况仅见于宋辽金元明的北方地区大中型墓。唐以后佛塔中也时常发现有铜镜出土。墓葬中的铜镜多数是单独放置的，也有些与其他器物搭配放置在一起。战国时期，秦墓和楚墓中墓主头前和腰侧的铜镜上面或旁边常见有带钩同出，汉唐时期各地墓葬都有此类现象发现。西晋以后，有些墓葬中墓主头前铜镜与匕首叠放一起，腰侧铜镜则与剑、刀等兵器叠放一起，这一现象在江汉一带最为多见。自战国以后，墓葬中铜镜置于奁、盒或匣中的情况逐渐增多。通过对历代墓葬中铜镜附着物和盛放器具的观察分析，有的墓葬中棺内的铜镜以布帛包裹，有的铜镜则置于棺内或棺外的容器中，还有的铜镜则悬挂于墓主头前、腰侧的带钩之上。❶

墓葬中铜镜的出土状态也间接地反映了古人平时使用与置放铜镜的方式。古人置放铜镜，一般有以下几种情况：一是用布帛做镜衣，在铜镜使用之后直接将其包裹起来存放；二是制作专门的容器存放，比如竹奁、漆奁、木匣、金属奁、瓷盒、镜箱等（如萧县汉墓 XZM9 和 XZM11 出土的铜镜外有漆皮或漆盒残迹）；三是为铜镜配备镜架；四是制作镜囊，随身携带。

墓葬中大量出土铜镜，也直接说明了铜镜除了具有日常照容的功能外，还具有一些特殊的用途，反映了古代的丧葬习俗、民俗观念和宗教信仰。古人崇尚"事死如事生"，将逝者生前使用过的东西作为随葬品，希望他们死后依然能享受生前的富庶物质生活。铜镜还被古人赋予驱鬼辟邪的功能，在汉代以后的文献中常有记载，这一功能主要体现在铜镜的特殊摆放位置上或与特定器物搭配摆放的方式上，比如将铜镜置放于甬道天井口下、墓室排水孔或悬于墓壁上，或与剪刀、兵器等搭配放在墓主人头前或腰侧（萧县汉墓中也有此种情况，如 XWM39 和 XCM3 出土的铜镜与铁刀放置在一起，XPM108 出土的铜镜与铁剑放置在一起，XCM7 出土的铜镜与铁削放置在一起）。墓室内出现莲花图案的藻井并于墓室内顶悬挂铜镜，以及铜镜纹饰中出现佛教和道教题材，则反映了墓主人的宗教信仰。

### 三、宿州市博物馆馆藏铜镜概况与研究

宿州市博物馆馆藏铜镜大多数是来源于考古发掘或移交，还有一些为社会征集的藏品。宿州地区能出土如此多的铜镜，这与宿州地区历史发展、建制沿革关系密切。宿州市博物馆馆藏铜镜 159 面。馆藏铜镜造型多样，纹饰精美，涵盖了多种表现题材，更有内容丰富、寓意深刻的铭文，时间跨度上涵盖了战国至明代这一漫长的历史时期，其中战国铜镜 4 面、汉代铜镜 119 面、西晋铜镜 1 面、隋代铜镜 1 面、唐代铜镜 9 面、宋代铜镜 12 面、辽代铜镜 1 面、元代铜镜 2 面，明代铜镜 10 面。从数量上看汉代铜镜数量最多、比重最大，其次是唐宋时期铜镜，由此也折射出宿州汉文化与唐宋时期运河文化的繁荣发展（表 4）。

铜镜是中国青铜器的一个重要门类，自成体系。中华人民共和国成立以后，人们对铜镜的重视度有了很大的提高，很多研究机构与专家学者都开展了对铜镜纹饰、成分、铸造技术等内容的专业研究，全面系统地阐释了铜镜所蕴含的文化价值与社会价值。

古代铜镜有很多种纹饰和不同的形状，为了方便鉴赏和收藏，我们把铜镜分为镜形、镜面、镜背、钮、钮座、内区、中区、外区、镜缘、镜铭、纹饰等。

#### 表 4　宿州市博物馆馆藏铜镜概况

| 序号 | 时代 | 馆藏铜镜数量（件） |
| --- | --- | --- |
| 1 | 战国 | 4 |
| 2 | 汉代 | 119 |
| 3 | 西晋 | 1 |
| 4 | 隋代 | 1 |
| 5 | 唐代 | 9 |
| 6 | 宋代 | 12 |
| 7 | 辽代 | 1 |
| 8 | 元代 | 2 |
| 9 | 明代 | 10 |
| | 合计 | 159 |

镜形：指镜子的平面形状。如圆形、方形、长方形、八角形、菱形、葵花形、桃形、钟形、亚字形、有柄圆形、有柄花叶形等形状。

镜面：指镜子的正面。镜面一般显微凸或平坦状，表面光洁平滑，以供照面之用。

镜背：即镜子的背面。铜镜的背面大致可分为有纹饰、无纹饰两种。无纹饰者称为素镜。

钮：指镜背中央有一凸出带有穿孔的物件，称之为钮。钮的作用可供系带悬挂固定或手持之用。有柄的铜镜没有钮。常见的钮有弓形钮、桥形钮、乳状钮、弦纹钮、半球形钮、兽形钮等。

钮座：指紧靠钮周围的纹饰称为钮座。常见的钮座有连珠纹钮座、圆形钮座、方形钮座、花边纹钮座等。

内区、中区、外区：靠近钮的为内区，靠近边缘的为外区，中间为中区。有的铜镜是以所铸纹饰划分不同的区域。有的镜背不分区域，以钮为中心，用各种形式的圆圈组成几个同心圆，也有仅分为内区和外区等。

镜缘：指镜背的边缘。常见的有卷缘、宽缘。靠近镜缘的纹饰称为镜缘纹饰。如素宽缘、三角锯齿纹缘等。

铭带：指镜背铸有铭文的部分。常见的有条状铭带、环状铭带等。

镜铭：指镜背上所铸的文字。

纹饰：指镜背上所铸的图案花纹。

铜镜的铸造一般采用范铸技术浇铸而成，"范"就是铸制青铜器、铜镜或铜钱的模具，主要有陶范、石范等（图4）。要铸制一面青铜镜，必须先制模，就是用木或陶先雕刻出一面"镜子"，用黏土和细砂包裹制成"范"。范为上下两块：一块是镜背有纹饰图案和镜钮的，一块是平整的镜面。范上面还要有浇口和冒口，以便于浇铸铜液和释放范芯里面的气体。将镜背与镜面合范焙烧之后，再经过修模处理，就可以用来浇铸铜镜，待铜液冷却，便破范取出铜镜。铸造好的铜镜再经过热处理，表面机械加工，如刮削、研磨和表面抛光处理等，就成为光可鉴人的实用器。

铜镜除去模范印制花纹之外，镜背面还采用其他装饰技术。铜镜的装饰技术是一项专门的技艺，以下是铜镜装饰中普遍使用的技法：

镂空（透雕），从传世和出土资料看此类镜采用方形的较多。由镜背与镜面相合而成，一般镜面为青铜，背面为模铸镂空式红铜，因此为"二重镜"。湖南长沙楚墓中出土有透雕蟠螭纹镜；四川涪陵战国早期墓出土有透雕双龙纹镜。流失于国外的镂空纹镜也不少，纹饰亦为蟠螭，还有四夔纹、嵌石变形

图4　《天工开物》中铜钱的制法

兽纹镜。

金银错，所谓金银错工艺是将金银一类的物料以条状、块状形式填入到铜器背面预先做好的凹槽内，再将其错磨平整。这种工艺大约在春秋时兴起，战国时有了较大的发展。最有名的错金银镜当属传河南洛阳金村出土的狩猎纹镜。

镶嵌式，镜背镶嵌绿松石、玉、琉璃等的工艺。山东淄博出土镜有 29.8 厘米，在粗线条的云纹上错以金丝，地上嵌绿松石，还嵌了 9 枚银质乳钉。传河南洛阳金村出土已流失于国外的嵌玉和琉璃镜亦十分华美，背面正中嵌一枚圆形蓝色琉璃，其外嵌素面白玉环，环外一周蓝色琉璃，最外为索纹玉环。

彩绘，使用色漆在铜镜背面素地上描绘花纹。河南信阳长台关战国早期楚墓中出土了几面彩绘镜。有以红、黑、银等彩色绘出的对称云纹镜，朱地上以黑、银灰、黄色绘出的蟠螭纹镜，绿、朱、褐等色绘出的云纹镜。湖南慈利楚墓出土了方形彩绘方格纹、圆形彩绘方格勾云纹镜，湖南长沙楚墓中四兽纹镜素缘绘有红色方连纹。另外已流失在国外的凤鸟纹镜上有敷彩的，此镜传为河南洛阳金村出土。

鎏金银，所谓鎏金银是用汞剂涂附法来外镀金银的工艺，一般是将水银与金粉或银粉和在一起研磨成汞剂，涂在处理干净的铜器表面，用一定方式加热器物，使汞剂中的汞挥发，留下金粉或银粉均匀地附在铜器表面。

金银平脱，金银平脱镜是将金片、银片裁剪成所需要的纹样，将其贴在填满胶漆的镜背上，然后在上面涂漆数重，待干后加以细细研磨，使贴上的金银饰片与漆面平齐，露出闪亮的纹饰。

螺钿，用螺蚌贝壳薄片造成所需要的图案，用漆贴在器物上的工艺。中国一般器物的螺钿工艺约始于商代，但唯铜镜的螺钿工艺盛于唐。

合金成分，青铜镜因其镜面需经打磨抛光以照容，因此其合金成分中，锡的比例相对其他青铜器要高些。从战国至唐五代，均属于高锡青铜；宋至明清之后，铜的含锡量减少，铅增多。《考工记·六齐》说："金有六齐，六分其金而锡居一，谓之钟鼎之齐；五分其金而锡居一，谓之斧斤之齐；四分其金而锡居一，谓之戈戟之齐；三分其金而锡居一，谓之大刃之齐；五分其金而锡居二，谓之削杀矢之齐；金锡半，谓之鉴燧之齐。"这"金"即是铜，"齐"同"剂"，表示剂量，全文说铜与锡有六种配比，可用来制作六种不同性能的器物。

受经济文化发展水平、地方考古工作开展以及资料公布不及时不完整等原因影响，铜镜研究成果也呈现出地区差异性。目前，宿州市内出土与收藏铜镜研究成果较少，已知的和铜镜有关的研究主要集中体现在以安徽省文物考古研究所为主编写的考古发掘报告中，如《安徽萧县陈沟墓群 ( 东区 ) 发掘简报》收录铜镜 4 面，《安徽萧县陈沟墓地 ( 西区 ) 发掘简报》收录铜镜 2 面，《安徽萧县西虎山汉墓清理简报》收录铜镜 5 面，《安徽萧县张村汉墓发掘简报》收录铜镜 7 面，《安徽宿州市骑路堌堆汉墓发掘简报》收录铜镜 2 面，《安徽宿州市邱园战国至汉代墓群发掘简报》收录铜镜 1 面，《灵璧县大李墓群发掘简报》收录铜镜 1 面，《萧县汉墓》收录铜镜 40 面。针对馆藏铜镜的研究，1998 年宿州市文物管理所的冀和先生发表了《安徽宿州市发现的唐宋铜镜》一文，详细地对其单位收藏的唐宋铜镜做了文化与艺术阐释。另外，《宿州文物》《宿州市博物馆文物集萃》也收录了部分精美的铜镜。

为大力推广铜镜文化，让大家更加深入了解铜镜背后的故事，以物观史，打破展览的空间与时间的局限性，我馆筹备出版《宿州市博物馆铜镜集萃》一书，此书收录馆藏精品铜镜 114 件，同时收录安徽省文物考古研究所宿州工作站考古发掘并收藏保管的宿州境内出土的精品铜镜 10 件。本书收录的铜镜，始于战国时期，终于明代，以时间为序，以纹饰归类，下面对收录的铜镜做些简要说明。

### 战国时期的铜镜

春秋战国时期由于社会制度和生产力的发展变化，人们的思想意识和生活习俗也发生了翻天覆地的变化，青铜工艺得到了迅速的发展，铜镜的生产规模扩大并快速流行与发展。这一时期的铜镜发展可分为三个阶段。春秋中晚期到战国早期，这一时期是铜镜工艺蓬勃兴起阶段，制作技法上仍有许多不足，铜镜在形制上小而薄，镜面平，平缘或微卷缘，小钮；在装饰技法上较为简单，一般采用素面或弦纹、连弧纹这样简单的单层纹饰，也有仅施羽状纹、云雷纹等地纹的铜镜。战国中期，制镜工艺显著提高，这一时期制造的铜镜，在形制上镜体增大增厚，素卷缘；在装饰技法上，一般采用主纹、地纹双层纹饰，装饰的图案内容丰富，与初期的铜镜有明显的差别。战国晚期，制镜工艺相对成熟。铜镜在形制上变大变厚，增强了其实用性与耐用性；在装饰技法上，纹饰层数及种类变多，新的制镜工艺不断涌现，出现了金银错、透雕、镶嵌等新工艺，铜镜制作达到了新高峰。根据纹饰，春秋战国时期的铜镜可分为素镜、纯地纹镜、花叶镜、山字镜、菱纹镜、禽兽纹镜、蟠螭纹镜、羽鳞纹镜、连弧纹镜、彩绘镜、透雕镜、金银错纹镜、多钮镜等。

本书辑录战国铜镜4件，包含了全素镜和山字纹镜。全素镜出现的时代最早，流行的时间较长。山字镜分布地区广泛，主要集中在两湖地区，安徽地区也有分布，如六安、淮南等地区。山字镜属于楚式镜比较典型的铜镜。

山字镜的主要特征是在羽状地纹上由三至六个斜形的类似于山字的纹样组成主题纹饰。山字有左旋和右旋两种，等距分布于钮座之外，山字之间装饰花瓣纹、叶纹、绳纹等。山字镜均为圆形，钮座分为方形钮座和圆形钮座，多数山字的底边与方形钮座的四边作平行线排列。少数山字的底边与方形钮座的四角处作错角状排列。山字镜分为三山镜、四山镜、五山镜和六山镜四种。四山镜较为常见，出土较多，三山镜和六山镜数量较少。我馆收藏三山镜和五山镜，均为圆形、三弦钮、圆钮座，其中三山镜为右旋式山字镜，五山镜为左旋式山字镜，是涉案移交文物，极为珍贵。

### 两汉时期的铜镜

公元前202年，刘邦建立汉朝，中国封建社会逐渐进入鼎盛时期。两汉时期，国家统一，经济文化空前发展繁荣，文化交流广泛。这种大一统的社会背景也推进了制镜业的高度发展与进步，铜镜进入了繁荣鼎盛阶段。西汉早期的铜镜仍较多保留沿用了战国时期的元素特点。西汉中晚期的铜镜有了较大的变化，出现许多新特点，如：许多铜镜采用四分法布局方式，以四乳钉为基点组织主题纹饰；更加突出显示主纹，且主纹逐渐趋于简单朴素化，地纹逐渐消失；铭文逐渐成为铜镜的重要纹饰之一等。西汉末到东汉前期，形象逼真的瑞兽禽鸟纹成为主题纹饰，铭文镜的种类也更加繁多，这一时期的铜镜也更加重视对镜缘的装饰，使铜镜更具有艺术性。东汉中晚期的铜镜，题材广泛，纹饰复杂，多以神兽纹为主，同时出现了有故事情节的画像镜，产生了浮雕式工艺新技法，开始运用了轴对称的纹饰布局方式。两汉时期流行的铜镜，大致可以分为以下几类：蟠螭纹镜、蟠虺纹镜、草叶纹镜、星云纹镜、铭文镜、四乳镜、规矩纹镜、多乳禽兽纹镜、连弧纹镜、变形四叶纹镜、神兽镜、画像镜、夔纹镜、龙虎纹镜等。

两汉时期宿地置有符离、竹、蕲、萧、夏丘等县，属沛郡。沛郡又是汉高祖刘邦的家乡，是汉室王朝起家地。宿州分布着大量汉代城址、遗址、墓葬，并出土大量反映汉代社会物质文化的文物，充分体现了两汉时期社会稳定、经济繁荣和人民生活富足。

汉代铜镜，是我馆铜镜收藏的重要内容。本书辑录汉镜88件，其中馆藏78件，安徽省文物考古研究所考古发掘10件。纹饰上，主要包含了蟠螭镜、星云纹镜、日光镜、昭明镜、四乳四虺镜、博局镜、四乳八鸟纹镜、多乳禽兽纹镜、连弧纹镜、神兽纹镜等。

星云纹镜出土分布广泛，始于汉武帝时期，在昭宣时期比较流行，之后迅速衰落，因其多乳钉且与星相图相似而得名，属于典型的高浮雕纹饰镜。本书收录星云纹镜4件，主要特征是圆形，多为连峰钮，主纹区采用四分法布局，一般是四乳钉划分四区，区间饰有许多小的乳钉，小乳钉间用曲线相连接，边缘由内向的连弧纹构成。星云纹镜的出现体现了汉代先民对天文星象的认知和对吉祥美好生活的向往。

日光镜是汉镜中出土数量多、流行范围广的镜类之一，镜铭非常富于变化，多以"见日之光"作为首句，最常见的是"见日之光，天下大明"。日光镜字铭间常以◖纹和◈纹间隔。本书辑录日光镜12件，形制相似，均为圆形、圆钮，钮座外饰内向八连弧纹一周，其中11件铭文相同，为"见日之光，天下大明"，字铭间均以◖纹和◈纹相隔，铭文圈带两侧各饰一周栉齿纹，还有一件铭文"见日之光，长不相忘"。

昭明镜也是出土数量多、流行范围广的汉代镜种之一，流行于西汉中后期，以西汉后期最盛行。根据镜子的大小，昭明镜常出现省字的情况，完整的铭文应是"内清质以昭明，光辉象夫分日月，心忽扬而愿忠，然雍塞而不泄"，字铭间以"而"字间隔。本书辑录昭明镜16件，均为省字昭明镜，分别为"内清以昭明，光象日月"，"内清以昭明，光象夫日月"，"内清以昭明，光日月"等。

四乳四虺镜出土较多，流行地区较广，流行时间较长，从汉武帝时期一直延续到东汉前期。该镜纹饰布局严谨，以四乳钉将镜背等分成四区，每区置一虺纹，以镜钮为中心，首尾相连，对称分布。四乳四虺铜镜是汉镜中最常见的品种之一，一般的四乳四虺镜将虺纹与雀鸟置于一处，也有的在虺的头尾部加上龙头，表现了从虺到龙的蜕变过程。本书辑录四乳四虺镜7件，形制基本相同，圆形、圆钮、圆钮座，以四乳钉分区，每区置一虺纹，以镜钮为中心，对称分布。

博局镜，也称规矩镜，主要特征就是镜背装饰图案中有"T""L""V"三种符号组成的博局纹。博局纹来源于六博棋局图像。西汉初期就出现了博局纹镜，一直流行到西汉晚期到东汉早期，尤其是在新莽时期极为盛行。东汉中晚期之后，博局纹趋向简化，发展到魏晋初期逐渐消失。"TLV"博局纹具有特殊文化内涵，一是这种图像被赋予了与仙人世界沟通联系的作用，二是反映了两汉时期独特的宇宙观念，包括阴阳五行、天圆地方、规矩、公平理念等。本书收录博局纹镜14件（其中2件为简化博局纹镜），分别在博局纹间搭配装饰四神纹、龙虎纹、禽鸟纹、羽人瑞兽纹等。

**隋唐时期的铜镜**

公元581年，隋朝建立，公元589年灭陈，结束了三百多年南北分裂的局面。唐朝时期，国家统一，封建政治经济文化高度发展，开创了一个繁荣强盛的历史时代。在社会稳定，经济高度发展的前提下，制镜业也进入了繁荣发展阶段，它以新颖的造型、丰富多彩的题材、精湛的铸造工艺，带来了中国铜镜史的新纪元。

对唐代铜镜的镜形、纹饰及铭文的变化，孔祥星、徐殿魁等学者进行了深入的研究。尤其是在铜镜的分期上存在三期说和四期说。

徐殿魁根据纪年唐墓出土铜镜的资料将唐镜的发展演变分为四个时期：第一期，初唐期，7世纪初至7世纪晚期，即唐高祖至唐高宗在位时期；第二期，盛唐期，7世纪晚至8世纪中期，即武则天光宅元年（684年）至玄宗开元年末（741年）；第三期，中唐期，8世纪中叶至9世纪初，即玄宗天宝年（742年）始至德宗贞元末年（805年）；第四期，晚唐期，9世纪初至10世纪初，即宪宗元和元年（806年）至唐末哀帝天祐四年（907年）。**⑫**

"三期说"**⑬**：第一期为隋至唐高宗时期，是铜镜承上启下的一个发展时期，这个时期的铜镜在沿袭传统的同时又在不断创新，铜镜开启了由拘谨板滞到自由写实、由纷繁杂乱到清新优雅的历史性转变，新的镜类和纹饰陆续出现，主题纹饰中花鸟植物纹逐渐增多，揭开了唐代铜镜以花鸟为主题的序幕。第二期为唐高宗到唐德宗时期，是唐式镜逐渐发展成熟的时期，也是中国铜镜史上又一鼎盛繁荣发展时期，在形制上，铜镜突破了圆形、方形的传统，出现了菱形镜、葵形镜等花式镜；在纹饰上，人物故事题材大量涌现，艺术表现手法和艺术样式多样化。第三期为唐德宗到晚唐五代时期，是隋唐铜镜急剧衰退的时期，这一时期的铜镜植物纹饰简单粗犷，盛行具有宗教意义的纹饰，形制上除圆形镜外还流行方形镜和亚方形镜，技法上采用细线浅雕或剔地成纹。

隋唐时期的铜镜种类多、纹饰复杂、形制多样，比较流行的有四神十二生肖镜、瑞兽镜、瑞兽葡萄镜、瑞兽鸾鸟镜、花鸟镜、瑞花镜、神仙人物故事镜、盘龙镜、八卦镜、万字镜、金银平脱镜、螺钿镜、贴金贴银镜等。

隋唐时期，也是宿州历史上一个十分重要的经济文化高度繁荣发展时期。公元605年，隋炀帝"发动河南诸郡男女百余万开通济渠"，这条水道自河南的开封折向东南，沿河南杞县、睢县、商丘、永城，经安徽的濉溪，宿州的埇桥区、灵璧、泗县，至江苏盱眙入淮。唐朝时期，人们称通济渠为"汴河""汴水"或"汴渠""隋堤"，由于这段运河流经范围广，因此人流量、物流量都很大，除战乱年代，其他时候都十分繁华热闹。宿州是唐代漕粮通过汴渠运道的必经之路，宰相李泌曾先后两次上言，反复强调其作为漕运咽喉的重要战略地位。伴随汴渠在南北经济交流中作用的日渐显露和增强，宿州的经济也逐渐繁荣起来。唐代宗大历十四年（779年），刘晏进行盐铁官营改革，曾于全国设置四大盐场、十监和十三巡院，宿州为十三盐铁巡院之一。唐廷据此以贮聚向当地人民和过往客商所征收的杂税、钱帛和物资，并借以加强对漕运、盐运的管理。唐德宗建中年间，为了保障运输物资不被劫掠，又调派猛将张万福驻守濠州，益兵屯守，保护埇桥。随着通济渠的开通，"扼汴水咽喉，当南北要冲"的埇桥小镇，已经无法承当自身的重任。为了防御淮西叛藩的审扰，保护汴河漕运，唐宪宗元和四年（809年），将徐州所属的符离县、蕲县和泗州所属的虹县割出，建立了宿州，宿州始名，治所最初定在虹（今泗县），后为了保护漕运，又于公元833年将治所迁到埇桥，这使埇桥不仅成为南粮北运的重镇，也一度成为繁华的关津渡口和兵家必争之地。公元868年，庞勋起义，攻占宿州，掳大船300艘来壮大自己的力量。在当时，能夜泊如此多数量的船只，足以体现当时的宿州已经发展成为一个大都会，埇桥也是汴渠上规模较大的港埠码头，"舳舻之会，舟车之要"，所言非虚，反映出宿州在唐代的经济地位之重要。经济和文化繁荣发展，促使铜镜制造技术与工艺也大大提高，在造型上突破了汉式镜，样式新颖、题材丰富。盛唐以后，图案以花为主，多为吉祥图案，自由豪放，清新活泼，表现了大唐帝国蓬勃向上的精神面貌。我馆馆藏的唐代铜镜，正是大唐繁荣景象的有力实证。

本书辑录唐镜8件，主要以花鸟为题材，包括瑞兽葡萄纹、瑞兽鸾鸟纹、双鸾衔绶纹、禽鸟纹、瑞花纹等。从形制上，圆形镜1件，葵形镜5件，菱形镜2件。

瑞兽葡萄镜，又称海兽葡萄镜，其纹饰复杂，从镜心密布至镜缘，层次清晰，刻画精密。纹饰主要由瑞兽和葡萄蔓叶果实组合，多以一周凸棱相隔，分内外二区。铜镜采用高浮雕手法使纹饰起伏，主次分明，立体感较强。瑞兽和禽鸟等姿态各异，雍容富丽。铜镜纹样受外来文化的影响，充分显示出唐代对外来文化的吸收与容纳，瑞兽表达了吉祥如意的美好寓意，葡萄被赋予多子的象征意义，再现了大唐浓厚的文化气息。本书收录的瑞兽葡萄镜虽然在造型上设计分区，但纹饰图案自由结合又显得浑然一体，呈现出由中央向外围缠绕放射状。虽然铜镜局部锈蚀，纹饰缺失，但是依然可以清晰地看到铜镜镜纹中的瑞兽造型呈奔跑跳跃状与外区的轻盈优美的蜂蝶与鸾鸟相呼应，使视觉效果由中心向外围舒展，呈现出由重到轻、由实到虚的延展。

本书辑录双鸾双瑞兽镜3面（其中双鸾衔绶纹样2面）。在形制上大致相同，八出葵花形，圆钮或拱形钮，八瓣莲花形钮座。镜面纹饰上下、左右对称布局。双鸾面对镜钮，左右分布，呈振翅状。双兽以镜钮为中心，上下分布。上方的瑞兽与下方的瑞兽，乍看相似，实则不同。上方的瑞兽，头有一角，似为独角兽。下方的瑞兽头似狮子，两侧各饰一花叶纹。两瑞兽均呈向右飞奔状。双鸾衔绶是古代中国吉祥图案，是唐代的一种流行纹饰。常见双鸾相对飞翔，口衔挽结长绶，配以鲜花祥云。鸾是中国民间传统中象征吉祥的飞鸟，"长绶"象征"长寿"(同音)，绶带挽结，表示永结同心。

雀绕花枝镜是唐代比较流行的一种镜型，形制上以菱形镜居多，纹饰布局以四只禽鸟绕钮同向排列，其间装饰花枝纹。本书收录的雀绕花枝镜，禽鸟为两雀两雁，间饰有叶有苞的小折枝花，近缘处配蜂蝶花枝纹，内外相映成趣，清新简洁。

宝相花铜镜是唐代极具代表性的铜镜之一，风格艳丽，形制多变，具有美好的象征意义，深受人们喜爱。宝相花，一般指的是"将某些自然形态的花朵（主要是荷花）进行艺术处理，变成一种装饰化的花朵纹样"，即将莲花、牡丹、月季等有美好象征意义的花朵进行艺术处理变成各种不同形象的花形。宝相花纹样之所以在唐代流行与当时佛教的盛行以及社会背景是分不开的。佛教在印度创立以前，莲花就被古印度人民当作圣物。佛教产生以后，人们把莲花的自然属性与佛教的教义、规则相类比美化，逐渐形成了对莲花的崇拜，将许多美好圣洁的事物以莲花做比喻。佛教传入中国之后，莲花纹逐渐演变为宝相花纹。莲花是佛教艺术中的经典形象，既有佛家莲花化生的思想，又结合其在中国吉祥、美好的寓意，在中国得到了极大的发展。宝相花铜镜在唐代的兴盛现象，反映了唐代人欣赏观念的转变，人们更加喜爱用植物、花卉作为装饰，揭开了唐代铜镜花鸟主题纹饰的序幕。本书收录宝相花纹镜1面，花瓣纹钮座，座外两种不同形花瓣六朵相间配列，花蕊花瓣端庄素雅，素缘。

唐朝灭亡后，中国历史进入了五代十国、宋、辽、金、元时期，这一时期历史局面复杂，社会动荡，政治经济发展不平衡，铜镜制造业日趋衰落。

### 宋辽时期的铜镜

宋朝时期的铜镜，工艺整体上处于缓慢发展阶段。五代到宋真宗时期，沿袭模仿唐代铜镜形制，但质量远不如唐镜，镜身也相对轻薄。宋神宗到北宋末期是铜镜短暂发展时期，铜镜质量有所提高，纹饰也相对精致细腻。南宋时期，铜镜在装饰艺术上处于衰落阶段，重实用不尚花纹，多为素地加制造者商标字号的铭文；在形制上，却是处于一个创新时期，除了常见的圆形、方形、菱形、葵形外，还出了一些特异的形制，如盾形、钟形、鼎形、长条形、扇形、瓶形、带柄形等。宋镜有三个特点，一是形制多样；二是题材集中，主要包括缠枝花草、有宗教色彩的神仙故事、以诗文题记的铭文；三是出现大量带有字号商标铭文的铜镜。宋代铜镜主要有以下几类，都省铜坊铭文镜、吉祥铭文镜、素镜、缠枝花草镜、花鸟镜、神仙人物故事镜、八卦镜、纪名号铭镜等。

北宋时期，宿州地区相对安定，交通发达，经济繁荣，已发展成为汴河上的繁华都会之一。南宋时期，宋金对峙，动乱频繁。绍兴十一年（1141年），宋金议和，以淮河为界，宿州划归金国统治。宋隆兴元年（1163年），宋金大战爆发，宋军先后收复灵璧、虹县，进据宿州城，与金军在符离鏖战数月，最终溃败，被迫议和，史称"隆兴和议"。此后，宋金两国维持了四十多年的和平。20世纪80年代在宿县图书馆发现的瞻宸楼记碑记载了金国统治下的宿州"政成民听，百废待兴"。

本书辑录宋代铜镜9面，从形制上主要分为葵形镜、圆形镜、执柄镜。纹饰简单，主要为素面镜、弦纹镜、玉兔捣药纹镜、湖州镜。

玉兔捣药纹镜，造型小巧，月桂树下一只玉兔站在长条石凳上，身子似人直立，翘着尾巴，认真捣药。该纹饰惟妙惟肖，十分有趣，活灵活现地展示了在民间广为流传的玉兔捣药的神话传说。玉兔捣药镜镜钮有别于本书收录的其他铜镜，它的镜钮是两个半环形钮，位于铜镜下方近缘处。此镜与湖南博物院收藏的一面玉兔捣药镜纹饰上基本相同，形制相似，唯一的区别是湖南博物院的玉兔捣药镜与其下方的支架是一体的，借鉴其造型，可以判断我馆馆藏的玉兔捣药镜在当时应该也是固定在一个三足支架上使用的。

湖州镜是宋代最流行的镜类之一，其命名与它的纹饰特征紧密相关，它的镜背带有"湖州"二字铭文，表明了其铸造生产地点在湖州。宋代的湖州是一个著名的制镜中心，铸镜商号店铺林立，能工巧匠众多。宋代湖州镜以轻纹饰为显著特点，不同于汉唐时期的复杂纹饰，宋代湖州镜虽然造型多样，有花形、圆形、方形及带柄镜，但是背面多为素面，且一般铸有作坊和商业铭文，个别铜镜会在背后刻上"长命富贵"等吉祥语，印证了湖州镜商品化的特征。本书收录湖州镜2面。一面圆形，银锭形钮两侧各有一个长方形框，框内铸铭文"湖州孙家青鸾宝鉴"，形制规整，铸造精细。一面六出葵花形，近似倒置的元宝形小圆钮，无钮座，镜背素地无纹饰，钮右侧有两行铭文"湖州真石家/念二叔照子"，呈长方形印戳式，钮左侧近缘处有笔划纤细的阴刻"徐州验记官"。据《金史》记载和文物考古材料证明，金人在民间实行极为严格的铜禁政策，对新旧铜器都要经官府验记后才能使用。根据本镜上的徐州地方官府验记花押证明它是由南方铸镜商营销到北方的，足见湖州镜在当时的市场上销售势头之强。❶

辽代因制镜工匠多来源于中原北方，所以多数铜镜风格与五代、宋一致，少数具有辽国自己的特色，如契丹文字镜。金代在铜镜制作上异军突起，在仿唐镜宋镜的同时，也创新了一些别开生面的纹饰，流行的镜类主要有双鱼镜、历史人物故事镜、盘龙镜、瑞兽镜、瑞花镜。

本书辑录辽代鱼龙变化镜1面，带柄莲花朵形。鱼龙变化纹样，取材于我国长期流传的鲤鱼跃龙门的传说，是一种中国传统的吉祥寓意纹。因民间常把科举及第称为"跃龙门""登龙门"，鱼龙变化纹样的流行与这种愿望亦有一定的关系。

**元明清时期的铜镜**

元明清时期是中国铜镜发展的衰落阶段。元代的金银细工制作有较高的水平，但是制镜业却相对落后，铸镜工艺粗糙，常见的铜镜有双鱼镜、缠枝牡丹纹镜、神仙人物故事镜、双龙镜等。明朝时期随着经济和手工业的繁荣发展、采矿和冶金技术的提高以及工匠制度改革，制镜业获得了很大的发展，这一时期是元明清时期铜镜发展相对繁荣阶段。明代的铜镜不仅是一种生活必备品，同时还兼具馈赠、祈福、辟邪等功用，社会需求量很大。在继承传统的同时，明代铜镜在纹饰和铭文上也有所创新。此外明代还大量流行仿古镜，以仿汉唐时期的铜镜为主。明代的铜镜，镜钮形式多样，除常见镜钮外，平顶圆柱形钮和银锭形钮也十分流行。平顶圆柱形钮是明代出现的一种新形制，上面常有铸镜工匠或作坊的戳记。在纹饰上，除龙纹、双鱼纹、花卉纹、人物故事纹等传统内容外，吉祥图案和吉祥文字成为这一时期最具特色的题材。清代中晚期，铜镜逐渐被玻璃镜所取代并退出了历史舞台。

明清时期，铜镜铸造既沿袭传统又开拓创新，尤其是出现了一些反映当时社会心态及文化信息的新花纹及铭文。随着玻璃镜的流行，铜镜已渐渐失去照容功能，虽仍有生产，但是多用于作为辟邪迎福的吉祥物使用。本书辑录明代铜镜 10 面，主要包括素面镜、弦纹镜、福寿吉语镜、五子登科镜。

吉语文字是明代铜镜上一种比较流行的纹饰。文字或按上下左右的位置环钮分布或在镜钮两侧布置，字体通常大而规整，以楷书和篆书为主。除长寿、富贵的内容外，还新出现了大量与科举有关的吉语，反映了明代科举制度的繁荣。五子登科镜就是明代出现的一个新镜种，是对当时科举政策的一种折射。五子登科本为中国民间谚语，最初来源于民间故事，话说五代后周时期，燕山府有个叫窦禹钧的人，他的五个儿子都品学兼优，先后登科及第，故称"五子登科"。五子登科后来成为中国传统吉祥图案，一般人家期望子弟都能像窦禹钧五子一样获得科考成功。

### 四、宿州市博物馆馆藏铜镜的保护与利用情况

随着历史的发展与社会生产力的不断提高，铜镜除了在形制、纹饰、工艺等方面具备时代特点外，其所含的金属成分也具有时代特征。经科学实验研究表明，古代青铜镜为铜锡铅三元合金，如果只用铜来铸镜，制出的镜子为红色，使用时映照效果会很模糊。随着锡含量的不断增加，合金的颜色会由红色变为黄色而逐渐至白色，当含锡量增加到 24% 左右时，铸制出的铜镜就有了今天的玻璃镜一样的映照效果了。早期的齐家文化镜至殷墟铜镜，都属于我国铜镜铸制技术的起始阶段，该时期的铜镜合金配比还没有形成规范。进入西周中期以后，我国的铸镜合金配比逐步有了规律而趋于成熟。商周时期的铜镜合金以红铜为主，锡、铅成分极少。红铜通常容易生锈，因此该时期的铜镜锈蚀较严重。春秋至战国时期，我国铜镜的合金配比及铜镜的范铸技术已完全成熟，此时的铜镜具有含铜量高，含锡量低，含铅量不固定的特点。经过两汉、三国、六朝至隋唐，一直保持着高锡青铜工艺技术至唐代晚期。汉代的铜镜合金成分铜、锡、铅三者适宜，合金比例比较稳定，含锡量比战国镜增高，因此汉镜较脆硬。唐镜比汉镜厚实，多呈银白色，铜、锡、铅的合金比例基本上与汉镜相同。宋代的铜镜合金成分发生了变化，含锡量明显减少，含铅量增多，锌的比例加大，所以宋镜质地不如唐镜，为黄中闪红铜质，镜体也比唐镜轻薄。宋代以后，铜镜合金里加入了大量的铅，明代铜镜合金里加入了一定量的锌，已不属于高锡青铜。❶⑤

习近平总书记在 2017 年 4 月 19 日广西考察工作时的讲话："中华民族历史悠久，中华文明源远流长，中华文化博大精深，一个博物馆就是一所大学校，博物馆建设要注重特色。""要让文物说话，让历史说话，让文化说话。要加强文物保护和利用，加强历史研究和传承，使中华优秀传统文化不断发扬光大。要增强文化自信，在传承中华优秀传统文化基础上发展社会主义先进文化，加快建设社会主义文化强国。"习近平总书记指出"让收藏在博物馆里的文物、陈列在广阔大地上的遗产、书写在古籍里的文字都活起来"，博物馆承担着文物保护和利用的重要使命。为更好地保护、宣传和展示我市历史文化，充分开发利用馆藏资源，2015～2016 年，宿州市博物馆申请保护修复馆藏 240 件（套）金属文物。这些文物为历年来征集和考古发掘出土，器型涵盖礼器、兵器、食器、铜镜等多个种类，时代跨度从战国至清代，是研究宿州地区古代政治、经济、文化发展十分珍贵的实物资料。由于年代久远以及出土后保存条件不好，这些青铜器大多锈蚀残破，存在不同程度的文物病害，其中有相当一部分已逐渐呈现濒危状态，亟待进行保护修复。为此，宿州市博物

馆委托安徽博物院文物科技保护中心和荆州文物保护中心承担此次青铜器保护修复方案的编制工作。在前期调研和检测分析的基础上，按照中国国家文物局颁发的《中华人民共和国文物保护法》《中华人民共和国文物保护法实施条例》等相关法律法规及文物保护修复技术规范要求，我们确定了保护修复目标和技术路线，编制了《宿州市博物馆馆藏金属文物保护修复方案》用于指导开展文物保护修复工作，使之达到保管和陈列的要求，并对未来的文物保护修复工作起到借鉴作用。此次文物保护修复项目，重点修复对象就是铜镜。在修复过程中，我们针对每件器物不同残损情况，"对症下药"，在对文物的病害进行科学分析研究的基础上，依据分析结论有针对性地采取物理、化学方法相结合的技术手段和方法对该文物进行清洗、去锈矫形、缓蚀、封护处理。考虑到文物个体本身的特殊性，以及文物本体对技术的制约性较大而会引起不可预见的不利因素，在实施过程中我们组织专家召开专家咨询会，全面把握技术的可行性和可操作性。

为保证修复工作的科学性、规范性与严谨性，2015 年 8 月，安徽博物院文物科技保护中心派遣专业技术人员赴宿州实地对文物进行了调查测绘，并采集了部分样品，送交中国科学技术大学科技史与科技考古系进行科学分析检测，并出具检测分析报告。分析测试项目主要包括超景深三维光学显微分析、X 射线荧光（XRF）分析、X 射线衍射（XRD）分析（表5；以下检测分析资料均来源于《宿州市博物馆馆藏金属文物保护修复方案》[16]）。

光学金相显微分析：超景深三维光学显微分析检测，利用超景深三维显微光学系统在 100 倍下观察金属样品的锈层以及锈蚀程度，通过观察检测，发现文物样品存在不同程度的腐蚀情况，锈层呈层状堆积，

### 表 5　样品测试信息表

| 样品名称 | 样品照片 | 样品特征 | 测试项目 |
| --- | --- | --- | --- |
| SZ1687 宋代 青铜镜残片 | | 样品为青铜，锈蚀严重，锈蚀物多呈绿色、褐色。 | |
| SZ1688 唐代青铜镜 | | 样品为青铜，有锈蚀产物，锈蚀物呈黑色。 | 1. 超景深三维光学显微分析 2. X 射线荧光（XRF）分析 3. X 射线衍射（XRD）分析 |
| SZ1692 铜镜残片 | | 样品为青铜，锈蚀相当严重，锈蚀物多呈黑色、绿色。 | |

表面有大量污染物或硬结物，有的样品甚至存在通体矿化现象（图5~10）。

X射线荧光分析检测：通过X射线荧光光谱仪，用X射线荧光分析金属样品中的元素及其含量，了解金属文物的组成成分、制作工艺等信息。我们在样品表面或断面进行无损分析，每件样品采集3个点的数据，每个点分析时间60s，采集的数据，仅保留主量元素信息，以此来判断每件样品中Cu、Pb、Sn的含量比例情况（表6）。

图5　样品SZ1687视频显微照片（锈层）

图6　样品SZ1687视频显微照片（锈层）

图7　样品SZ1688视频显微照片（锈层）

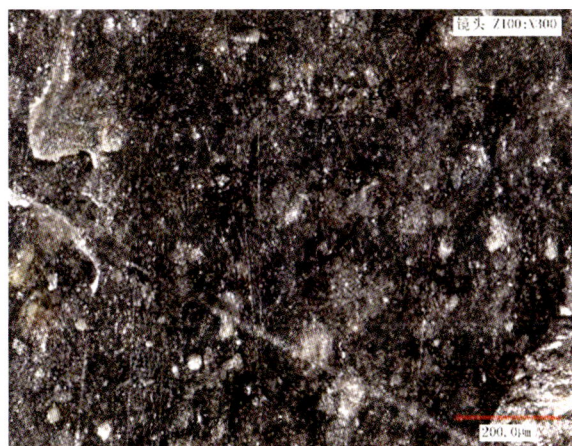

图8　样品SZ1688视频显微照片（锈层）

图9　样品SZ1692视频显微照片（锈层）

图10　样品SZ1692视频显微照片（锈层）

## 表6 铜镜样品 XRF 分析结果

| 元素含量<br>样品编号 | Cu（mt） | Pb（mt） | Sn（mt） |
|---|---|---|---|
| SZ1687 | 75.07% | 4.43% | 20.51% |
| SZ1688 | 67.40% | 29.27% | 3.34% |
| SZ1692 | 66.42% | 5.63% | 27.95% |

X 射线衍射分析检测：利用 X 射线衍射分析金属样品中锈蚀产物的物相结构，了解金属文物的病害状况，为金属文物的保护修复提供基础资料。通过检测，我们发现样品中主要腐蚀产物为 $Cu_2O$、$CuO$、$CuCO_3 \cdot Cu(OH)_2$、$CuCl$、$PbCO_3$。光学金相显微分析检测，利用金相显微镜对样品组织、均匀度以及夹杂物形貌、特征、分布等进行观察与研究，研究金属的金相结构，判断其保存状况并推测其制作工艺。通过对文物样品进行这几项科学检测分析，揭示了其保存状况以及材料、工艺等信息，为下一步修复工作的实施提供科学依据（图 11～13）。

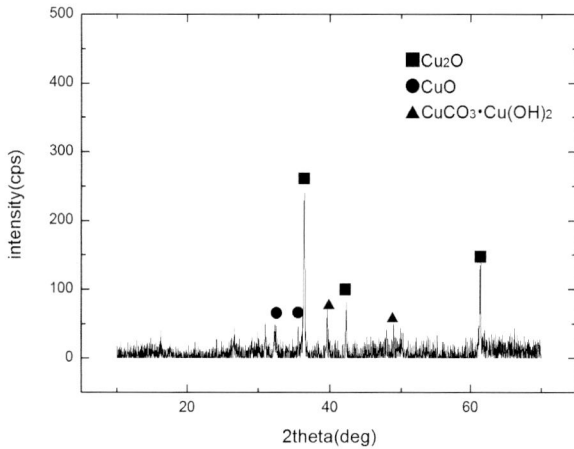

图 11 青铜样品 SZ1687XRD 物相分析图

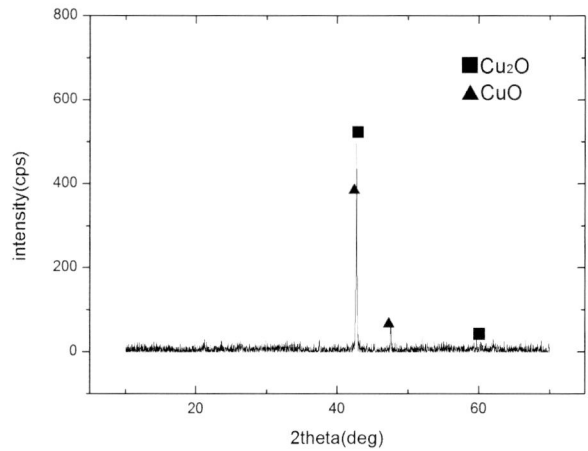

图 12 青铜样品 SZ1688XRD 物相分析图

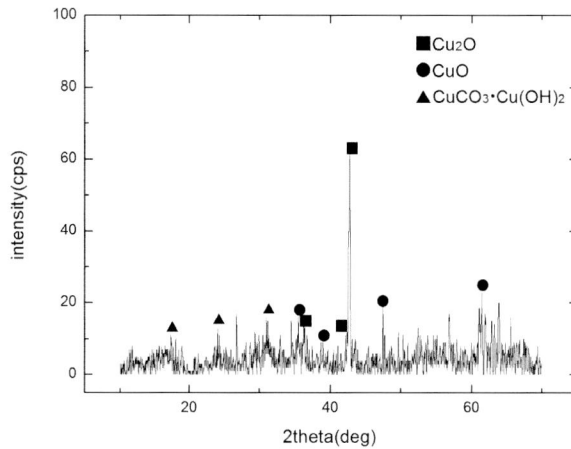

图 13 青铜样品 SZ1692XRD 物相分析图

在实施文物修复工作中，我们严格履行保护修复方案中的各项技术要求，能够小修解决的问题不作大修处理，不扩大保护修复范围，合理和慎重使用化学试剂。保护修复技术路线科学合理，保护修复材料安全并具有可逆性。针对文物保存状况，在尊重文物的原状、保持原有的气韵色调的基础上，进行焊接（黏结）、补缺、作色，使修复部分与本体从视觉效果上协调。经过修复与除锈，很多铜镜被覆盖的纹饰显露出来，其中不乏精品，既丰富了展陈内容，又为我们开展历史文化研究提供了有力的物质支撑（图14）。

修复前　　　　　　　　　　　　　　　　　　修复后

图14　唐代缠枝莲花镜修复前后对比图

为利于文物的长久保存，巩固保护修复成果，我们为修复后的文物配备了无酸纸囊匣，同时使用调湿材料，如变色硅胶等控制文物柜，为其创建稳定的保存小环境。在大环境的管理上，通过安装空调系统，使用温湿度调控设备，如柜式恒温恒湿机、除湿机等来调控大环境的温湿度。虽然我们已经开展了文物的保护修复工作，但是文物本体的老化变质是自然规律，不可避免，任何干预措施都只是希望延缓其蜕变速度，不可能一劳永逸。保护修复工作只是在一定程度上的防护或将有害影响因素减弱，其保存状况与其保存环境依然有着紧密的联系，病害状态仍旧时刻处于变化之中，保护修复材料本身也存在环境适用性和老化问题。因此，维护保养工作就显得格外重要。加强文物的日常维护与保养，合理利用文物资源，是我们的一项长期且十分重要的工作。

铜镜作为古代较为常见的日用器具之一，能够最直观地反映古人对生活的美好想象，折射出当时社会的经济状况和文化面貌。铜镜背面的装饰在不同的历史时期都有着鲜活的时代印记，其发展历史也是中华优秀传统文化富有生命力的缩影。为了提升文物资源利用率，充分发挥铜镜的文化价值，传承中华优秀传统文化，展示文物修复成果，2019年我们甄选百余枚铜镜，举办了"宿州市博物馆馆藏铜镜展"，展览诠释了战国至明清时期铜镜的历史文化演变，解读铜镜的常见类别，讲述了铜镜背后的历史故事。本次展览主题鲜明，定位准确，用讲故事的方式来阐述和演绎中国古代铜镜的内涵，较好地展示了各个时代铜镜的文化特征。在展览的形式设计上，采用虚实对比提升展陈形式，用一幅幅古代照镜整妆的场景画与展出的实物做一个虚实对比，运用铜镜拓片局部放大的手法与实物展品形成虚实对比，使观众对铜镜中的纹饰有了更深刻的解读。文物与辅助展品的密切配合，新颖的艺术展示手法彰显了铜镜的历史发展过程及文化价值。除了推出铜镜专题展外，我们还精挑细选出比较具有代表性的铜镜用于常设展览的展陈提升中，目前常设展览中包含战国铜镜 2 面，汉代铜镜 50 面，隋代铜镜 1 面，唐代铜镜 6 面，宋代铜镜 4 面，辽代铜镜 1 面，元代铜镜 1 面，明代铜镜 5 面（表 7）。

　　在展陈设计中，我们注重提升展览的学术性、知识性、艺术性、普及性和可看性。根据铜镜本身特点，展览中合理使用灯光、展台、托架、标签等辅助设施，突出铜镜纹饰特点（图 15）。在展品的选用中不以

**表 7　展出铜镜概况**

| 时代 | 纹饰类别 | 数量 |
| --- | --- | --- |
| 战国 | 山字镜 | 2 |
| 汉代 | 神兽纹镜 | 10 |
| | 星云纹镜 | 3 |
| | 昭明镜 | 10 |
| | 日光镜 | 4 |
| | 家常富贵镜 | 3 |
| | 席纹镜 | 1 |
| | 长宜子孙镜 | 2 |
| | 几何纹镜 | 1 |
| | 连弧纹镜 | 3 |
| | 铭文镜 | 1 |
| | 博局纹镜 | 6 |
| | 四乳八鸟纹镜 | 3 |
| | 四乳四虺纹镜 | 3 |
| 隋代 | 双龙镜 | 1 |
| 唐代 | 花卉纹镜 | 3 |
| | 雀绕花枝镜 | 1 |
| | 双鸾双兽镜 | 2 |
| 宋代 | 玉兔捣药镜 | 1 |
| | 飞凤纹执镜 | 1 |
| | 四乳八鸟纹镜 | 1 |
| | 湖州镜 | 1 |
| 辽代 | 鱼龙变化纹镜 | 1 |
| 元代 | "马小山造"铭文镜 | 1 |
| 明代 | 八卦镜 | 1 |
| | 五子登科镜 | 2 |
| | 弦纹镜 | 1 |
| | 福寿双全镜 | 1 |

数量为标准，甄选展出纹饰清晰、时代特征突出的精品铜镜，尽量避免过多地选用纹饰重复的铜镜，防止观众审美疲劳。在知识的宣传推广上，注重展板的设计，巧妙地将铜镜的历史、制作工艺、功能及其内含的文化传达给观众。展陈提升后的铜镜板块，整体以文物本体为主，以知识宣传介绍为辅，观众只要从中看懂自己能懂的元素和意境，被其中某个知识点所吸引，就达到了展览的宣传目的和审美愉悦的效果。通过推出常设展览和临时展览，观众可以更好地了解中国古代铜镜所承载的历史信息和文化内涵，以此发挥博物馆弘扬传统文化、增强文化自信的社会功能。

图 15  《女史箴图》（局部）

　　"以铜为镜，可以正衣冠；以古为镜，可以知兴替；以人为镜，可以明得失"。铜镜不仅是人们日常生活中的照容器物，它还具有装饰居所、记事言情、祈福辟邪的作用和文化内涵。铜镜是中国宝贵历史文化遗产中的重要组成部分。铜镜虽小，却能真实地反映出古代政治、经济、思想文化、社会生活、宗教信仰等方方面面的内容，是当时社会的一个缩影，是研究古代文化的重要物质载体。以物观史，镜鉴古今，今后我们将继续对铜镜开展科学文化研究，不断发掘其文化艺术内涵，让其文化璀璨之光，永留在人们的记忆之中。衷心希望本书的出版能够引导观众深入了解中国古代铜镜文化的发展历史和文化内涵，更加深刻理解我们祖先的伟大创造力，坚定文化自信，为建设社会主义文化强国凝聚力量。

# 注释

❶ 安徽省萧县博物馆、萧县文物管理所：《安徽萧县西虎山汉墓清理简报》，《东南文化》2007年第6期（总第200期）。

❷ 安徽省文物考古研究所：《安徽萧县张村汉墓发掘简报》，《江汉考古》2000年第3期。

❸ 安徽省文物考古研究所、安徽省萧县博物馆：《萧县汉墓》，文物出版社，2008年。

❹ 安徽省文物考古研究所、宿州市文物管理所：《安徽宿州市骑路堌堆汉墓发掘简报》，《华夏考古》2002年第1期。

❺ 安徽省文物考古研究所：《萧县陈沟墓地（西区）发掘简报》，《南方文物》2013年第3期。

❻ 安徽省文物考古研究所、安徽省萧县博物馆，《安徽萧县陈沟墓群（东区）发掘简报》，《东南文化》2013年第1期（总第231期）。

❼ 安徽省文物考古研究所、安徽省萧县博物馆：《萧县汉墓》，文物出版社，2008年。

❽ 安徽省文物考古研究所、安徽省萧县博物馆：《萧县汉墓》，文物出版社，2008年，第258页。

❾ 安徽省文物考古研究所、安徽省萧县博物馆：《萧县汉墓》，文物出版社，2008年，第35页。

❿ 安徽省文物考古研究所、安徽省萧县博物馆：《萧县汉墓》，文物出版社，2008年，第129页。

⓫ 王锋钧、杨宏毅：《铜镜出土状态研究》，《中原文物》2013年第6期。

⓬ 徐殿魁：《唐镜分期的考古学探讨》，《考古学报》1994年第3期。

⓭ 管维良：《中国铜镜史》，群言出版社，2013年。

⓮ 冀和：《安徽宿州市发现的唐宋铜镜》，《华夏考古》1998年第3期。

⓯ 董亚巍：《论古代铜镜合金成分与镜体剖面几何形状的关系》，《中国历史博物馆馆刊》2000年第2期。

⓰ 《宿州市博物馆馆藏金属文物保护修复方案》，安徽博物院，2016年。

# OVERVIEW

## 1. Historical evolution of Suzhou

Suzhou is located in the hinterland of the Huanghuai Plain, in the northeast of Anhui Province, and is also the junction of Jiangsu, Shandong, Henan and Anhui provinces. Now it has jurisdiction over Dangshan County, Xiao County, Lingbi County, Si County and Yongqiao District, with a total area of 9,939 square kilometers.

The history of Suzhou can be traced back to the Neolithic period 8000 years ago, with rich prehistoric cultural relics, represented by the Xiaoshankou site and the Gutai Temple site in the early stage, and more sites in Dawenkou Culture period and Longshan Culture period. At the same time, there are several Yueshi cultural relics.

During the Shang and Zhou dynasties, Suzhou belonged to the influence of Yi, and tribes such as Huai Yi and Xu Yi thrived here. From the Western Zhou Dynasty to the Spring and Autumn Period, Suzhou was mostly a dependency of the Song Dynasty. In the 14th year of King Zhouzhuang (683 BC), the State of Song moved the State of Su, which is located in Dongping, Shandong Province, to the territory as a vassal. This is the first time that the word "Su" as a place name has entered the history of Suzhou.

Suzhou belonged to Chu in the late Warring States Period. Chu was a big country in the Jianghuai areas. After a long war with the State of Qin, the political center was gradually forced to move from west to east, and the Huai regions became its most important base. Therefore, Suzhou during the Warring States Period was deeply influenced by the Chu culture. After the unification of China, the Qin Dynasty established many counties. Most of the counties in Suzhou city belong to Sishui County, and Dangshan in the northwest belongs to Dang County.

During the Western Han Dynasty, the counties and districts of Suzhou respectively belonged to Linhuai County and Chu State of Xuzhou History Department, Liang State of Yanzhou History Department, and Pei County of Yuzhou History Department. During the Eastern Han Dynasty, Suzhou belonged to the states of Pei and Liang, and Pengcheng State and Xiapi State in Xuzhou.

Sui Dynasty unified the whole country, set up Pengcheng County and includding Fu Li County, Qi County and Xiao County; Xiaqiu County (now it is Si County); and Dangshan County, Liang County. With the prosperity of the Bian River, in the fourth year of the Tang Dynasty (809), in order to protect the grain transport of the Bianhe River, Suzhou was built, including Fuli County, Qi County and Hong County, and Suzhou also ushered in the development peak in history.

During the Five Dynasties and Ten Kingdoms, Suzhou once again fell into the division between the north and the south. In the Northern Song Dynasty, Suzhou was divided into Jingdong West Road and Huainan East Road. In the first year of Yuanyou (1086) of Song Zhezong, the town of Lingbi, which belongs to Hong County, was established as a county. In the seventh year of Song Huizong Zhenghe (1117), Lingbi County was changed into Lingbi County. At this time, Suzhou belongs to Huainan East Road, managing four counties of Fuli, Qi, Lingbi, Linhuan, while the rest of Xiao County and Dangshan belong to Xuzhou and Shanzhou of Jingdong West Road. In the 11th year of Song Gaozong(1141), Song and Jin negotiated peace, and Suzhou became the southern territory of Jin.

During the Yuan Dynasty, Suzhou belonged to Guide Prefecture and Huaian Road in northbound Henan Province and Jining Road in Zhongshu Province, in which Suzhou, Lingbi and Xiao County belonged to Guide Prefecture, Hong County belonged to Sizhou of Huaian Road, and Dangshan belonged to Jining Road. During the Ming Dynasty, Suzhou was under the jurisdiction of Nanjing District, in which Suzhou, Lingbi and Hong county all belong to Fengyang Prefecture, and Dangshan and Xiao county all belong to Xuzhou. In the sixth year of Kangxi's reign (1667), Jiangnan Province was divided into Jiangsu and Anhui provinces, and Suzhou belonged to Fengyang Prefecture of Anhui Province. In the forty-second year of Qianlong

(1777), the state was moved to Hong County, and then Hong County was abolished and merged into Sizhou. Dangshan and Xiao county are under the jurisdiction of Xuzhou Prefecture of Jiangsu Province.

Suzhou has a long history and rich cultural relics. In recent years, the archaeological cause in Suzhou has been developing rapidly and has made abundant archaeological achievements.

## 2. Discovery and research of bronze mirror in Suzhou area

In the process of the rapid economic development of Suzhou, in order to cooperate with the engineering construction, the Anhui Provincial Institute of Cultural Relics and Archaeology, the cultural relics and protection departments of Suzhou city and the counties under its jurisdiction have successively excavated a number of Han tombs, and unearthed a large number of exquisite bronze mirrors, such as:

In 1985, Longcheng found a number of ancient tombs when burning bricks and collecting soil from a kiln built at the foot of Hushan 1.5 kilometers west of Xiao County, which aroused the great attention of the local government, and promptly organized professionals to take rescue cleaning and excavation of the tomb. Excavated three sarcophagus tomb in the western Han Dynasty, unearthed 61 cultural relics, including 5 bronze mirrors.[1]

From January to April 1999, Anhui Provincial Institute of Cultural Relics and Archaeology conducted a rescue excavation of the Western Han Dynasty graveyard on the hillside in the north of Zhang Village, Baitu Town, Xiao County. A total of 22 tombs were excavated, unearthed more than 170 cultural relics, including 7 bronze mirrors. Among them, the mirror unearthed from the no. 9 tomb has nearly square lacquer chips and rotten wood traces found around it. There is another trace, one end is oval and the other end contracting into a bundle, looks like a bag which is used to hold the mirror. A bronze mirror unearthed from Tomb No.18 is located near the head, and an iron sword is placed next to the mirror.[2]

From 1999 to 2001, in conjunction with the construction of the Lianhuo Expressway, the Anhui Provincial Institute of Cultural relics and Archaeology, together with the cultural relics departments of Suzhou City and its subordinate counties, excavated the Han Dynasty tombs found in the construction of the first-line expressway in Xiao County. A total of 151 tombs of the Han Dynasty were excavated, of which 40 of them were buried with bronze mirrors, and 46 bronze mirrors were unearthed.[3]

Qilugudui is a neolithic site. In order to cooperate with the railway construction, the Provincial Institute of Cultural Relics and Archaeology carried out archaeological excavation of the site from June to July 2000, excavated 3 Han tombs, including 2 Han tombs buried with bronze mirrors, and 2 bronze mirrors were unearthed.[4]

From August to October 2010, in order to cooperate with the estate vocational construction project, the Anhui Provincial Institute of Cultural Relics and Archaeology carried out rescue excavation of ancient tombs within the scope of the construction land, cleared 63 tombs and unearthed 203 various precious cultural relics, including 2 bronze mirrors.[5]

From November 2010 to January 2011, departments excavated the eastern area of the Chengou tombs, and a total of 61 tombs were excavated, including 56 tombs in the Han Dynasty. 206 pieces of precious cultural relics were unearthed, including 2 bronze mirrors.[6]

The following is a brief analysis of the bronze mirror unearthed in Suzhou, taking the Han tombs excavated in Xiao County from 1999 to 2001 as an example[7] (Form 2).

Among the tombs, one tomb of the Han Dynasty was buried with 3 bronze mirrors, four tombs of the Han Dynasty were buried with 2 bronze mirrors, and the other tomb of the Han Dynasty were buried with 1 bronze mirror, with a total of 46 bronze mirrors were unearthed (Form 1; Fig1-3).

**Form 1  Comparison table of unearthed bronze mirrors**

| The bronze mirror unearthed in the same tomb | One bronze mirror was unearthed | Two bronze mirrors were unearthed | Three bronze mirrors were unearthed |
|---|---|---|---|
| Number of tombs | 35 | 4 | 1 |

# Form 2  Statistical table of copper mirror unearthed situation

| Number | Tomb number | Number of unearthed bronze mirrors (pieces) | Bronze mirror number | The decoration of bronze mirror | Whether there are any attachments when unearthed | The position of the bronze mirror when unearthed | remarks |
|---|---|---|---|---|---|---|---|
| 1 | XZM7 | 1 | XZM7：4 | Mirror with design of four nipples and eight animals | | | The tomb passage was disturbed and the position was moved |
| 2 | XZM8 | 1 | XZM8：3 | Bo-Ju mirror with design of interlaced hydras | | Buried with the coffin | |
| 3 | XZM9 | 1 | XZM9：15 | Mirror with design of four nipples and two dragons | There are lacquer chips marks outside the mirror | Burial with the coffin | |
| 4 | XZM11 | 1 | XZM11：3 | Mirror with design of simple interlaced hydras | The unearthed fashion in a square lacquer box, which is rotten and difficult to extract | With the burial pottery at the north end of the tomb | |
| 5 | XZM14 | 1 | XZM14：23 | Mirror with design of nebula | | Buried with the coffin, near the head | |
| 6 | XZM16 | 1 | XZM16：1 | Zhao-Ming mirror | | Burial with the coffin | |
| 7 | XZM18 | 1 | XZM18：1 | Bo-Ju mirror with design of four deities | | Buried with the coffin, near the head | |
| 8 | XFM38 | 1 | XFM38：5 | Bronze mirror | | East of the tomb | Residues into fragments |
| 9 | XFM58 | 1 | XFM58：3 | Sunlight mirror | | South end of the tomb bottom, near the head | |
| 10 | XFM65 | 1 | XFM65：5 | Bo-Ju mirror with design of four deities | | South of the tomb bottom, near the head | |
| 11 | XFM85 | 1 | XFM85:1 | Zhao-Ming mirror | | The southern end of the tomb | |
| 12 | XWM39 | 3 | XWM39：4 | Bo-Ju mirror with design of four deities | | The southern end of the tomb | |
| | | | XWM39：6 | Mirror with linked arcs desgin | | The southern part of the tomb | With the iron knife |
| | | | XWM39：13 | Mirror with linked arcs desgin | | South of the tomb | With the iron knife |
| 13 | XPM65 | 1 | XPM65：5 | Bronze mirror | | The northern part of the tomb | Residues into fragments |
| 14 | XPM66 | 1 | XPM66：3 | Zhao-Ming mirror | | Buried with the coffin, near the head | |
| 15 | XPM72 | 1 | XPM72：1 | Sunlight mirror | | Buried with the coffin, near the head | |
| 16 | XPM73 | 1 | XPM73：2 | Sunlight mirror with linked arcs desgin | | The northern part of the tomb | |
| 17 | XPM75 | 1 | XPM75：2 | Mirror with design of four nipples and eight animals | | Near the head | |
| 18 | XPM87 | 1 | XPM87：1 | Sunlight mirror with linked arcs desgin | | Northeast of the tomb | |
| 19 | XPM93 | 1 | XPM93：1 | Mirror with design of four nipples and four hydras | | The northern part of the tomb | |
| 20 | XPM94 | 1 | XPM94：1 | Mirror with design of four nipples and four hydras | | In the middle of the tomb | |

| Number | Tomb number | Number of unearthed bronze mirrors (pieces) | Bronze mirror number | The decoration of bronze mirror | Whether there are any attachments when unearthed | The position of the bronze mirror when unearthed | remarks |
|---|---|---|---|---|---|---|---|
| 21 | XPM108 | 2 | XPM108：1 | Mirror with design of grass and leaf | | North of the tomb near the head | |
| | | | XPM108：2 | Mirror with ground of cloud-thunder and design of interlaced hydras | | North of the tomb near the head | There is an iron sword next to it |
| 22 | XPM111 | 1 | XPM111：7 | Mirror with ground of cloud-thunder and design of interlaced hydras | | At the bottom of the tomb | |
| 23 | XPM112 | 1 | XPM112：6 | Bronze mirror | | At the south side of the tomb | Rusting into several pieces, irreparable |
| 24 | XPM121 | 1 | XPM121：3 | Bronze mirror | | At the south side of the tomb | Rusting into several pieces, irreparable |
| 25 | XPM128 | 1 | XPM128：1 | Mirror with design of four nipples and four hydras | | Outside the coffin, north of the tomb | |
| 26 | XPM145 | 1 | XPM145：2 | Mirror with design of grass and leaf | | Burial with the coffin | |
| 27 | XPM150 | 1 | XPM150：1 | Bo-Ju mirror with design of cloud | | Near the head | |
| 28 | XPM158 | 2 | XPM158：10 | Sunlight mirror with linked arcs desgin | | Inside the coffin, near the head | |
| | | | XPM158：1 | Sunlight mirror withlinked arcs desgin | | Inside the coffin, near the head | |
| 29 | XPM163 | 1 | XPM163：13 | Zhao-Ming mirror withlinked arcs desgin | | At the southwest side of the tomb | |
| 30 | XPM164 | 1 | XPM164：1 | Mirror with design of four leaves and interlaced hydras | | At the east side of the tomb | |
| 31 | XPM166 | 1 | XPM166：2 | Mirror with design of four nipples and two dragons | | At the east side of the tomb | |
| 32 | XPM170 | 2 | XPM170：1 | Mirror with design of nebula | | Buried with the coffin, near the head | |
| | | | XPM170：2 | Bronze mirror | | Buried with the coffin, near the head | Broken, unknown shape |
| 33 | XPM171 | 1 | XPM171：1 | Bo-Ju mirror | | The northern part of the tomb | The position is disturbed |
| 34 | XPM173 | 2 | XPM173：1 | Mirror with inscription of "Good for posterity" | | West of the bottom of the tomb | The position is disturbed |
| | | | XPM173：2 | Mirror with design of four nipples and four animals | | West of the bottom of the tomb | The position is disturbed |
| 35 | XCM3 | 1 | XCM3：2 | Bo-Ju mirror with design of four deities | | Near the head | There is an iron book knife |
| 36 | XCM4 | 1 | XCM4：10 | Zhao-Ming mirror | | Near the head | |
| 37 | XCM7 | 1 | XCM7：2 | Bo-Ju mirror | | West side of tomb chamber | With iron knife |

| Number | Tomb number | Number of unearthed bronze mirrors (pieces) | Bronze mirror number | The decoration of bronze mirror | Whether there are any attachments when unearthed | The position of the bronze mirror when unearthed | remarks |
|---|---|---|---|---|---|---|---|
| 38 | XCM11 | 1 | XCM11：1 | Zhao-Ming mirror | | Near the head | With bronze brush |
| 39 | XCM20 | 1 | XCM20：4 | Mirror with design of four nipples and four hydras | | West of the tomb | |
| 40 | XCM41 | 1 | XCM41：9 | Bronze mirror | | East of the tomb | Severe rust, the shape is unknown |
| total | There are forty tombs and forty-six bronze mirrors. | | | | | | |

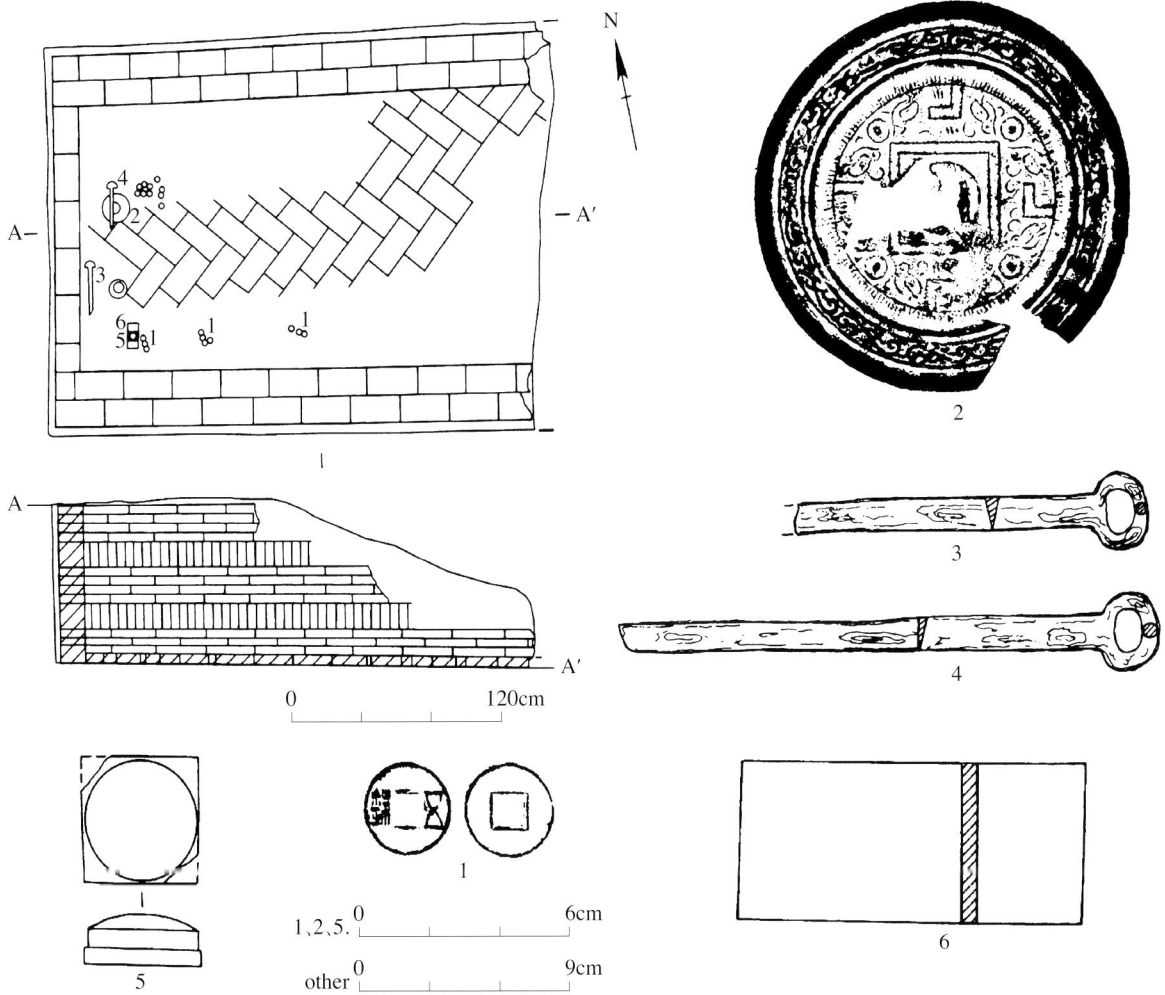

Fig.1 XCM7 Distribution map of funerary objects[8]

Southwest of the excavation area of Cheniufan tombs in the east hillside of Cheniufan village, Dulou town, Xiaoxian County, Anhui province

(Excavated in September 2000 to April 2001)

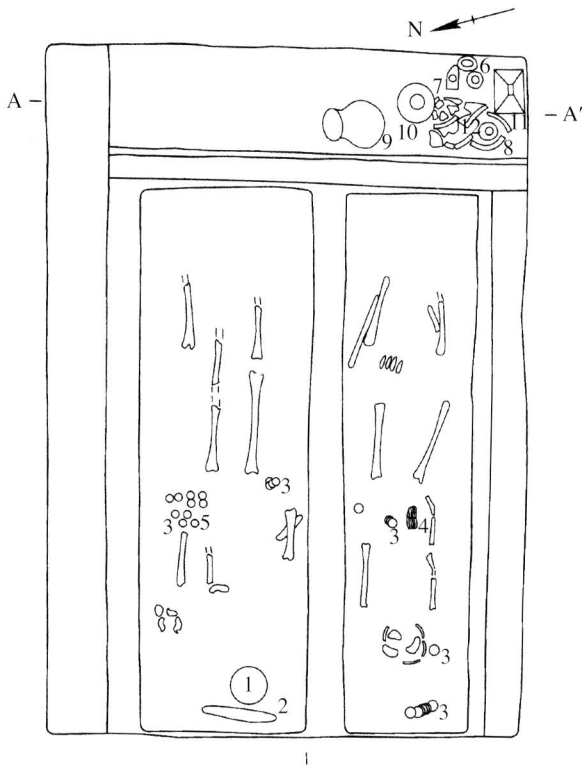

Fig.2  XZM18 Distribution map of funerary objects[9]

North of the excavation area of Zhangcun tombs in the north slope
of Zhangcun village, Baitu town, the Southeast of Xiaoxian County
(Excavated in January to April in 1999)

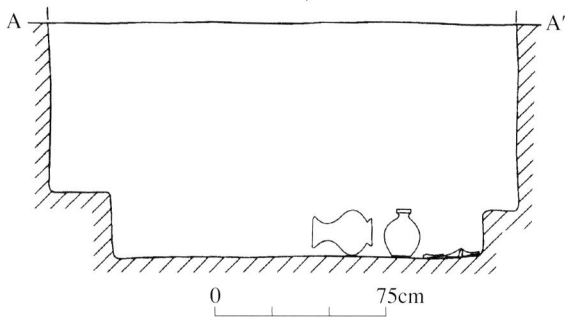

Fig.3  XPM75 Distribution map of funerary objects[10]

The middle of the excavation area of Poge tombs in the southeast hillside
of Poge village, Sunweizi town, southwest of Xiaoxian county
( December 1999 to April 2000)

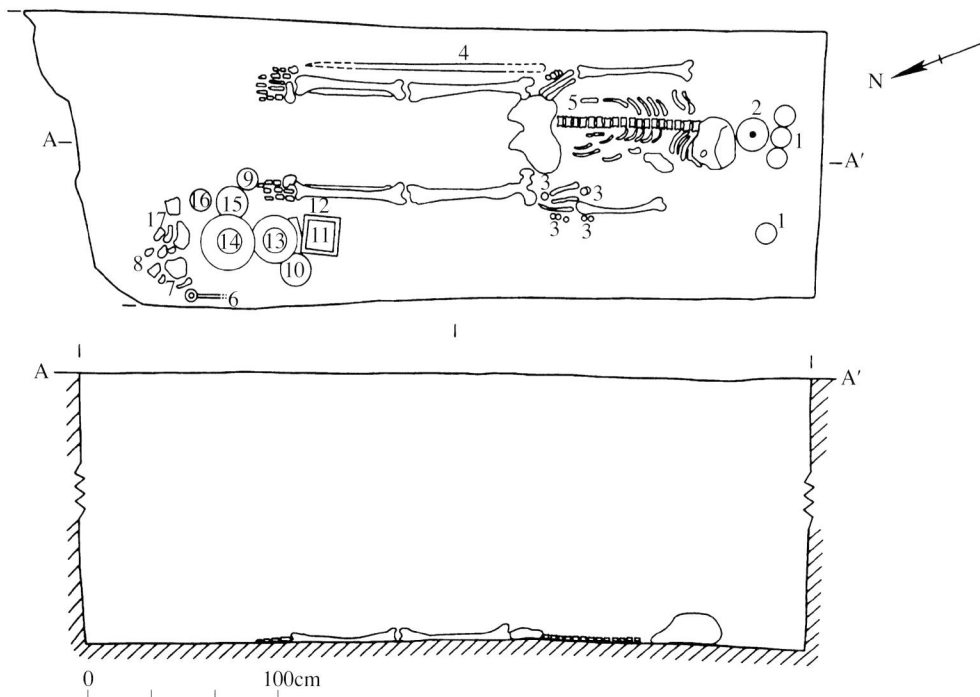

Through the analysis of archaeological materials, it is found that the bronze mirrors in the tombs are relatively fixed, most of them are buried with the coffin or near the head, a few are placed on the chest, which are also in the same way with the burial objects. Because some of the tombs were disturbed, the position of the bronze mirrors changed. Among the forty-six bronze mirrors, thirty-seven are well preserved, although the three pieces are damaged, most of them still exist, and the six pieces are seriously corroded, unable to distinguished. Most of them are exquisite, pure in color, decorated with patterns or inscriptions. Some of them are also attached with fine silk patterns such as rotten wood and cloth when unearthed (Form 3).

The ornamentation is mainly divided into 9 categories which were popular in the Han Dynasty.

The burial mode of the mirror also indirectly reflects the funeral culture and religious belief of the society at that time. At present, most of the researches on bronze mirrors focus on the ornamentation, shape and casting technology, but less research on the unearthed status of them. Mr.Wang Fengjun once published the article "Research on the Unearthed State of Bronze Mirrors". Combined with archaeological excavation and literature data, he studied the state of bronze mirrors in various periods and summarized the way of ancient placing them and the ideas, beliefs and customs reflected by the burial method. In terms of the position and method of placing bronze mirrors, he pointed out that the unearthed state of mirrors in tombs in different periods showed different characteristics. Through the research, it was found that most of them buried in all dynasties came from the coffin and relatively few outside the coffin. The bronze mirrors in the coffin are mainly distributed next to the head, chest, abdomen, crotch, waist, hands, feet, mask, coffin wall and so on. About half of them in the research are next to the head of the tomb owner. In the tombs from the Western Zhou Dynasty to the Tang Dynasty, they can also be seen at the waist side or behind the feet. In the tomb of the Han Dynasty in Jiangsu province, the deceased can be seen holding the mirror in hand or with the mirror embedded in the mask plate. It can be seen in the tombs of the Tang Dynasty and the Ming Dynasty at the back of the waist or waist pit. The position of bronze mirrors outside the coffin also has the characteristics of the times and regions, mirrors in the Chu tombs of the Warring States Period were mostly

**Form 3  Statistical table of unearthed bronze mirror decoration patterns**

| Order number | Decoration category | Number of bronze mirrors (piece) | remarks |
|---|---|---|---|
| 1 | Mirror with design of interlaced hydras | 5 | Two mirrors with ground of cloud-thunder and design of interlaced hydras, one mirror with design of four leaves and interlaced hydras, one mirror with design of simple interlaced hydras |
| 2 | Mirror with design of leaves | 2 | |
| 3 | Mirror with design of four nipples and two dragons | 2 | |
| 4 | Mirror with design of nebula | 2 | |
| 5 | Sunlight mirror | 6 | |
| 6 | Zhao-Ming mirror | 6 | |
| 7 | Mirror with design of four nipples and animals | 7 | Four mirrors with design of four nipples and interlaced hydras, one mirrors with design of four nipples and four animals, two mirrors with design of four nipples and eight animals |
| 8 | Bo-Ju mirror | 7 | Four Bo-Ju mirrors with design of four gods , one Bo-Ju mirror with design of cloud, two Bo-Ju mirrors |
| 9 | Mirror with desgin of linked arcs | 3 | Two mirrors with desgin of linked arcs, one mirror with inscription of "Good for posterity" and inked arcs pattern |
| 10 | Bronze mirror (Unknown style) | 6 | Severe rust, the shape is unknown |
| | total | 46 | |

placed in the head box, and a few in the edge box; mirrors in the the tombs of the Qin Dynasty were often placed in the middle of the head niche.

After the Han Dynasty, the bronze mirrors outside the coffin in large and medium-sized tombs were mostly placed in the tomb chamber with other burial goods, and some of them were placed under the corridor or patio. The mirror hanging on the top of the tomb is only seen in the large and medium-sized tombs in the northern areas of the Song, Liao, Jin, Yuan and Ming dynasties. After the Tang Dynasty, they were often found unearthed in the stupas. Most of them were placed separately, and some were placed together with other objects. During the Warring States Period, hooks were often found beside the mirrors in front of the head and waist of the dead in the tombs of the Qin and Chu dynasties. After the Western Jin Dynasty, some bronze mirrors in front of the tomb owner were stacked together with daggers, and some were stacked together with swords, knives and other weapons, which were common in the Jianghan area. Since the Warring States Period, the number of mirrors placed in the mirror cases, boxes or caskets in the tombs had gradually increased. Through the analysis, some mirrors were wrapped in cloth or placed in the container inside or outside the coffin, and some were hanging in front of the the hook.[1]

The unearthed state of the bronze mirrors also indirectly reflects the way the ancients usually used and placed them: one is to use silk to wrap them after the use; the other is to make special containers, such as bamboo box, lacquer box, wooden box, metal box, porcelain box, mirror box, etc., (for example, the bronze mirrors unearthed in XZM 9 and XZM 11 of the Han Tomb have traces of lacquer); the third is to frame the bronze mirrors; the fourth is to make mirror bags and carry them.

A large number of bronze mirrors unearthed in the tombs also directly show that they not only have the function of daily use, but also reflect the ancient funeral customs, folk concepts and religious beliefs. The ancients advocated that "death is like life", and used the things used by the deceased as burial objects, hoping that they could still enjoy the rich material life after they died. The mirror was also endowed with the function of exorcising ghosts and evil spirits, which was often recorded in the literature after the Han dynasty, this function was mainly reflected in the special position of the bronze mirror or in the way it was arranged with specific objects, such as placing the mirror under the entrance of the corrido patio or hanging on the wall or in combination with scissors, weapons and other collocation near the tomb master head or waist (This is also the case in the Han tomb in Xiao County. Bronze mirrors unearthed from XWM39 and XCM3 was placed with iron knives, bronze mirrors unearthed from XPM108 was placed with iron swords, and bronze mirrors unearthed from XCM7 was placed with iron knives). The ceiling with lotus pattern appeared in the tomb and the mirrors with ornamentation of Buddhist and Taoist motifs, reflected the religious belief of the tomb owner.

### 3. Overview of the bronze mirror in Suzhou Museum

Most of the bronze mirrors in Suzhou Museum are from archaeological excavations, and a few are handed over or collected by the society. So many bronze mirrors unearthed in Suzhou area is closely related to the historical development and organizational evolution. Suzhou Museum has 159 bronze mirrors. They are diverse in shape, decorated exquisitely, covering a variety of themes, as well as rich and profound inscriptions, containing the long historical period from the Warring States period to the Ming Dynasty, including 4 bronze mirrors of the Warring States period, 119 bronze mirrors of the Han Dynasty, 1 bronze mirror of the Western Jin Dynasty, 1 bronze mirror of Sui Dynasty, 9 bronze mirrors of Tang Dynasty, 12 bronze mirrors of Song Dynasty, 1 bronze mirror of Liao Dynasty, 2 bronze mirrors of Yuan Dynasty, and 10 bronze mirrors of Ming Dynasty. In terms of the number, the mirrors in the Han Dynasty had the largest number and proportion, followed by the the Tang and Song Dynasties, which also reflected the prosperity and development of the Han culture and the canal culture in the Tang and Song dynasties (Form 4).

Bronze mirror is an important category of Chinese bronze ware. After the founding of the People's Republic of China, people have paid great importance to it, many research institutions and experts and scholars have carried out professional research on the ornamentation, composition, casting technology and other contents of bronze mirror, comprehensively explained the cultural and social value contained in them.

The ancient bronze mirrors had many kinds of patterns and shapes. We divided the bronze mirrors into shape, surface,

**Form 4  overview of bronze mirror in the museum**

| Order number | Times | Number of bronze mirrors in the collection (pieces) |
| --- | --- | --- |
| 1 | Warring States | 4 |
| 2 | Han Dynasty | 119 |
| 3 | the Western Jin Dynasty | 1 |
| 4 | Sui Dynasty | 1 |
| 5 | Tang Dynasty | 9 |
| 6 | Song Dynasty | 12 |
| 7 | Liao Dynasty | 1 |
| 8 | Yuan Dynasty | 2 |
| 9 | Ming Dynasty | 10 |
| total | | 159 |

ground, knob, knob base, inner area, middle area, outer area, rim, inscription, ornamentation and other parts.

Shape: The flat shape of the mirror. Such as round, square, rectangular, octagonal, water chestnut shaped, mallow-shaped, peach-shaped, bell-shaped, like the word of "ya" shaped, round shape with a handle, flower and leaf shape with a handle, and other shapes.

Surface: The front side of the mirror. It is generally slightly convex or flat, the surface is smooth for use.

Ground: The back of the mirror.

Knob: There is a protruding object with a perforation in the center of the back of the mirror, which is called a knob. It can be used for hanging of hand holding. The common ones are arcuate shaped, bridge shaped, nippple shaped, string shaped, hemisphere shaped and so on. Bronze mirror with a handle has no knob.

Knob base: Common ones are bead shaped, circular, square, flower and leaf pattern shaped and so on.

Inner, central and outer area: the inner area near is the button; the outer area is near the edge; the middle is the central area. Some bronze mirrors are divided into different areas with cast patterns. Some mirror back is not divided into regions, with the knob as the center, with various forms of circles to form several concentric circles.

Rim: The edge of the back.

Band of inscription: The part with inscriptions on the back of the mirror.

Inscription: The words cast on the back of the mirror.

Ornamentation: The pattern cast on the back.

The casting of bronze mirror is generally made by mold casting technology. "Fan" is the mold of bronze ware, bronze mirror or copper coin. The main materials are pottery, stone and so on (Fig.4). The first step is to use wood or pottery to carve out a "mirror", and use clay and sand to make "Fan", which is made of two pieces: one is the mirror ground with the decorative pattern and knob, and the other is a flat mirror. There are holes on the mold in order to cast copper liquid and release the gas inside the mold core. After the ground of the mirror is roasted in conjunction with the surface, and the mold is repaired, "Fan" can be used to cast the liquid copper. When the liquid copper cools, the mirror will be baked out, and then after heat treatment, surface mechining, such as scraping, grinding and surface polishing treatment, it will become a smooth practical device.

The decoration technology of bronze mirror is a specialized skill. The following are the techniques commonly used in the decoration of bronze mirror:

Hollow out carving, this type of mirror is mostly in square shape. It is formed by the combination of the ground and surface of the mirror, the surface is generally bronze, and the back is molded hollow red copper, so it is called "double mirror". The bronze mirrors unearthed in the Chu tombs in Changsha, Hunan Province have the interlaced hydras desgin,

Fig.4  The method of copper coins

and the mirrors unearthed in the tombs of the early Warring States period in Peiling, Sichuan Province have the desgin of double dragons. There are also many hollowed-out mirrors have been lost abroad, decorated with interlaced hydras and other animals.

Gold and silver grinding, the materials such as gold and silver are filled into the pre-made grooves on the ground of the mirror, and then polished and smoothed. This process sprang up in the Spring and Autumn period and developed greatly in the Warring States period. The most famous grinding gold and silver mirror is the hunting pattern mirror unearthed in Jin Village, Luoyang, Henan Province.

Inlay, the ground of mirror is inlaid with turquoise, jade, colored glass and so on. The unearthed mirror in Zibo, Shandong province is 29.8 cm, with gold filled in the thick lines of cloud pattern, turquoise and 9 silver nails on the bottom. The inlaid jade and glass mirrors unearthed in Luoyang, Henan province, which have been lost abroad, are also very beautiful, with a round blue glass embedded in the middle of the ground, a plain white jade ring, and a blue glass outside the ring, the outermost is a corded jade ring.

Coloring, using colored paint to paint the pattern on the back of the bronze mirror. Several painted mirrors were unearthed from the Chu tomb in the early Warring States Period in Xinyang. There are mirrors with desgin of nebular painted in red, black and silver; mirrors with desgin of dragon painted in black, silver, gray and yellow. Square check painted mirrorss and circular check painted mirrors with cloud pattern were unearthed from the tomb of Cili Chu in Hunan province. The mirrors with desgin of four animals in the Chu tomb in Changsha, were painted with red square lines. In addition, the mirror with phoenix desgin that had been lost abroad was covered with pigments, was unearthed in Jin Village, Luoyang, Henan Province.

Gilding, gilding gold and silver is the process of plating gold and silver with mercury agent. Generally, mercury and gold powder are ground together to form a mixture, which is coated on the surface of clean copper ware and heated in a certain way, so that the mercury in the mixture agent volatile, leaving gold powder or silver powder evenly attached to the surface of the bronze.

Flat stripping of gold and silver, it refers to cutting gold and silver into the required pattern, paste it on the ground of the mirror filled with glue lacquer, then paint on it several times, carefully grindding it after drying, so that the gold and silver ornaments are flush with the lacquer surface, revealing glittering decoration.

Mother-of-pearl inlay, which is a process of using thin slices of conch shells to create the desired pattern, affixing them to objects with lacquer. The craft of mother-of-pearl inlay in China began in the Shang Dynasty, but the use in bronze mirror flourished in the Tang Dynasty.

The bronze mirror needs to be polished to shine, so the proportion of tin is higher than that of other bronze ware. From the Warring States to the Tang and Five Dynasties, they all had a high tin content; after the Song, Ming and Qing dynasties, the tin content of copper decreased and the lead increased.

<Examination of the work>: "Bronze wares have six formulations for blending the proportion of copper and tin: when tin accounts for 1/6, which is the proportion of casting bell or tripod; when tin accounts for 1/5, which is the proportion of axe making; and tin, which accounts for 1/4, is the proportion of making long weapons; when tin accounts for1/3, which is the proportion of casting heavy weapons; when tin accounts for2/5, which is the proportion of casting small weapons;

when tin accounts for1/2 can only be used for making vessels for drawing fire or water." It is said in this paper that there are six kinds of ratios of copper and tin, which can be used to make six kinds of bronzes.

Influenced by the level of economic and cultural development and local archaeological work, the research results of bronze mirror also show regional differences. At present, there are few research achievements on bronze mirrors unearthed and collected in Suzhou, the known studies related to bronze mirrors are mainly reflected in the archaeological excavation reports compiled by the Anhui Provincial Institute of Cultural Relics and Archaeology. For example, "Brief report on the excavation of Chengou Tombs (East District) in Xiao County, Anhui Province" contains four bronze mirrors; "Brief report on the excavation of Chengou Tombs (Wast District) in Xiao County, Anhui Province" contains two bronze mirrors; "Brief report on the  excavation of Xihu Mountain Han Tomb in Xiao County, Anhui Province" contains five bronze mirrors. "Brief report on the excavation of Han Tombs in Zhangcun, Xiao County, Anhui Province" contains seven bronze mirrors. "Brief report on the excavation of Han Tombs in Qilugudui, Suzhou City, Anhui Province" contains two bronze mirrors. "Briefreport on the excavation of tombs from Warring States to Han Dynasty in Qiuyuan,Suzhou City, Anhui Province" contains one bronze mirror; "Lingbi County Dali Tomb excavation brief" contains one bronze mirror, "Xiao County Han Tomb" contains forty bronze mirrors. In view of the study of mirrors in the museum, Mr.Ji He, published the article "Bronze mirrors of Tang and Song dynasties discovered in Suzhou, Anhui province" in 1998, which is a detailed cultural and artistic interpretation of the mirrors. In addition, "Suzhou Cultural Relics", "Suzhou Museum Cultural Relics Collection" also included some exquisite bronze mirrors.

To promote the culture of bronze mirror, let the public have in-depth understanding of it, and break the limitations of space and time, we are going to publish the book "Collection of Bronze Mirror of Suzhou Museum", it contains one hundred and fourteen bronze mirrors collected by Suzhou Museum, as well as ten precious bronze mirrors unearthed by Suzhou workstation of Anhui Institute of Archaeology.

The bronze mirrors included in this book began in the Warring States Period and ended in the Ming Dynasty. They are classified by time order and ornamentation. The following is a brief explanation.

**The Bronze mirror in the Warring States Period**

During the Spring and Autumn Period and the Warring States Period, due to the development of social system and productive forces, people's ideology and living customs have undergone earth-shaking changes. The bronze craft has developed rapidly, and the production scale of bronze mirrors has expanded rapidly. The development can be divided into three stages. From the middle and late Spring and Autumn Period to the early Warring States Period, the bronze mirror technology was booming, there were still many deficiencies in production techniques, mirror was small and thin in the shape, with smooth surface, flat or micro-roll edge and small knob; the decoration was relatively simple, generally using single ornamentation, there were mirrors which only used feather, cloud-thunder and other patterns. In the middle of the Warring States Period, the mirror making technology was significantly improved, and the mirrors were bigger and thicker, with simple curling edges; in the decorative techniques, the double-layer patterns were generally used, and the patterns were rich in content, which were obviously different from the initial mirrors. In the late Warring States Period, technology was relatively mature, the shape became larger and thicker, which enhanced their practicality and durability; new processes appeared, such as gold and silver grinding, hollow out carving, mosaic and so on, the production had reached a new peak. According to the ornamentation, mirrors in the Spring and Autumn and the Warring States Period can be divided into the mirror without design, the mirror with plain pattern as ground motif, the mirror with motif of leaves and flowers, the mirror with inscription of "Shan", mirror with animal patterns, mirror with desgin of linked arcs, mirror with color painting, mirror with hollow out carving, mirror with multi-knob, and so on.

This book records the bronze mirrors of the Warring States Period, including the mirror without desgin and the mirror with inscription of "Shan". The mirror without desgin appeared at the earliest and was popular for a long time. The distribution area of the mirror with inscription of "Shan" is wide, mainly concentrated in Hunan Province, Hubei Province and Anhui area, such as Lu'an, Huainan and other areas. It belongs to the typical bronze mirror of the State of Chu. The main feature is the theme decoration, which is composed of three to six oblique patterns similar to the inscription of "Shan" on the feathery background pattern. There are two kinds of inscription: left-handed and right-handed, which are evenly distributed outside the knob base, and decorated with design of petal, leaf and so on. Their shapes are round, and the knob seats are divided into square seats and round seats, and the bottom edges of most inscriptions are parallel to the four sides of the square seat. The bottom edge of a few inscriptions are arranged in a staggered angle with the four corners of the seat. The mirrors are divided into three inscriptions, four inscriptions, five inscriptions and six inscriptions, the mirror with four inscriptions of "Shan" is more common. Our museum collects the mirror with three inscriptions and five inscriptions of "Shan", all of which are round in shape, have knob with three-string design on round base, transferred from the cultural relics case and are extremely precious.

**Bronze mirror in the Han Dynasty**

In 202 BC, Liu Bang established the Han Dynasty, and China's feudal society gradually entered its heyday. During the Han Dynasty, the country was unified, the economic and cultural development were unprecedented, and the cultural exchanges were extensive. This unified social background also promoted the high progress of the mirror industry. The bronze mirrors in the early Western Han Dynasty still retained the elements of the Warring States period. Great changes had taken place in the middle and late Western Han Dynasty with many new features, such as: many of them were divided into four equals parts, with four nails as the theme decoration; the main pattern was more prominent and gradually tended to be simple, and without ground pattern; the inscription gradually became one of the important ornaments. From the end of the Western Han Dynasty to the early Eastern Han Dynasty, the vivid auspicious animals became the theme decoration, and the types of the mirrors with inscription were more various, mirrors in this period also paid more attention to the decoration of the edges, which made them more artistic. In the middle and late Eastern Han Dynasty, the bronze mirrors had a wide range of themes and complex patterns, most of which were mainly immortal animals, while portrait mirrors with storylines appeared, which produced relief techniques, and began to use axisymmetric decorative layout. The popular bronze mirrors in the Han Dynasty can be roughly divided into the following categories: mirror with design of interlaced hydras, mirror with design of serpent, mirror with design of leaf, mirror with nebula pattern, mirror with inscription, mirror with Bo-Ju pattern, mirror with linked arcs design, mirror with auspicious animal design and so on.

During the Han Dynasty, there were Fuli, Zhu, Qi, Xiao, Xiaqiu and other counties, belonging to Pei County. Pei County was the hometown of Liu Bang, Emperor Gaozu of the Han Dynasty, and was the birthplace of the Han Dynasty. There are a large number of Han Dynasty city sites and tombs in Suzhou, and many culture relics reflecting the culture of the Han Dynasty, which fully reflect the social stability, economic prosperity and people's rich life during this period.

Bronze mirror in this period is an important part of the collection in our museum. This book contains mirrors of the Han Dynasty, including the collection, archaeological excavation of Anhui Provincial Institute of Cultural Relics and Archaeology. In terms of decoration, it mainly includes mirror with design of interlaced hydras, mirror with nebula pattern, mirror Sunlight, mirror with design of four nipples and four serpents, Bo-Ju mirror, mirror with linked arcs design and so on.

The mirror with nebula pattern is widely distributed, and started in the period of Emperor Wudi of the Han Dynasty, relatively popular in the Zhaoxuan period, then declined rapidly, there are many nails similar to the star chart, which belongs to the typical high relief decorative mirror. The mirrors with nebula pattern in this book, most of them are round in shape, with a Boshan-incense-burner-shaped knob. The main pattern is divided into four areas with four dotted nails, decorated with many small nails connected by curves, the edge is composed of introverted arcs. The appearance of this mirror reflects the cognition of astronomical stars and yearning for auspicious.

Sunlight mirror has a large number and a wide range. The inscription is varied, and often separated by ᄃ patterns and ◈ patterns. The Sunlight mirrors in this book, all of which are round in shape, have a round knob on a round base, outside the base are surrounded with a band of eight linked arcs, in which the inscription is the same, each side of the the band of inscription is decorated with fine-toothed pattern.

Mirror in the type of "Zhao Ming" has a large number of unearthed, which was popular in the middle and late Western Han Dynasty. According to the size of the mirror, the inscriptions are often incomplete and separated by the word "Er". Zhao Ming mirrors in this book have the inscriptions of, "Nei Qing Yi Zhao Ming, Guang Xiang Ri Yue" (piece), which can be translated as "The quality is noble and clean and honest, the loyalty is equal to the sun and moon."

The mirrors with four nipples and four serpents desgin, which are basically the same shape, with a round knob on a round base, divided by four nails, each area with one serpent pattern, symmetrical distributed with the knob as the center. The Four nipples and Four serpents Mirror has been unearthed extensively and has been popular for a long time, from the period of Emperor Wu of Han to the early Eastern Han Dynasty. The layout of the mirror decoration is rigorous, with four nails dividing the back of the mirror into four areas, with one serpent pattern placed in each area, centered around the mirror button, connected head to tail, and symmetrically distributed.The four nipples and four serpents bronze mirror is one of the most common varieties in Han mirrors. Generally, the four nipples and four serpents mirror places serpents patterns with birds, and some also add dragon heads to the head and tail of serpents, depicting the transformation process from serpents to dragons.

Bo-ju mirror, also known as Gui-Ju mirror, the main feature is the decorative pattern with T, L, V symbols. The Bo-Ju pattern comes from the Liu-bo chess game image. In the early stage of the Western Han Dynasty, the Bo-ju mirror appeared, which was popular until the late Western Han Dynasty to the early Eastern Han Dynasty, especially in the Xin Mang period. After the middle and late Eastern Han Dynasty, the Bo-Ju pattern tended to be simplified and gradually disappeared in the early Wei and Jin Dynasties. The "TLV" pattern has special cultural connotation. First, it is endowed with the role of communication with the immortal world. Second, it reflects the unique cosmic concept of the Han Dynasty, including Yin and Yang elements, the rules and the concept of fairness. The Bo-Ju mirrors in this book (two of which are simplified Bo-ju mirrors), which are respectively matched with four gods pattern, dragon and tiger pattern, bird pattern, flying fairy and auspicious animal pattern, etc.

### Bronze mirror in the Sui and Tang Dynasties

In 581 AD, the Sui Dynasty was established and Chen was destroyed in 589 AD, ended the split between the north and the south for more than 300 years. During the Tang Dynasty, the country was unified and the politics, economy and culture developed highly, created a prosperous historical era. The mirror making industry had also entered the stage of prosperity and development. It brought a new era of Chinese bronze mirror history with its novel shapes, rich and colorful themes and exquisite casting technology.

Kong Xiangxing, Xu Diankui and other scholars have deeply studied the changes of shapes, patterns and inscriptions of the bronze mirrors in the Tang Dynasty. Especially in the stage of the development of mirror, there are three-stage theory and four-stage theory.

According to the data of bronze mirrors unearthed from Tang tombs, Xu Diankui divided the development and evolution into four periods: The first period, the early Tang Dynasty, the beginning of the seventh century to the late seventh century; the second period, the prosperous Tang Dynasty, from the first year of Guangzhai of Wu Zetian period (684) to the end of Kaiyuan of Xuanzong period (741); The third period, the mid-Tang period, from the reign of Tianbao of the Emperor Xuan Zong (742) to the last year of Zhenyuan of Dezong period (805); the fourth stage, the late Tang Dynasty, from the first year of Yuanhe of Xianzong period (806) to the fourth year of Tianyou of the Emperor Aidi period (907).[⑫]

The "three-stage period"[⑬] : The first period,from the Sui Dynasty to Gaozong of the Tang Dynasty period, was a development period, the bronze mirrors in this period continued to innovate while following the tradition. Bronze mirrors had opened a historic transformation from rigid to free realism, from complex to fresh and elegant. New mirrors and ornaments emerged one after another, and the flower bird and plant patterns in the theme decoration gradually increased. It opened the prelude to the theme of flowers and birds in the bronze mirror of the Tang Dynasty. The second period:from Tang Gaozong to Tang Dezong, the Tang style mirror gradually developed and matured, and it was also another period of prosperity in the history of Chinese bronze mirrors. In form, the bronze mirror broke through the tradition of round and square, and fancy mirrors such as flower of water chestnut shaped mirror and mallow-shaped mirror appeared; in the decoration, a large number of character stories emerged, and the artistic expression techniques and styles were diversified. The third period: from Tang Dezong to the late Tang and Five dynasties, bronze mirrors declined sharply. The plant patterns of bronze mirrors in this period were simple and rough, and religious ornamentation prevailed. In addition to circular mirrors, square mirrors were also popular in shape, thin lines were carved shallowly or carved the back into patterns in techniques.

In the Sui and Tang dynasties, there were many kinds of bronze mirrors with complex patterns and various shapes. The popular ones were mirror with design of four gods and twelve Symbolic Animals, mirror with design of auspicious animals and grapes, mirror with flowers and birds design, mirror with eight diagrams design, mirror with gold and silver flat stripping, mirror with Mother-of-pearl inlaid and so on.

The Sui and Tang dynasties was a very important period of high economic and cultural prosperity and development in the history of Suzhou. In 605 AD, Emperor Yang of the Sui Dynasty "mobilized more than one million of men and women in the counties to open the TongJi canal". This waterway turned from Kaifeng to the southeast, along Qixian, Suixian, Shangqiu, Yongcheng, and through Suixi, Yongqiao, Lingbi, Sixian, to Xuyi in Jiangsu Province to enter the Huaihe River. During the Tang Dynasty, people called the Tongji Canal as "Bian He", "Bian Shui" or "Bian Qu", the flow of people and goods was very large because of the wide range of the canal. Suzhou was the only way through the Bian canal in the Tang Dynasty. Prime Minister Li Bi once spoke up twice, emphasized its important position as the throat of grain transport. With the  important position of Bian canal between north and south, the economy of Suzhou gradually prospered. In the 14th year of Dali period of Daizong in the Tang Dynasty (779 AD), Liu Yan carried out the reform of salt and iron official camp. He set up four major salt farms, ten supervisoryorganizations and thirteen inspectorate organizations in the country, and Suzhou was one of the thirteen inspectorate organizations. Accordingly, the Tang Dynasty collected taxes, money, and materials from the local people and past merchants to strengthen the management of grain and salt transport. During the reign of Emperor Dezong of the Tang Dynasty, in order to protect the transportation materials from being looted, Zhang Wanfu was dispatched to garrison Haozhou and to defend the troops to protect the Yongqiao town. With the opening of the Tongji Canal, the Yongqiao town was unable to bear its responsibility. In order to prevent the harassment and protect the water transport, in AD 809, Fuli County and Qi County which belonged to Xuzhou、 Hong County which belonged to Sizhou, were cut out and established Suzhou. Suzhou was originally located in Hong (now is Si County), in order to protect water transport, it was moved to Yongqiao in AD 833, which made Yongqiao not only an important town for the transportation from the south to the north, but also once became the bustling ferry and the battleground for soldiers. In 868, Pang Xun rose up, captured Suzhou, and captured 300 large ships to enlarge his strength. At that time, such a large number of ships showed that Suzhou had developed into a metropolis, and Yongqiao was also a large port and wharf on the Bian canal. "Ships meet here, vehicles go through " reflected the importance of Suzhou in the Tang Dynasty. The prosperity and development of economy and culture had greatly improved the manufacturing technology of bronze mirror, and broke through in the shape, with novel styles and rich themes. After the prosperity of the Tang Dynasty, the patterns were mainly flowers, mostly were auspicious patterns, showing the vigorous and upward mental outlook of the Tang Empire. The bronze mirrors of the Tang Dynasty collected in our museum are a strong demonstration of the prosperity of the Tang Dynasty.

This book contains eight pieces of mirrors of Tang Dynasty, mainly with flowers and birds as the theme, including animals and grapes pattern, phoenixes with ribbon pattern, birds pattern and so on. There are in round shape, sunflower shape or diamond shape.

The mirror with design of auspicious animals and grapes, which decoration is complex, with clear layers and precise depiction from the center to the edge of the mirror. The ornamentation is mainly composed of the auspicious animal and grape vine and fruit, separated by a convex edges and divided into two areas. The mirror uses high relief technique to make the ornamentation fluctuate, The auspicious animals and birds have different postures. The pattern shows the absorption and accommodation of foreign cultures in the Tang Dynasty, the auspicious animals expresses the meaning of luck, and the grapes are endowed with the symbolic meaning of multiple children, reproducing the strong cultural atmosphere of the Tang Dynasty. Although the mirrors included in this book has a zoning in shape, the free combination of ornamentation appears to be integrated, showing a radial shape from the center to the periphery.The mirrors are partially corroded, it can still be clearly seen that the animals are running and jumping, echoing with the butterflies and birds in the outer area, which making the visual effect stretch from the center to the periphery, showing an extension from real to virtual.

This book collects three mirrors with design of double phoenixes and double animals. Roughly the same in shape, with eight-petal mallow shaped, have round knob or arch knob on the eight-petal lotus shaped base. Two phoenixes flutter their wings to face the knob. Two animals are distributed up and down with the knob as the center. The auspicious animals above are similar to those below, but in fact they are different. The auspicious animal above has a horn on its head and the below looks like a lion. Both auspicious animals are running to the right. The phoenix with ribbon is a popular pattern in the Tang Dynasty. It is common for two phoenixes to fly relative to each other, with long ribbons tied to the mouth. "Luan" is a symbol of auspicious birds in Chinese folk tradition. The "long ribbon" symbolizes "longevity", and ribbons tied with the knot indicating that they are of one mind forever.

Mirror with design of sparrows winding flower branches is a popular type in the Tang Dynasty, mostly is in shape of flower of water chestnut, and the knob is arranged by four birds in the same direction, during which decorated with flower branches. The mirror in this book shows that birds are two finches and two geese, decorated with flowers and buds, and branches with bee and butterfly near the edge, which are fresh and simple.

The mirror with Baoxiang flowers desgin was one of the most representative bronze mirrors in the Tang Dynasty, with gorgeous style and beautiful symbolic meaning, and was deeply loved by people. Baoxiang flowers desgin generally refers to the "the artistic treatment of some natural flowers into a decorative flower pattern", the lotus, peony, rose and other flowers are artistically treated into a variety of flower patterns with different images. The popularity of this pattern was inseparable from the prevalence of Buddhism and social background at that time. Before the founding of Buddhism in India, the lotus was regarded as sacred object by ancient Indian people. After Buddhism came born, people compared the natural attributes of lotus with the teachings and rules of Buddhism, gradually formed the worship of lotus, and compared many beautiful and holy things to lotus. After the introduction of Buddhism into China, the lotus pattern gradually evolved into the Baoxiang flowers pattern. Lotus is a classic image in Buddhist art, which not only has the thought of Buddhist lotus transformation, but also combined with traditional auspicious meaning, and has achieved great development in China. The proseperity of the mirror reflected the change of appreciation concept in the Tang Dynasty. This book includes one mirrors with Baoxiang flowers desgin, petal patterns on the knob base, six flowers of two different shapes are arranged alternately, it has a rim without design.

After the fall of the Tang Dynasty, Chinese history entered the Five Dynasties and Ten Kingdoms, Song, Liao, Jin and Yuan dynasties, during this period, the historical situation was complicated, political and economic development was unbalanced, and the bronze mirror industry began to declined gradually.

**Bronze mirror in the Song and Liao Dynasties**

In the Song Dynasty, the bronze mirror was in a slow development stage. From the Five Dynasties to the period of Song Yingzong, it followed the imitation of the bronze mirror of the Tang Dynasty, and the mirror was relatively thin. The period from Song Shenzong to the end of the Northern Song Dynasty was a short period of development, the quality of bronze mirrors was improved, and the decoration was relatively delicate. In the Southern Song Dynasty, the bronze mirror was in the decline of the decorative art, emphasizing practicality but not the pattern, most of the inscription were manufacturer's trademark; the shape was in a period of innovation, in addition to the common round, square, flower of water chestnut, mallow shapes, there were also some special shapes, such as shield-shaped, bell-shaped, tripod-shaped, long strip-shaped, fan-shaped, bottle-shaped and so on. The mirror of the Song Dynasty had three characteristics: diverse shapes; the subject matter was concentrated, including flowers and plants, fairy stories with religious background, and inscriptions in poems; there were numerous bronze mirrors with inscriptions of brand name.

During the Northern Song Dynasty, Suzhou area was relatively stable, with developed transportation and prosperous economy, which had developed into one of the prosperous capitals on the Bianhe River. During the Southern Song Dynasty, the Song and Jin dynasties faced off and caused frequent disturbances. In the eleventh year of Shaoxing (AD 1141), the Song and Jin discussed harmony, with the Huai River as the boundary, and Suzhou was under the rule of the State of Jin. In the year Longxing of the Song Dynasty (AD 1163), the war between the Song and Jin dynasties broke out, the Song army recovered Lingbi and Hong county and entered Suzhou. They fought with the Jin army in Fuli for several months, and were finally defeated and forced to make peace, which was known as "Longxing Harmony" in history. After that, the Song and Jin dynasties had maintained peace for more than 40 years. The monument of Zhanchen Building found in Suxian Library in the 1980s recorded that Suzhou under the rule of Jin Dynasty was "The government listens to the voices of the people, and everything is waiting for prosperity".

This book contains nine bronze mirrors in the Song Dynasty, which are divided into mallow-shaped, round, mirror with handle. The decoration is simple, mainly for mirror without design, mirror with design of bow string, mirror with Jade Hare pattern and mirror with inscription of "Hu Zhou".

The shape of the mirror with Jade Hare smashes medicine design is small, under the laurel tree, a rabbit stands on a long stone bench like a man, tilting a tail and pounding medicine. The decoration vividly shows the myth widely spread in the folk. The mirror knob is different from the others included in this book, it has two half-ring knobs, located near the edge. This mirror is basically the same as the mirror in Hunan museum, except that the mirror in Hunan museum is integrated with the bracket below it, we can judge that the mirror in our museum, should also be fixed on a three-legged support at that time.

Mirror with inscription of "Hu Zhou" is one of the most popular mirrors in the Song Dynasty and its name is closely related to the decorative features. The back of the mirror is inscribed with the words "Hu Zhou", indicating that it was produced in Huzhou. Huzhou was a famous mirror making center with many casting shops and skilled craftsmen in the Song Dynasty. This mirror in the Song dynasty is characterized by simple ornamentation, which is different from the complex pattern of the Han and Tang dynasties. It has various shapes, but the back is mostly without design, and generally cast with workshop and commercial inscriptions, a few of it engraved with auspicious words such as "longevity and wealth", confirming the characteristics of the commercialization of Huzhou mirror. This book includes two mirrors from Huzhou. One is round in shape, and there is a rectangular frame on both sides of the ingot-shaped knob, with the inscription of "Huzhou Sun Jia Qing Luan Bao Jian", which is regular in shape.The other is in shape of six-petal mallow and has inverted ingot shaped small round knob without base, and no patterns on the back. On the right side of the knob, there are two inscriptions "Huzhou Zhen Shi Jia, Nian Er Shu Zhao Zi", which looks like a rectangular stamp, the left edge of the knob has a slender intaglio "Xuzhou inspector". According to the records in the History of the Jin Dynasty and the archaeological materials, people implemented a very strict policy of copper, and bronzes could only be used after being recorded by the government. According to the inspection record of Xuzhou local government on this mirror, it is proved that it was marketed by the southern casting mirror business to the north, which shows the strong sales momentum in the market at that time.[①]

Most of the mirror craftsmen in the Liao Dynasty came from the north of the Central Plains, so the style of most bronze mirrors were consistent with those of the Five Dynasty and Song Dynasty, while a few had their own national characteristics of the Liao state, such as the Khitan literary mirror. The Jin Dynasty made a sudden rise in the production of bronze mirrors, while imitating the Tang mirror and Song mirror, it also innovated some unique decorations, the popular mirrors mainly included double-fish mirror, historical Fig.story mirror, coiling dragon mirror, auspicious animal mirror and auspicious flower mirror.

This book contains a fish-dragon change mirror with a handle in the shape of lotus in the Liao Dynasty. The pattern is based on the legend of carp leaping over Dragon Gate, is a traditional Chinese auspicious pattern. The imperial examination often called "leaping lover Dragon Gate", "jumping Dragon Gate", the popularity of this pattern also has a certain relationship with this desire.

**Bronze mirror in the Yuan Ming and Qing Dynasties**

The Yuan, Ming and Qing dynasties were the decline stage of bronze mirrors. The gold and silver processing level of the Yuan Dynasty was relatively high, but the mirror industry was backward, casting technology was rough. In the Ming Dynasty, with the prosperous development of economy and handicraft industry, the improvement of mining and metallurgical technology and the reform of the craftsman system, the mirror industry achieved great development. This period was the relatively prosperous stage of bronze mirror development in the Yuan, Ming and Qing Dynasties. The bronze mirror in this time was not only a necessary product in life, but also had the functions of blessing and ward off evil spirits. While inheriting the tradition, the bronze mirror of the Ming Dynasty was also innovated in the ornamentation and inscriptions. In addition, a large number of archaistic mirrors were also popular in the Ming Dynasty, mainly imitating the bronze mirrors of the Han and Tang dynasties. The bronze mirror of the Ming Dynasty had various forms, such as the flat-top cylindrical shaped knob and the silver ingot shaped knob. The flat-top cylindrical was a new shape appeared in the Ming Dynasty, which was often stamped by a mirror craftsmen or workshop, in addition to the traditional contents such as dragon, fish, flower, character story, auspicious patterns and characters became the most distinctive themes in this period. In the middle and late Qing Dynasty, it was gradually replaced by the glass mirror.

During the Ming and Qing dynasties, casting technology not only followed the tradition but also innovated, especially new patterns and inscriptions, reflecting the social mentality and cultural information at that time. With the popularity of glass mirrors, bronze mirrors gradually lost daily use function, mostly used as a mascot to ward off evil spirits and express blessings. This book includes ten bronze mirrors of the Ming Dynasty, mainly including mirror without design, mirror with design of bow string, mirror with inscription of blessing, mirror with inscription of "Wu Zi Deng Ke".

Blessing words were popular decoration on the mirror in the Ming Dynasty. The inscription was distributed around the mirror knob, the font was usually large and neat, mainly used regular script and seal script. In addition to the contents of longevity and wealth, a large number of new auspicious languages related to the imperial examination also appeared, reflecting the prosperity of the imperial examination system. The mirror with inscription of "Wu zi Deng ke" was a new category appeared in the Ming Dynasty, which was a reflection of the imperial examination policy at that time. "Wu zi Deng ke" was originally a Chinese proverb derived from folk stories, in the Five Dynasties, the five sons of Dou Yujun were both won the civil examinations successively, hence the name of "Wu Zi Deng ke". It later became a traditional Chinese auspicious pattern, which expressed the good wish for the high offical.

## 4. Protection and utilization of bronze mirrors in the museum

With the development of history and social productivity, the shape, ornamentation, casting technology and the metal composition of mirror also has the characteristics of times. The scientific experiments show that the ancient bronze mirror is a alloy of copper、 tin and lead. If only use copper to cast the mirror, the mirror is red and the surface is blurred. With the increasing content of tin, the color will change from red to yellow and white, when the tin content increases to about 24%, the mirror is brilliant enough to use. The mirrors from Qijia culture to Yinxu cultural belonged to the initial stage, and the ratio of alloy had not formed a standard. After entering the middle of western Zhou Dynasty, the proportion of alloy gradually became regular and tends to mature. The alloy in the Shang and Zhou dynasties was mainly red copper, with little tin and lead, red copper was easy to rust, so most of the copper mirrors in this period were corroded. From the Spring and Autumn Period to the Warring States Period, the alloy ratio of mirrors and the casting technology had been fully mature, the mirrors had high copper content, low tin content and unfixed lead. The technology of high tin bronze was maintained from to Han Dynasty to the late Tang Dynasty. The copper mirror alloy composition of the Han Dynasty was relatively stable, and proportion of tin was higher, so it's more brittle and hard. The bronze mirrors of the Tang Dynasty were silvery white, which were thicker than those in the Han Dynasty, and the proportion of alloy remained basically unchanged. The tin content of the bronze mirror in the Song Dynasty decreased significantly, the lead content increased, and the proportion of zinc increased, so the texture of the mirror was thinner and lighter than it in the Tang Dynasty. After the Song Dynasty, a large amount of lead was added to the mirror, and a amount of zinc was added to the mirror in the Ming Dynasty, which no longer belonged to high tin bronze.[1]

In order to protect, publicize and display our city's history and culture, and make full use of the collection resources, from 2015 to 2016, Suzhou Museum applied for the protection and restoration of 240 pieces (sets) of metal relics. These cultural relics were collected and excavated over the years, including ceremonial instruments, weapons, utensils, bronze mirrors and so on, spanning from the Warring States Period to the Qing Dynasty. They were precious physical materials to study the ancient political, economic and cultural development in Suzhou area. Due to the long age and poor preservation conditions after excavation, most of these bronzes were corroded and broken, and had varying degrees of diseases, a considerable part of them had gradually become endangered and were in urgent need of protection and repair. To this end, Suzhou Museum entrusted Anhui Museum Cultural

Relics Science and Technology Protection Center and Jingzhou Cultural Relics Protection Center to undertake the preparation of the bronze protection plan. On the basis of preliminary research, according to the relevant laws and regulations, we had determined the protection and restoration target and technical route, compiled the "Protection and Restoration of Metal Cultural relics in Suzhou Museum" to guide the protection work, to achieve the requirements of storage and display, and play a reference for the future protection and restoration of cultural relics. The key restoration object of this project was the bronze mirror. In the process of repair, we applied the right remedy to the different damage of each artifact, on the basis of scientific analysis on the diseases of cultural relics, a variety of technical methods were adopted to clean rust and correct, inhibit corrosion, sealing treatment. Considering the particularity of individual cultural relics and unforeseeable unfavorable factors, we organized experts to hold consultation meeting in the implementation process to fully grasp the feasibility and operability of technology.

In order to ensure the scientific, standardization and rigor of the repair work, in August 2015, Anhui museum sent professional and technical personnel to Suzhou, to investigate、 survey and draw the relics, and collected some samples, which were sent to the Department of Science and Technology History and Archaeology of the University of Science and Technology of China for scientific analysis, and issued analysis report. The analysis items mainly include ultra-depth microscope, XRF, XRD （Form 5; The following test analysis data are from *Conservation and restoration plan for the metal relics of Suzhou Museum*[16]).

Optical microscopic analysis: the rust layer and corrosion degree of metal samples were observed by ultra-depth microscopic optical system at 100 times, through observation, it was found that the rust was layered and had a large number of pollutants or hard junction on the surface, some samples were even mineralized (Fig.5-10).

**Form 5**

| Name | Picture | Characteristic | Test project |
|---|---|---|---|
| Bronze mirror fragment of Song dynasty | | The sample is bronze, the corrosion is serious, and the rust is mostly green and brown. | 1. ultra-depth microscope<br>2. XRF<br>3. XRD |
| Bronze mirror fragment of Tang dynasty | | The sample is bronze with black rust. | |
| Bronze mirror fragment | | The sample is bronze, the corrosion is serious, and the rust is mostly green and black. | |

Fig.5 The Video micrograph of copper rust layer of sample of SZ1687

Fig.6 The Video micrograph of copper rust layer of sample of SZ1687

Fig.7 The Video micrograph of copper rust layer of sample of SZ1688

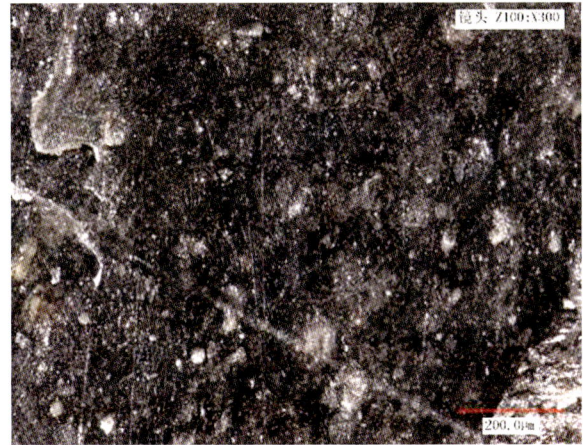

Fig.8 The Video micrograph of copper rust layer of sample of SZ1688

Fig.9 The Video micrograph of copper rust layer of sample of SZ1692

Fig.10 The Video micrograph of copper rust layer of sample of SZ1692

## Form 6  XRF analysis of bronze mirror samples

| Element contene<br>Number | Cu（mt） | Pb（mt） | Sn（mt） |
|---|---|---|---|
| SZ1687 | 75.07% | 4.43% | 20.51% |
| SZ1688 | 67.40% | 29.27% | 3.34% |
| SZ1692 | 66.42% | 5.63% | 27.95% |

XRF: It's used to analyze the elements and content of metal samples to understand the composition and production process of metal cultural relics. We conducted nondestructive analysis on the surface or section of the sample, collected the data of 3 points for each sample, and the analysis time of each point was 60s. Only the main quantity element information was retained, so as to judge the proportion of Cu, Pb and Sn in each sample (Form 6).

XRD: using XRD to analyze the structure of rust products in metal samples, to clear the disease status, and provide basic data for the protection and restoration. By the detection, we found that the main corrosions in the sample were $Cu_2O$, CuO, $CuCO_3 \cdot Cu(OH)_2$, CuCl, $PbCO_3$. Optical metallographic detection, use metallographic microscope to observe the sample and analyze its metallographic structure, estimate its preservation status and speculate the production process. Through the detection and analysis of the cultural relic samples, provides a scientific basis for the implementation of the next restoration work (Fig.11-13).

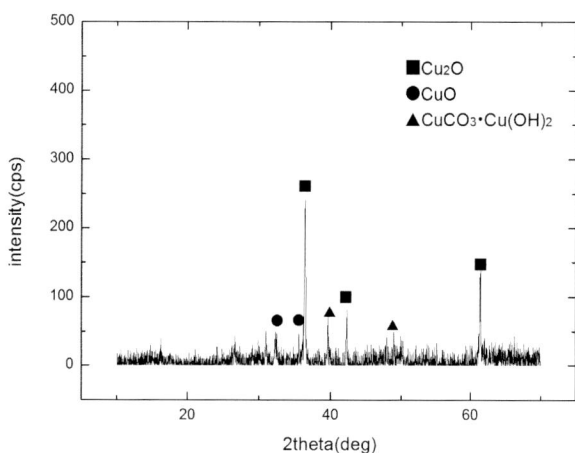

Fig.11  SZ1687 XRD phase analysis diagram

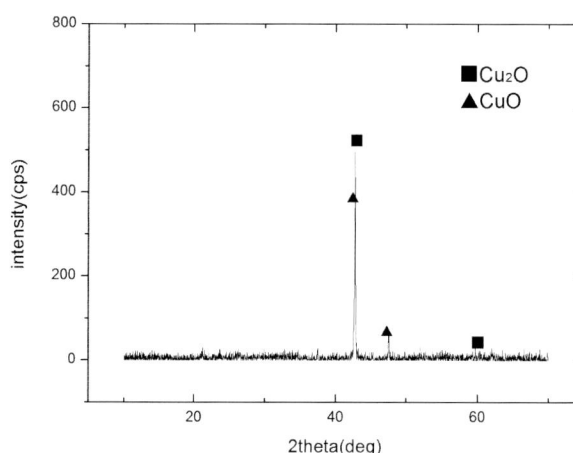

Fig.12  SZ1688 XRD phase analysis diagram

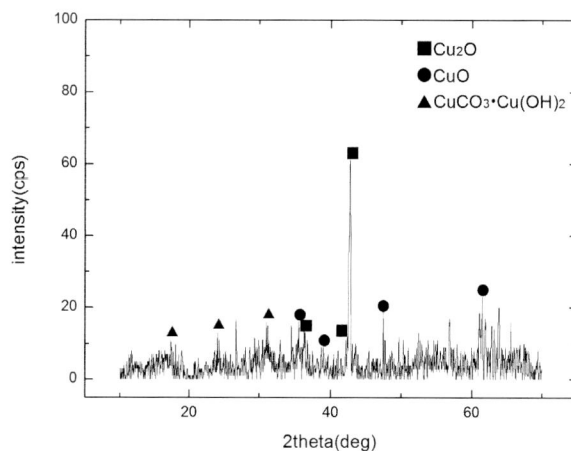

Fig.13  SZ1692 XRD phase analysis diagram

In the implementation of restoration work, we strictly implemented the technical requirements in the plan, did not overhaul the problems that can be solved by minor repairs, did not expand the scope of protection and restoration, and used chemical reagents prudently. The technical route of restoration was scientific, and the materials were safe and reversible. According to the preservation status of cultural relics, welding (bonding), filling gaps and coloring were carried out on the basis of respecting the original tone, so that coordinated the visual effect between the restoration part and the original part. After restoration and rust removal, the covered high-quality ornamentations were showed out, which enriched the the exhibition content, and provided a strong support to carry out historical and cultural research (Fig.14).

Before repair                                        After repair

Fig.14 Comparison before and after repair

In order to facilitate the long-term preservation of cultural relics and consolidate the achievement of protection, we equipped acid-free paper for the restored relics, and used the humidifying materials such as discolored silica gel to control cabinets to create a stable environment. In the management of the environment, through the installation of air conditioning system, temperature and humidity control equipment to control the temperature and humidity. The deterioration is a natural law, and any intervention measures only slow the speed of its transformation, and cannot be done once and for all. The protection work only weakens the harmful factors to a certain extent, and its preservation condition is still closely related to environment, the disease state is still changing all the time, and the protection materials also have environmental applicability and aging problems. Therefore, the maintenance work is particularly important. It is a long-term and important task for us to strengthen the daily maintenance of cultural relics and make rational use of cultural relics resources.

As one of the common daily utensils in ancient times, the bronze mirrors can intuitively reflect the imagination of the ancients, the economic situation and cultural appearance of the society. The decoration has a vivid mark in different historical periods, and its development is also the epitome of excellent traditional Chinese culture full of vitality. In order to enhance the utilization of cultural relics resources, inherit Chinese excellent traditional culture, and display the achievements of cultural relics restoration, we selected hundreds of bronze mirrors in 2019 and held the "Exhibition of Bronze Mirrors in Suzhou Museum", the exhibition interpreted the history and cultural evolution of mirrors from the Warring States to the Ming and Qing dynasties, and the common categories of bronze mirror, presented the historical story behind the bronze mirror. The exhibition had a distinct theme, with the way of storytelling to explain and deduce the connotation of ancient Chinese bronze mirrors, and showed the cultural characteristics of the bronze mirrors of various times. In the form design of the exhibition, the comparison between the virtual and the real was adopted to enhance the exhibition form, and the paintings of the ancients using mirror were compared with the real objects on display, so that the audience had a deeper interpretation of the ornamentation in the bronze mirror. With the close cooperation of cultural relics and auxiliary exhibits, and the artistic display techniques, highlighted the historical development process and cultural value of the bronze mirror. In addition to launching the temporary exhibition, we have also selected representative bronze mirrors for permanent exhibition, the permanent exhibition contains two bronze mirrors of the Warring States period, fifty bronze mirrors of the Han Dynasty, one bronze mirror of the Sui Dynasty, six bronze mirrors of the Tang Dynasty, 1 bronze mirror of the Song Dynasty, one bronze mirror of the Yuan Dynasty, five bronze mirrors of the Ming Dynasty (Form 7).

Form 7  Overview of bronze mirrors on exhibition

| Times | Decoration category | Quantity |
|---|---|---|
| Warring States | Mirror with inscription of "Shan" | 2 |
| Han Dynasty | Mirror with mythical animals design | 10 |
| | Nebula design | 3 |
| | Zhao-Ming mirror | 10 |
| | Mirror with inscription of "Sunlight mirror" | 4 |
| | Mirror with inscription of "Homely riches and honour" | 3 |
| | Mirror with desgin of mat | 1 |
| | Mirror with inscription of "Good for posterity" | 2 |
| | Mirror with desgin of geometric | 1 |
| | Linked arcs | 3 |
| | Mirror with inscription | 1 |
| | Gambling desgin Bo-Ju patterns | 6 |
| | Mirror with design of four nipples and eight birds | 3 |
| | Mirror with design of four nipples and four serpents | 3 |
| Sui Dynasty | Mirror with two dragons desgin | 1 |
| Tang Dynasty | Mirror with design of flowers | 3 |
| | Mirror with design of interlocking flowers and birds | 1 |
| | Mirror with doubble phoenixes and auspicious animals | 2 |
| Song Dynasty | Mirror with desgin of jade rabbit pounding medicine | 1 |
| | Mirror with motif of phoenix | 1 |
| | Mirror with design of four nipples and eight birds bird | 1 |
| | Huzhou mirror | 1 |
| Liao Dynasty | Mirror with design of fish and dragon | 1 |
| Yuan dynasty | Mirror with inscription of "Made by Ma Xiaoshan" | 1 |
| Ming Dynasty | Mirror with design of the Eight Diagrams | 1 |
| | Mirror with inscription of "Five sons passing the imperial examination" | 2 |
| | Mirror with design of string | 1 |
| | Mirror with inscription of "Happiness and longevity" | 1 |

We pay attention to improving the academic nature, knowledge, artistry, popularity and visibility of the exhibition. According to the characteristics of the mirror, the auxiliary facilities such as lights, booths, brackets and labels reasonably used in the exhibition to highlight characteristics of the ornamentation (Fig15). We select bronze mirrors with clear patterns and prominent characteristics of the times, so as to avoid repeated patterns and prevent the aesthetic fatigue of the audience. In the promotion of knowledge, we pay attention to the design of the exhibition boards, and skillfully convey the history, production technology, function and culture of the mirrors to the audience. After the promotion, the bronze mirror exhibition is mainly based on cultural relics, supplemented by introduction, as long as the audiences understand the elements and artistic conception they can understand, and attracted by some points, it has achieved the publicity purpose and aesthetic pleasure. Through the introduction of permanent and temporary exhibitions, audiences can better understand the historical information and cultural connotation of ancient mirrors, so as to give full play to the social function of the museum to carry forward the traditional culture and enhance the cultural confidence.

Fig.15 Admonitions Scroll

"With bronze as the mirror, you can dress properly; with history as the mirror, you can know the rise and falls; with people as the mirror, you can see the gains and losses." Bronze mirror is not only used in Daily life, but also has the function of decorating residence, praying for fortune and repelling evil. It is an important part of Chinese precious historical and cultural heritage. Although it's small, it can truly reflect the ancient politics, economy, ideological culture, social life, religious belief and so on. It is an epitome of the society at that time and an important material carrier for the study of ancient culture. In the future, we will continue to carry out scientific and cultural research on the bronze mirror and explore its cultural and artistic connotation, so that it will remain in people's memory forever. We sincerely hope that the publication of this book can guide the audiences to have a deep understanding of the development history and cultural connotation of the ancient Chinese bronze mirror, better understand the great creativity of our ancestors promote traditional culture, strengthen cultural confidence.

# Notes

❶ Xiaoxian Municipal Museum of Anhui Province, Xiaoxian County Heritage Management Institute: *Excavation of Han tombs at Xihu Mountain, Xiaoxian County, Anhui province*, *Southeast Culture* Issue 6, 2007(Total No.200).

❷ Institute of Culture Relics and Archaeology of Anhui Province: *Excavation of Han tombs at Zhangcun, Xiao County, Anhui province*, *Jianghan archaeology*, Issue 3, 2000.

❸ Institute of Culture Relics and Archaeology of Anhui Province, Xiaoxian Municipal Museum of Anhui Province: *Han Tombs in Xiaoxian County*, 2008.

❹ Institute of Culture Relics and Archaeology of Anhui Province, Suzhou Heritage Management Institute: *Excavation of the Han tomb at Qilugudui, Suzhou, Anhui Province*, *Chinese Archaeology*, Issue 1, 2002.

❺ Institute of Culture Relics and Archaeology of Anhui Province: *Excavation Report of Chan Gou Cemetery (Western District), Xiaoxian County*, *Southern Antiquities*, Issue 3, 2013.

❻ Institute of Culture Relics and Archaeology of Anhui Province, Xiaoxian Municipal Museum of Anhui Province: *Excavation Report of the Chengou tomb complex (Eastern District) in Xiaoxian County, Anhui province*, *Southeast Culture* Issue 1, 2013(Total No. 231).

❼ Institute of Culture Relics and Archaeology of Anhui Province, Xiaoxian Municipal Museum of Anhui Province: *Han Tombs in Xiaoxian County*, 2008.

❽ Institute of Culture Relics and Archaeology of Anhui Province, Xiaoxian Municipal Museum of Anhui Province: *Han Tombs in Xiaoxian County*, 2008, Page 258.

❾ Institute of Culture Relics and Archaeology of Anhui Province, Xiaoxian Municipal Museum of Anhui Province: *Han Tombs in Xiaoxian County*, 2008, Page 35.

❿ Institute of Culture Relics and Archaeology of Anhui Province, Xiaoxian Municipal Museum of Anhui Province: *Han Tombs in Xiaoxian County*, 2008, Page 129.

⓫ Wang Fengjun, Yang Hongyi: *Study on the unearthed state of Copper Mirror*, *Central Plains Cultural Relics*, Issue 6, 2013.

⓬ Xu Diankui: *An archaeological study of Tang Jing stages*, *Journal of Archaeology*, Issue 3, 1994.

⓭ Guan Weiliang: *History of Chinese Bronze Mirrors*, Qunyan Press, 2013.

⓮ Ji He: *Tang and Song dynasty bronze mirrors found in Suzhou, Anhui Province*, *Chinese Archaeology*, Issue 3, 1998.

⓯ Dong Yawei: *The relationship between the alloy composition of ancient bronze mirrors and the geometrical shape of the mirror body section is discussed*, *Journal of Chinese History Museum*, Issue 2, 2000.

⓰ *Conservation and restoration plan for the metal relics in the Suzhou Museum*, Suzhou Muscum, 2016.

图版 Plates

# 1. 素面镜

战国

2009 年涉案移交

直径 10.5 厘米，厚 0.1 厘米

　　圆形，三弦钮，镜背素面无纹。镜身较薄，质地粗糙。

　　春秋晚期、战国早期的全素镜，形体较小，无钮座，制作粗糙。战国晚期的全素镜，数量甚少，形体比春秋晚期、战国早期的要大一些。

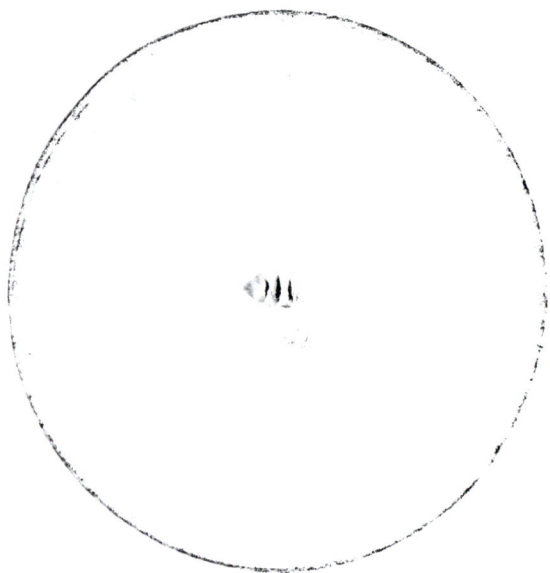

# 1. Mirror without design

Warring States

It was transferred in the case in 2009

Diameter: 10.5cm. Thickness: 0.1cm

Circular, three stringed button, with a plain surface on the back of the mirror without any pattern. The mirror body is relatively thin and has a rough texture.

The mirrors without design in the late Spring and Autumn period and early Warring States period have a smaller size, no button base, and rough production. The total number of pure mirrors in the late Warring States period is very small, and their shape are larger than those in the late Spring and Autumn period and early Warring States period.

## 2. 素面镜

战国

旧藏

直径 12.2 厘米，厚 0.2 厘米

　　圆形，三弦钮，素镜背，形体较小，镜身轻薄，制作工艺比较粗糙。

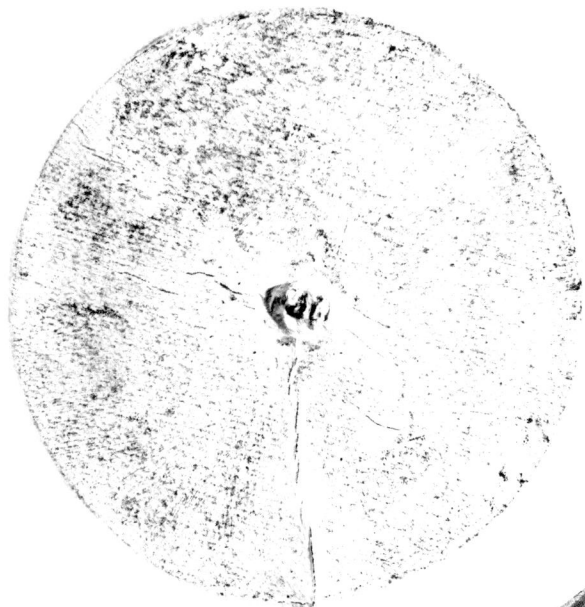

## 2. Mirror without design

Warring States

Old collection

Diameter: 12.2cm. Thickness: 0.2cm

Circular, three stringed button, plain mirror back, small in shape, light and thin in body, and rough in production process.

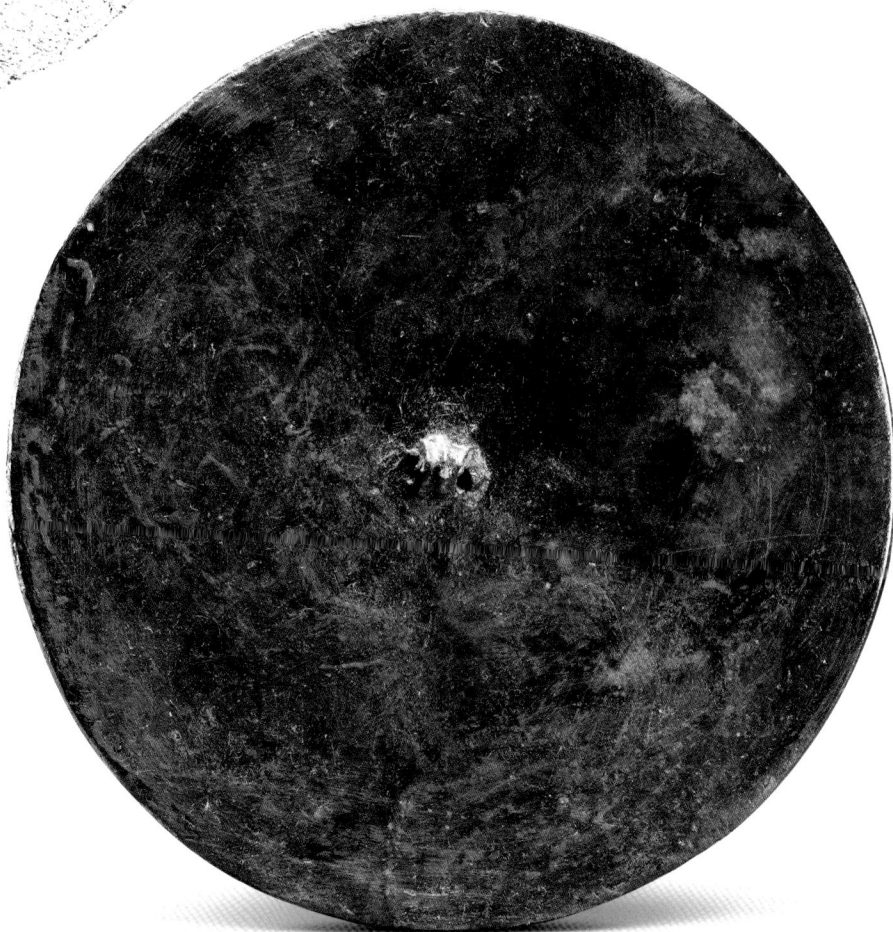

## 3. 三山纹镜

战国
2009 年涉案移交
直径 9.7 厘米，厚 0.35 厘米

　　圆形，三弦钮，圆钮座，外围重缘凹面形圈带一周。纹饰由主纹和地纹组成，三个右旋山字纹等距分布于钮座之外，细密的羽状地纹铺满镜背，外围弦纹圈一周。素卷缘。山字镜主要流行于战国，是比较常见的镜式之一。

## 3. Mirror with inscription of three "Shan" characters

Warring States
It was transferred in the case in 2009
Diameter: 9.7cm. Thickness: 0.35cm

The mirror is circular, with three string buttons, a circular button seat, and a concave ring with a double edge on the periphery. The decoration consists of a main pattern and a ground pattern, with three right oblique "Shan" characters patterns evenly distributed outside the button seat. The fine feather shaped ground pattern covers the back of the mirror, and the outer string pattern is circled around it. Plain rolled-up edge. The mirror with inscription of "Shan" characters was mainly popular in the Warring States period and is one of the more common mirror styles.

# 4. 五山纹镜

战国

2001 年 8 月从蕲县镇白陈村江得胜文物案件中追缴

直径 16.4 厘米，缘厚 0.6 厘米

　　圆形，三弦钮，圆钮座，外围重缘凹面形圈带一周。纹饰由主纹和地纹组成，圈带外等间距各向外延伸出两个连贯式花瓣纹，五组花瓣纹将铜镜分为五个区，每区各饰一左旋山字纹，每个山字纹中竖直抵接近镜缘的弦纹圈，山字纹右上侧各饰一花瓣纹，镜背铺满细密的羽状地纹。素卷缘。

# 4. Mirror with inscription of five "Shan" characters

Warring States

Recovered from the Jiangdesheng Cultural Relics Case in Baichen Village, Qixian Town in August 2001

Diameter: 16.4cm. Edge thickness: 0.6cm

The mirror is circular, with three string buttons and a circular button seat, with a concave ring around the outer edge. The decoration consists of a main pattern and a ground pattern, with two consecutive petal patterns extending outward at equal intervals outside the band. The five petal patterns divide the bronze mirror into five zones, each with a left sloping "*Shan*" characters. The vertical direction of each "*Shan*" character is directly connected to the string pattern which is close to the edge of the mirror. The upper right side of the "*Shan*" character is adorned with a petal pattern, and the back of the mirror is covered with fine feather shaped ground patterns. Plain rolled edge.

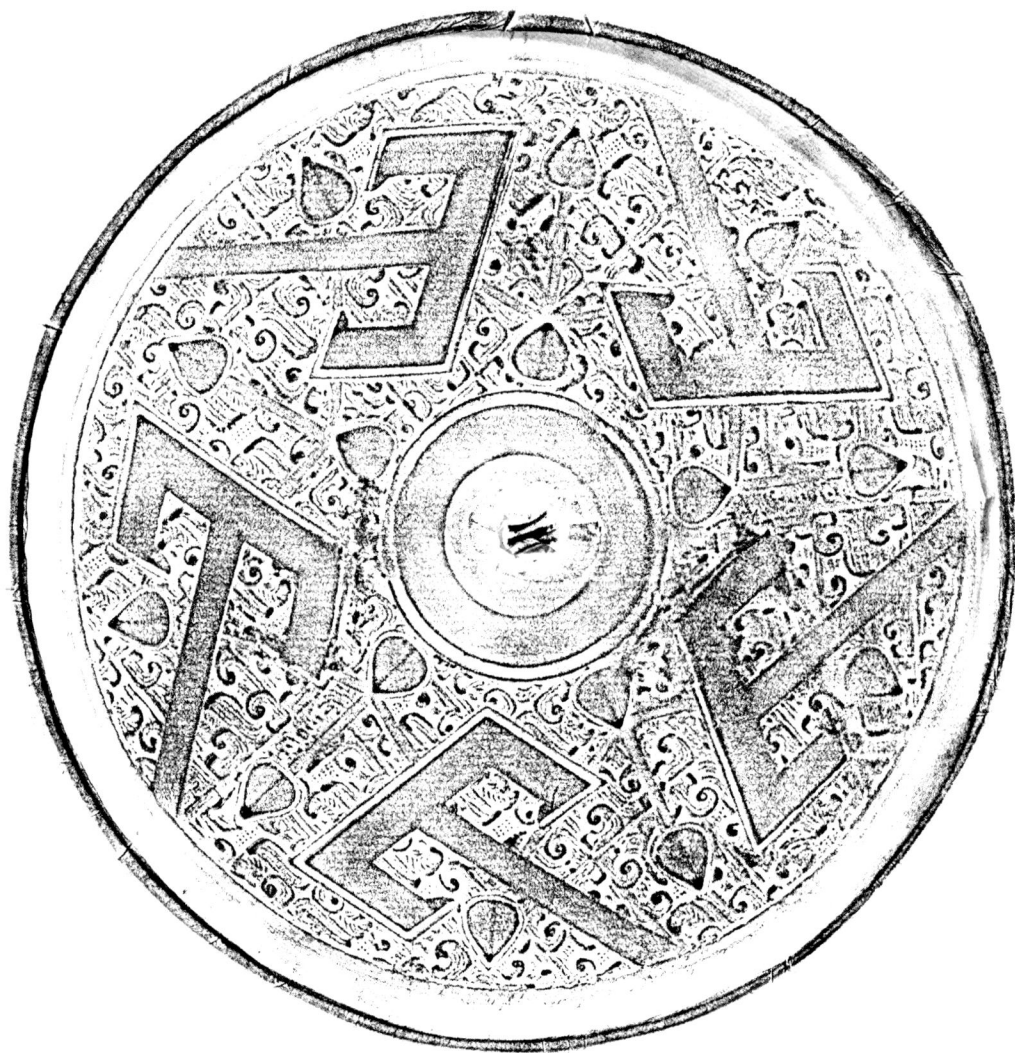

# 5. 蟠螭纹镜

汉

旧藏

直径 8 厘米

　　圆形，桥形钮，蟠螭钮座，外有一周铭文带，铭文模糊，难以辨识，主纹区饰线条勾勒的蟠螭纹，镜缘外沿上卷。

　　蟠螭纹镜纹饰一般由主纹和地纹组成，主纹多为三个或四个蟠螭纹，地纹为云雷纹，到西汉中后期地纹逐渐消失。钮座外有的为几重同心圆圈带，有的为方形格。

# 5. Mirror with design of interlaced hydras

Han Dynasty

Old collection

Diameter: 8cm

The mirror is round in shape. It has a bridge-shaped knob on a interlaced-hydras design base. Outside the base is a band of inscription, the inscription were indistinct and hard to read. The major motif is design of interlaced-hydras. The outer edge of the rim is rolled up.

The ornamentation consists of the ground motif and the major motif. The major motif is three or four interlaced-hydras patterns. The ground motif is the design of cloud and thunder, and gradually disappeared in the middle and the late Western Han Dynasty. Some buttons have concentric circles on the outside, while others have square boxes.

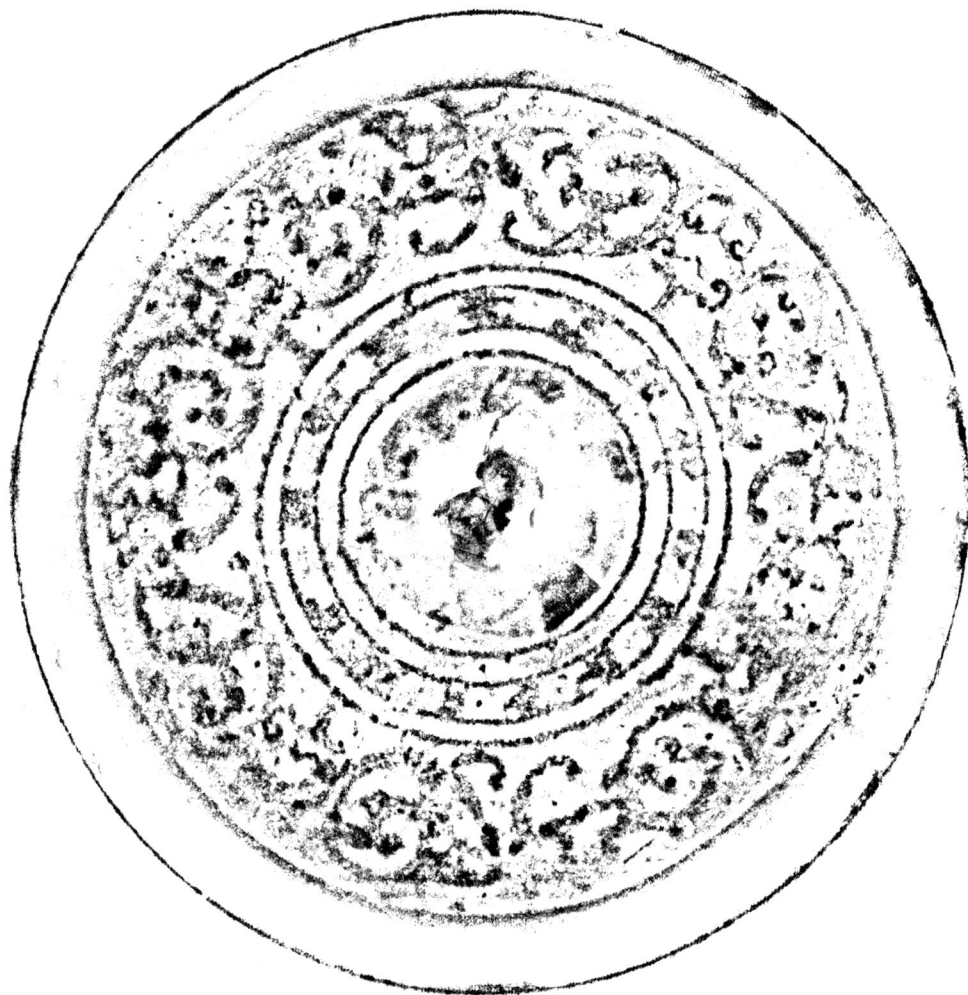

# 6. 四叶四螭纹镜

汉

萧县出土

直径 10.7 厘米，缘厚 0.5 厘米

　　圆形，三弦钮，蟠螭钮座。圈带铭文模糊，难辨识。主纹区以四株三叠式花瓣纹等分四区，每区内饰蟠螭纹，多层式四叶由花苞与草叶纹构成。蟠螭头近镜缘，翘角，张嘴，身躯呈"S"形勾卷，肢爪屈伸。素卷缘。

# 6. Mirror with design of four-leaf and interlaced hydras

Han Dynasty

Unearthed in Xiao County

Diameter: 10.7cm. Thickness: 0.5cm

The mirror is round in shape. It has a three-string knob on a base with interlaced-hydras design. The inscription is unclear and, difficult to distinguish. The main pattern area has four leaves and four hydras arranged in alternating rings, and the multi-layer four leaves are composed of flower buds and grass leaf patterns. The hydras's head is close to the edge of the mirror, its horns are raised, its mouth is open, its body is curled in an S-shape, and its limbs and claws are bent and extended. Plain rolled-up edge.

## 7. 蟠螭纹镜

汉

萧县植物园出土

直径 11.8 厘米，缘厚 0.5 厘米

　　圆形，三弦钮，蟠螭钮座。钮座外一周铭文圈带，铭文"大乐富贵，千秋万岁，宜酒食"。主纹区采用间隔式布局的方法，四株多层式花叶与四组蟠螭相间环绕。蟠螭身躯蟠屈缭纠，曲线流转，细腻繁缛。素卷缘。

## 7. Mirror with design of interlaced hydras

Han Dynasty

Unearthed in Xiaoxian Botanical Garden

Diameter: 11.8cm. Thickness: 0.5cm

The mirror is round in shape. It has a three-string knob on a base with interlaced-hydras design. On the outside of the button seat, there is an inscription circle with the inscription "Rich and prosperous, longevity, suitable for drinking and eating". The main pattern area adopts a spacing layout method, with four multi-layer flowers and leaves surrounded by four groups of interlaced hydras. The body of the hydra is convoluted and tangled, with curves flowing and delicate and intricate. Plain rolled edge.

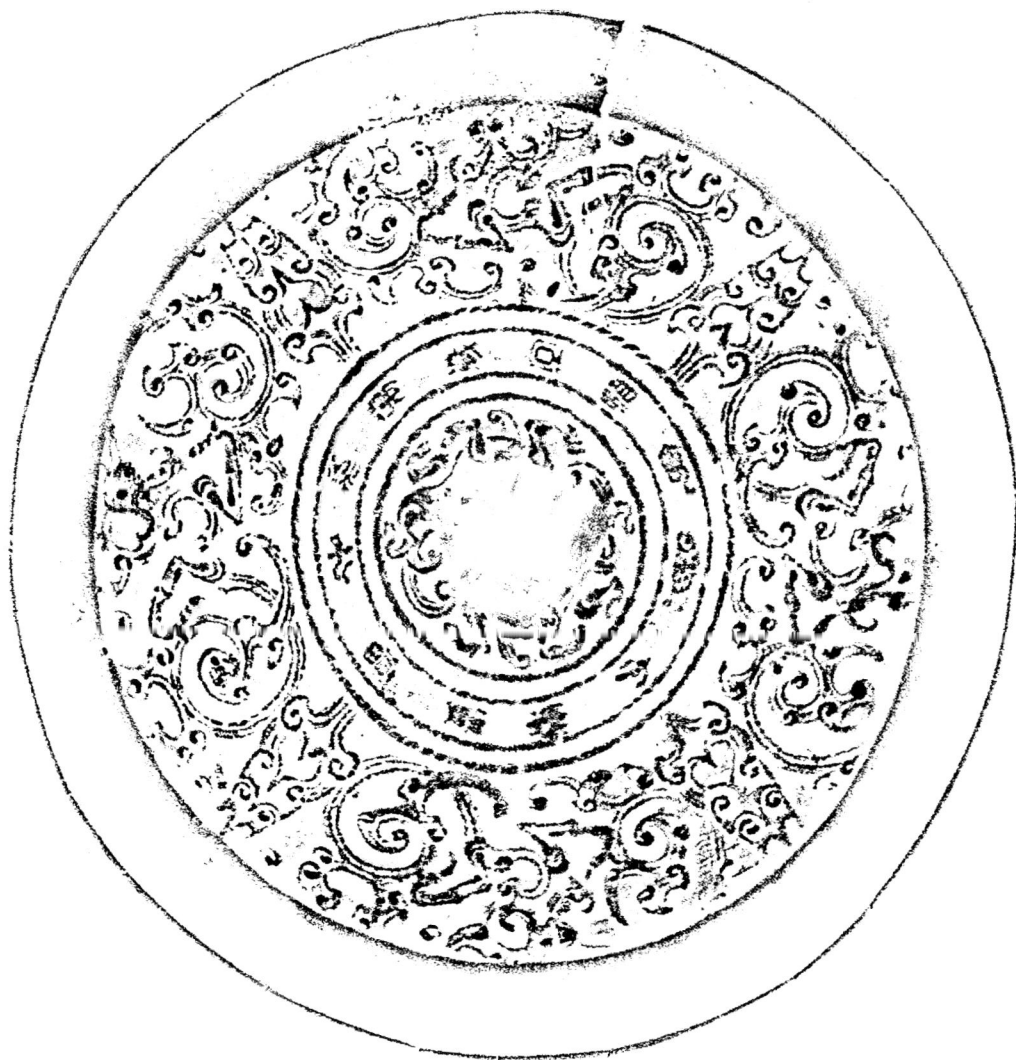

## 8. 蟠螭纹镜

## 8. Mirror with design of interlaced hydras

汉

埇桥区征集

直径 8.3 厘米，厚 0.4 厘米

Han Dynasty

The cultural relics was collected in Yongqiao District

Diameter: 8.3cm. Thickness: 0.4cm

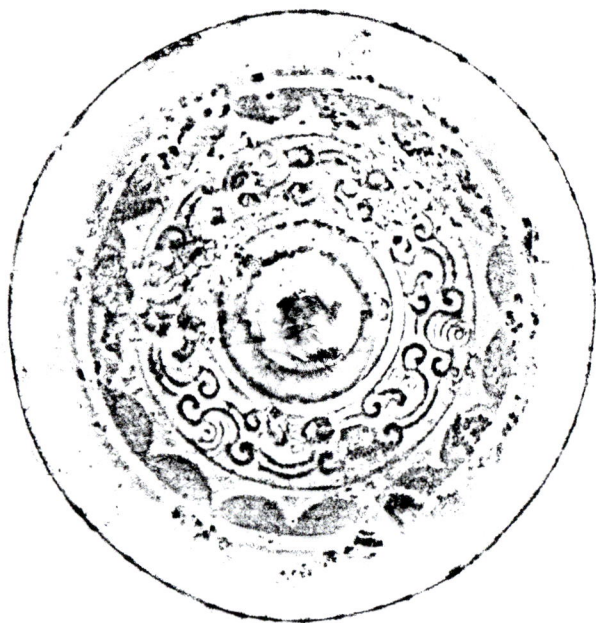

　　圆形，三弦钮，外围一周宽圈带。纹饰由地纹与主纹构成。以涡纹为地纹，"S"形蟠螭相间环列。其外一周十六内向连弧纹。宽素缘，缘边上卷。

The mirror is round in shape. It has a knob with three-string design, outside the base is a broad band. The ground motif is design of vortex with interlaced hydras pattern among them. Outside the groud is adorned with sixteen linked arcs inward. The broad rim is without design and outer edge is rolled up.

## 9. 四乳蟠螭连弧纹镜

## 9. Mirror with design of four nipples, interlaced hydras and linked arcs

汉

2009 年涉案移交

直径 8.3 厘米，厚 0.25 厘米

Han Dynasty

It was transferred in the case in 2009

Diameter: 8.3cm. Thickness: 0.25cm

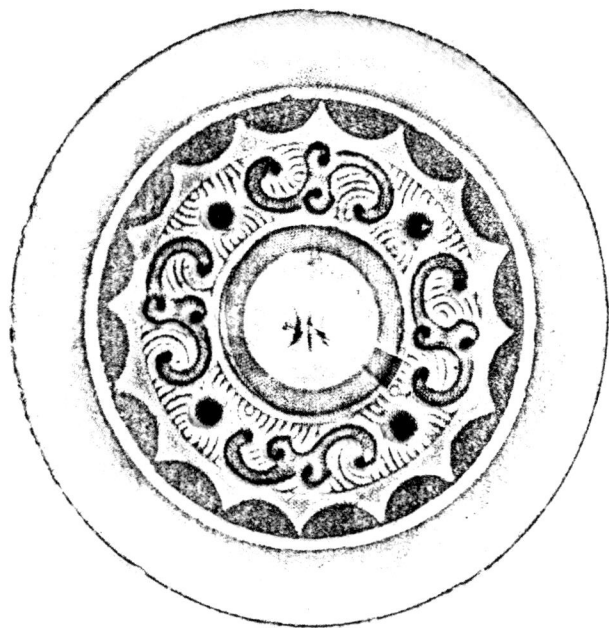

　　圆形，三弦钮，圆钮座，外环一周宽弦纹带。主纹区以短线纹为地纹，等距分布四个乳钉纹，乳钉纹间各置一个"S"形蟠螭纹，近缘处饰一周内向十六连弧纹。宽素缘，缘边上卷。

Circular, three string button, round button seat, with a wide string pattern around the outer ring. The main pattern area consists of short line patterns as the ground pattern, with four evenly spaced breast nail patterns. Each breast nail pattern is interspersed with an S-shaped interlaced hydra, and the near edge is decorated with sixteen linked arcs inward. Wide plain edge, edge curled up.

## 10. 星云纹镜

汉

2009 年涉案移交

直径 9.8 厘米，厚 0.3 厘米

　　圆形，连峰钮，圆钮座。钮座外饰一周较为粗糙的内向连弧纹。十六内向连弧纹镜缘。主纹饰区布满由小乳钉纹组成的星云纹。

　　星云纹镜又称为"百乳鉴"或"星云百乳鉴"。星云纹因其多乳钉且与星相图相似而得名，属于高浮雕纹饰镜。

## 10. Mirror with nebular design

Han Dynasty

It was transferred in the case in 2009

Diameter: 9.8cm. Thickness: 0.3cm

Circular, continuous peak button, round button seat, sixteen inward continuous arc pattern mirror edges. The main decorative area is covered with nebula patterns composed of small breast nail patterns.

The nebula pattern mirror is also known as the Hundred Breast Mirror or the Nebula Hundred Breast Mirror. The nebula pattern is named because of it has many breast nail patterns and similarity to the star phase diagram. It belongs to the category of high relief decorative mirrors.

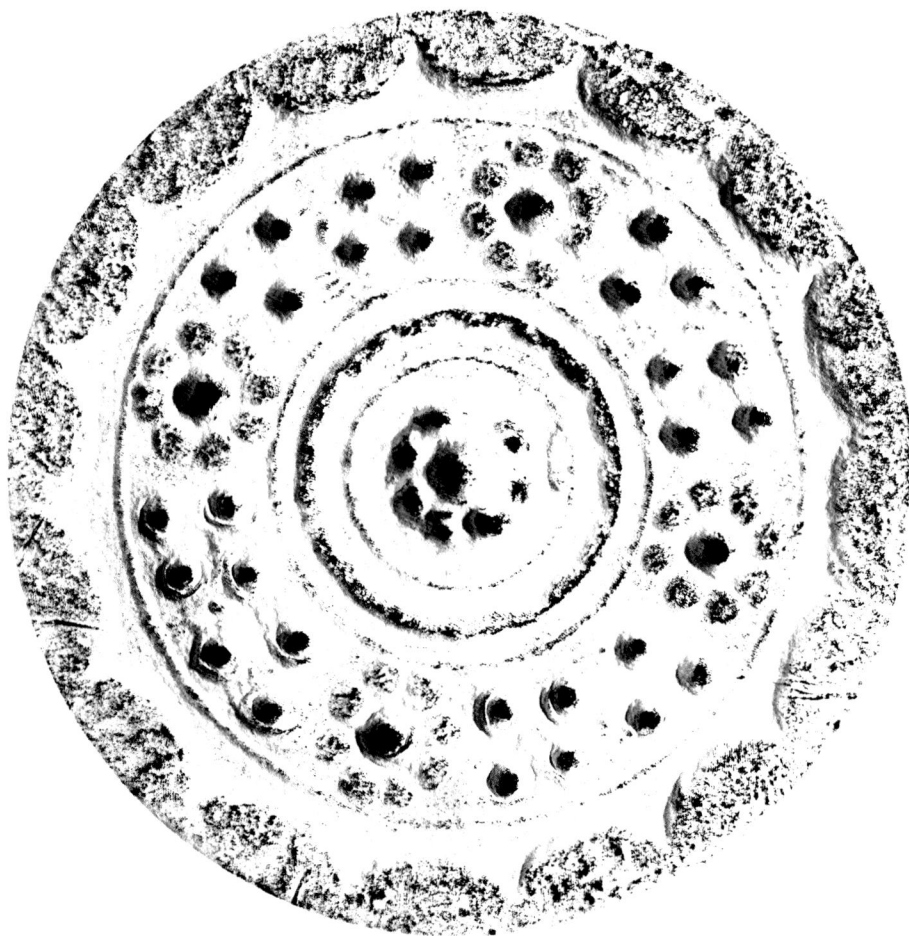

## 11. 星云纹镜

汉

2009 年涉案移交

直径 9.7 厘米，缘厚 0.3 厘米

　　圆形，连峰钮，圆钮座。钮座外饰一周内向十六连弧纹。四个圆座乳钉纹等距分布，将主纹区分为四区，每区内饰一组由小乳钉纹组成的星云纹、近缘处饰一周弦纹。镜缘上饰一周内向十六连弧纹。

　　星云纹镜的主要特征是圆形，连峰钮（有的为圆钮）。主纹区采用四分法布局，一般是四乳钉划分四区，区间饰有许多小的乳钉，小乳钉间用曲线相连接，边缘由内向的连弧纹构成。

## 11. Mirror with nebular design

Han Dynasty

It was transferred in the case in 2009

Diameter: 9.7cm. Edge thickness: 0.3cm

Circular, continuous peak-shaped button, circular button seat. The outer decoration of the button seat has sixteen linked arcs inward. Four circular breast nail patterns are evenly distributed, dividing the main pattern into four zones. Each zone covered with nebular patterns composed of small breast nail patterns, a circumferential string pattern near the edge. On the edge of the mirror, there are sixteen linked arcs inward.

The main characteristics of nebula mirrors are circular, with continuous peaks (some are circular). The main pattern area adopts a quartering layout, usually divided into four areas by four breast nails, with many small breast nails decorated in the interval. The small breast nails are connected by curves, and the edges are all composed of inward continuous arc patterns.

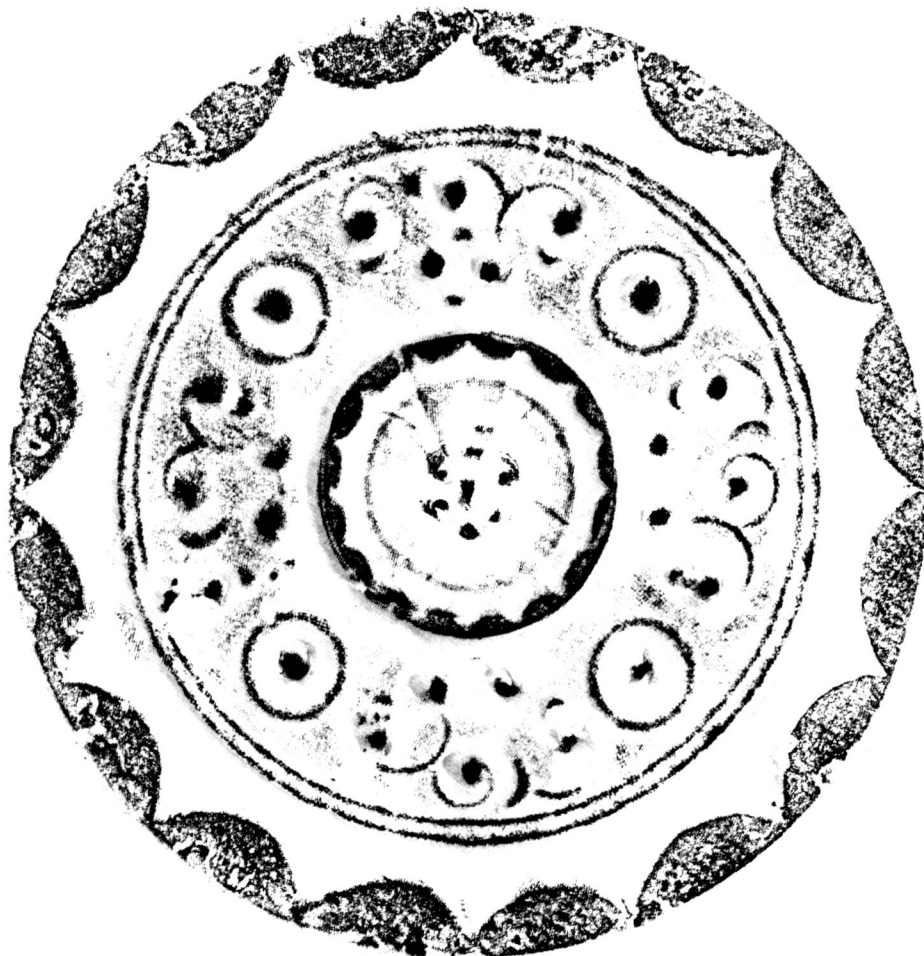

## 12. 星云纹镜
## 12. Mirror with nebular design

汉

2009 年涉案移交

直径 10 厘米，缘厚 0.3 厘米

Han Dynasty

It was transferred in the case in 2009

Diameter: 10cm. Edge thickness: 0.3cm

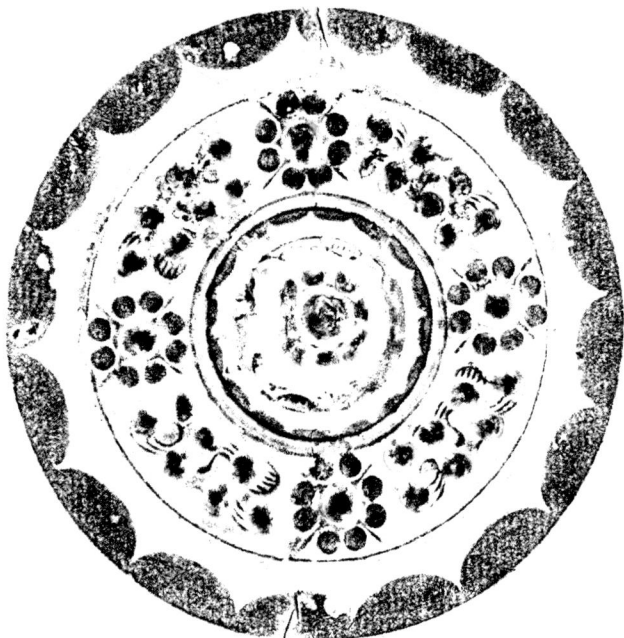

圆形，连峰钮，圆钮座。钮座外饰一周内向十六连弧纹。十六内向连弧纹镜缘。主纹饰区布满由小乳钉纹组成的星云纹。

星云纹镜的云纹变化多端，云纹之上的乳钉个数有多有少，有的比较繁缛，云纹纠缠在一起，似螭纹，乳钉小而多，多配以花叶乳钉分区；有的比较简洁，云纹相对简化，似虺纹，乳钉大而少，多以带座乳钉分区。

Circular, continuous peak-shaped button, round button seat with sixteen linked arcs inward, sixteen inward continuous arc pattern mirror edges. The main decorative area is covered with nebula patterns composed of small breast nail patterns.

The cloud patterns of the nebula pattern mirror vary greatly, with varying numbers of breast nails above the cloud patterns, some of which are quite complicated. The cloud patterns are intertwined like dragon patterns, and the breast nails are small and numerous, often paired with flower leaf breast nails for zoning; Some are relatively simple, with cloud patterns being relatively simplified, resembling cobra patterns. Breast nails are large but few, often divided into zones with a base.

## 13. 星云纹镜

汉

2009 年涉案移交

直径 10.5 厘米，厚 0.4 厘米

　　圆形，连峰钮，圆钮座，外饰一周内向连弧纹。十六内向连弧纹镜缘。主纹饰区布满由小乳钉纹组成的星云纹。

　　经考古发掘研究，星云纹镜出现于汉武帝时期，流行于西汉的昭宣时期，西汉中期以后比较少见。

## 13. Mirror with nebular design

Han Dynasty

It was transferred in the case in 2009

Diameter: 10.5cm. Thickness: 0.4cm

Circular, continuous peak-shaped button, round button seat with inward continuous arc pattern, sixteen inward continuous arc pattern mirror edge. The main decorative area is covered with nebula patterns composed of small breast nail patterns.

Through archaeological excavation and research, the nebula patterned mirror appeared during the reign of Emperor Wu of Han and was popular during the Zhaoxuan period of the Western Han Dynasty. It was relatively rare after the middle of the Western Han Dynasty.

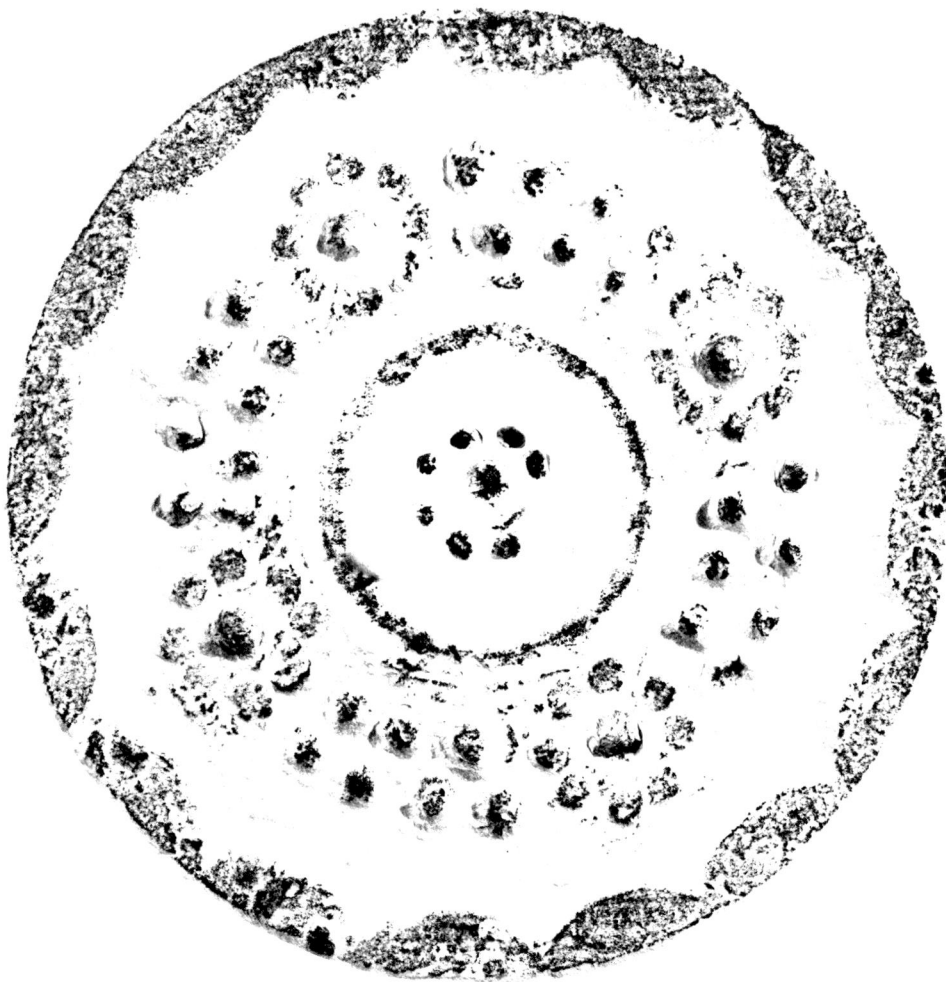

## 14. 四乳铭文镜

## 14. Mirror with design of four nipples and inscription

---

汉

*2009 年涉案移交*

*直径 7.4 厘米，厚 0.3 厘米*

Han Dynasty

It was transferred in the case in 2009

Diameter: 7.4cm. Thickness: 0.3cm

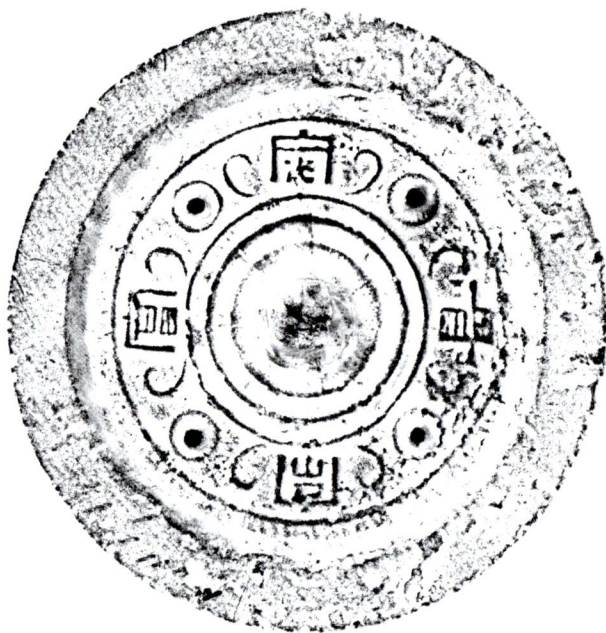

　　圆形，半球钮，圆钮座。四个等距分布的圆座乳钉将主纹区分为四区，每区内置一铭文，铭文"家常贵富"，每个铭文两侧各饰一弧线纹。主纹区两侧各置一周栉齿纹。宽平缘。

Circular, hemispherical button, round button seat. Four evenly spaced circular breast nails divide the main pattern into four zones, with each zone containing an inscription that can be translated as "Homely riches and honour". Each inscription is adorned with an arc pattern on either side. There is a band of fine-toothed pattern on both sides of the main pattern area. Wide flat edge.

## 15. 四乳铭文镜
## 15. Mirror with design of four nipples and inscription

———

汉

2009 年涉案移交

直径 6.1 厘米，厚 0.4 厘米

Han Dynasty

It was transferred in the case in 2009

Diameter: 6.1cm. Thickness: 0.4cm

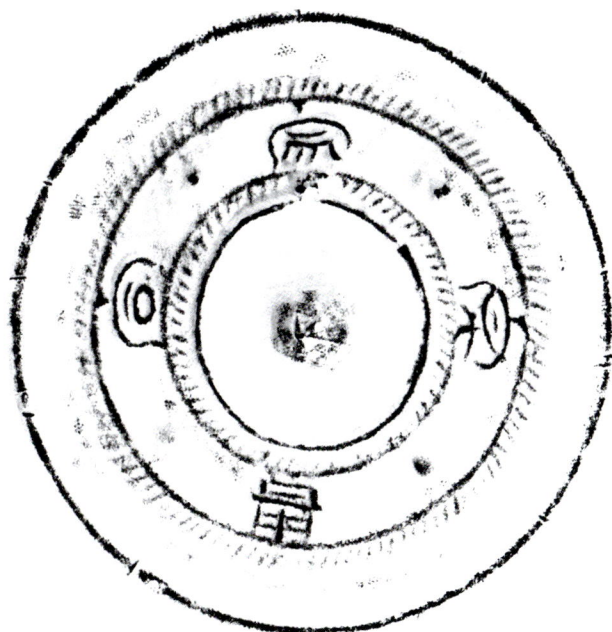

　　圆形，半球钮，圆钮座。主纹区以两周栉齿纹为廓，其内四字铭文与四个圆座乳钉相间分布，铭文"家常贵富"，卷缘。

Circular, hemispherical button, circular button seat. The main pattern area is outlined by two bands of fine-toothed pattern, with four character inscriptions and four circular breast nails distributed alternately. The inscription can be translated as "Homely riches and honour" and rolled-up edges.

# 16. 四乳铭文镜

汉

2009 年涉案移交

直径 7.5 厘米，厚 0.2 厘米

　　圆形，圆钮，圆钮座。钮座外环饰一周宽带纹，其上分布若干短弧线纹。主纹区以两周栉齿纹为栏，四个圆座乳钉等距分布，将主纹区分为四区，每区内饰一铭文，依次为"家常富贵"。宽素缘。

# 16. Mirror with design of four nipples and inscription

Han Dynasty

It was transferred in the case in 2009

Diameter: 7.5cm. Thickness: 0.2cm

Round, round button, round button seat. The outside of the button seat is decorated with a wide band pattern, with several short arc lines distributed on it. The main pattern area is divided into four areas, with two bands of fine-toothed pattern as columns and four circular breast nails evenly distributed. Each area has an inscription on the interior, which means "Homely riches and honour" in order. Wide margin.

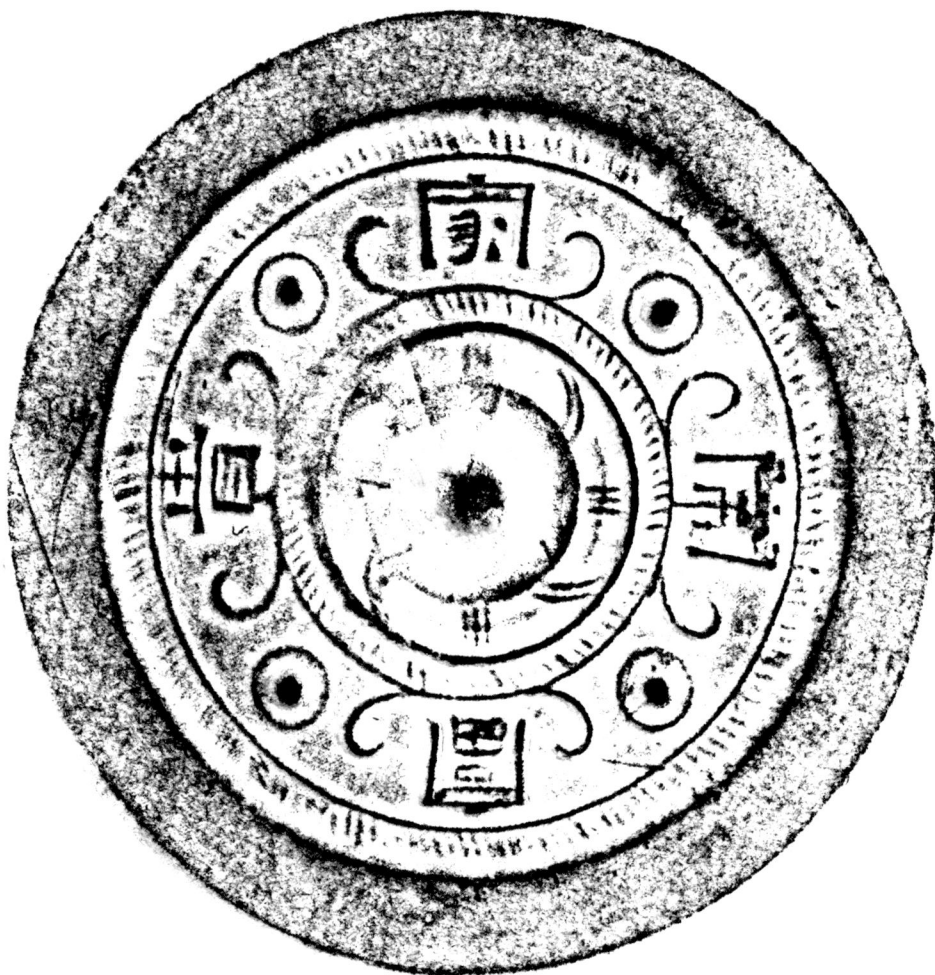

## 17. 连弧纹日光镜

汉

2009 年涉案移交

直径 7.6 厘米，厚 0.25 厘米

　　圆形，圆钮，圆钮座，钮座外环一周内向八连弧纹，与钮座之间饰若干短直线纹。主纹区以两周栉齿纹为廓，内饰铭文一圈，铭文"见日之光，天下大明"，字铭间间隔 ℮ 纹和 ◈ 纹，宽素缘。

　　日光镜流行于西汉中晚期到东汉中期，纹饰简明清新，是汉镜中出土数量多，流行范围广的镜类之一。日光镜是指镜背装饰中包含有"见日之光"或者由其衍生出的各类组合而成的铭文，均可称为日光镜。

## 17. Sunlight mirror with linked arcs design

Han Dynasty

It was transferred in the case in 2009

Diameter: 7.6cm. Thickness: 0.25cm

Round, round button, round button seat, surrounded by eight inward consecutive arc patterns onthe outside, and several short straight lines decorated between the button seat and it. The main pattern area is outlined by two bands of fine-toothed pattern, with a circle of interior inscriptions, with the inscription "See the light of the sun, the world is bright". The characters have spacing ℮ patterns and ◈ patterns between the inscriptions, with a wide plain edge.

Sunlight mirrors were popular from the mid to late Western Han Dynasty to the mid Eastern Han Dynasty, with concise and fresh patterns. They are one of the mirror types with a large number of unearthed and widespread popularity in the Han Dynasty. Sunlight mirror refers to the inscription on the back of the mirror that contains "See the light of the sun" or various combinations derived from it, and can be called a sunlight mirror.

## 18. 连弧纹日光镜

汉

2009 年涉案移交

直径 7 厘米，厚 0.3 厘米

　　圆形，半球钮，圆钮座。钮座外环一周内向八连弧纹，与钮座间饰 ℮ 纹和变形山字纹。主纹区为一周铭文圈带，铭文"见日之光，天下明大"，铭文间以圆座乳钉间隔。近缘处，饰一周栉齿纹。素缘。

## 18. Sunlight mirror with linked arcs design

Han Dynasty

It was transferred in the case in 2009

Diameter: 7cm. Thickness: 0.3cm

Circular, hemispherical button, circular button seat, surrounded by eight inward consecutive arc patterns on the outside, with decorative ℮ patterns and deformed mountain shaped patterns between the button seat. The main pattern area is a circular inscription band, with the inscription which can be translated as "See the light of the sun, the world is bright", and the inscriptions are separated by circular breast nails. Near the edge, adorned with a band of fine-toothed pattern. Plain margin.

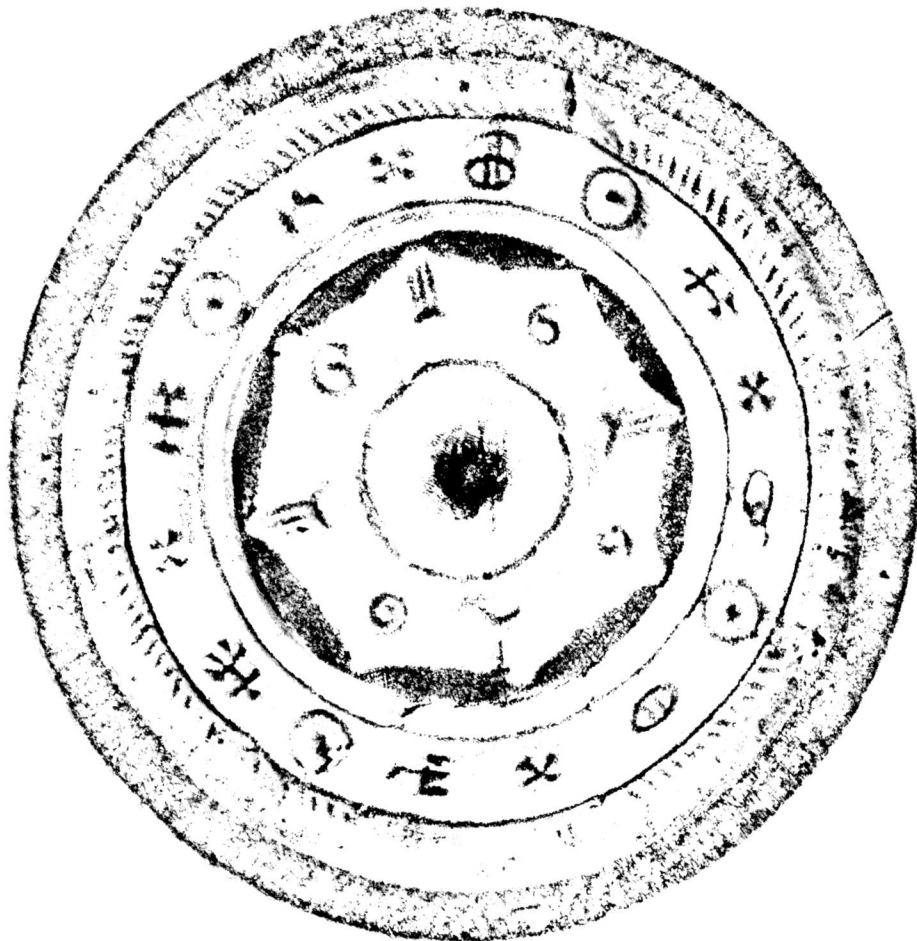

## 19. 连弧纹日光镜

汉

2000 年埇桥区公安分局移交

直径 8.2 厘米，厚 0.3 厘米

　　圆形，半球钮，圆钮座。钮座外饰一周内向八连弧纹，与钮座之间饰若干短线纹。主纹区以两周栉齿纹为栏，间饰一周铭文圈带，铭文"见日之光，天下大明"，字铭间以 ℮ 纹与 ◈ 纹相间。宽素缘。

　　部分镜缘及主纹区锈蚀严重，附着绿色锈蚀物。

## 19. Sunlight mirror with linked arcs design

Han Dynasty

It was transferred from the Yongqiao District Public Security Branch in 2000.

Diameter: 8.2cm. Thickness: 0.3cm

Circular, hemispherical button, circular button seat, surrounded by eight inward consecutive arc patterns on the outside, with several short lines between it and the button seat. The main pattern area is outlined by two bands of fine-toothed pattern, with a circle of inscriptions between them. The inscription can be translated as "See the light of the sun, the world is bright", and the inscriptions alternate with ℮ and ◈ patterns. Wide margin.

Part of the mirror edge and main pattern area are severely corroded, with green rust adhering.

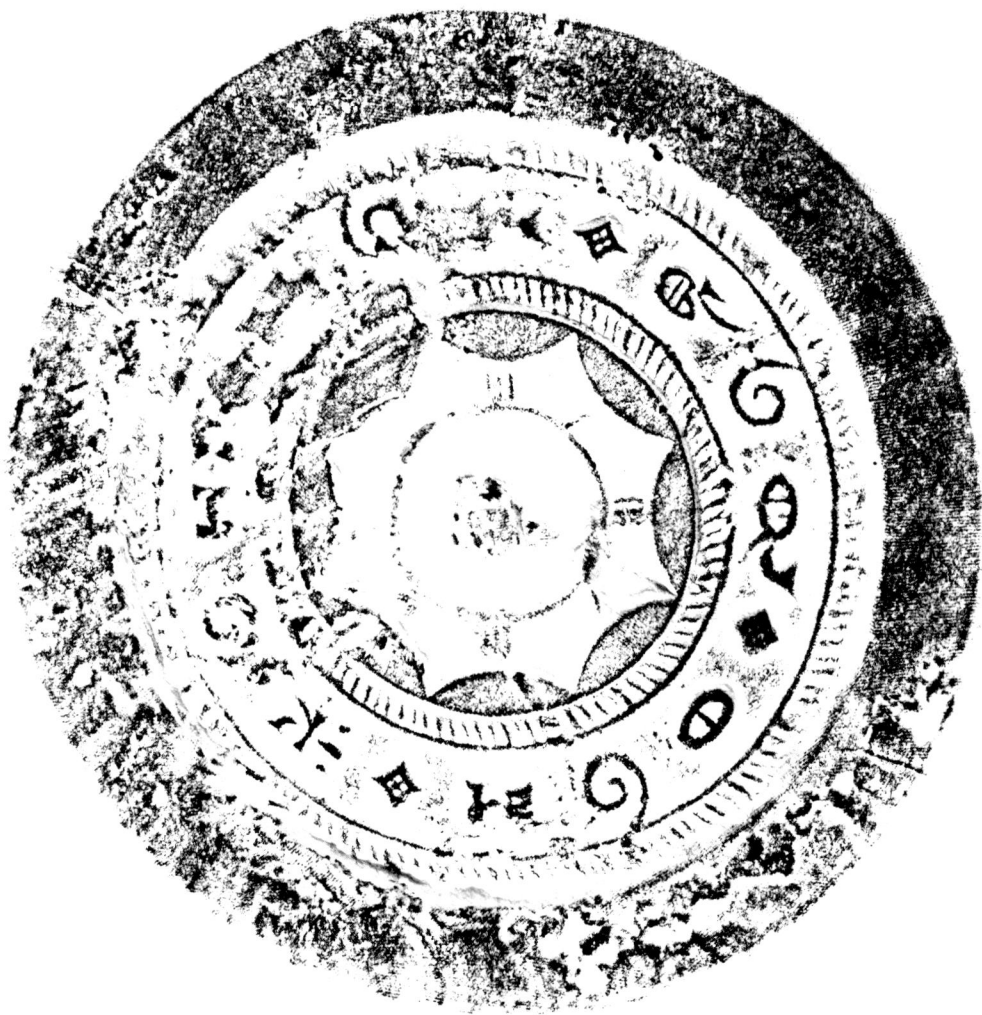

## 20. 连弧纹日光镜
## 20. Sunlight mirror with linked arcs design

汉

1979 年征集

直径 7.6 厘米，厚 0.5 厘米

Han Dynasty

It was collected in 1979

Diameter: 7.6cm. Thickness: 0.5cm

　　圆形，半球钮，圆钮座，钮座外环一周内向八连弧纹，与钮座之间饰若干短线纹。主纹区以两周栉齿纹为廓，间饰一周铭文圈带，铭文"见日之光，天下大明"，字铭间饰 ℮ 纹和 ❖ 纹。素宽缘。

Circular, hemispherical button, circular button seat, surrounded by eight inward consecutive arc patterns on the outside, and several short line patterns decorated between the button seat and it. The main pattern area is outlined by two bands of fine-toothed pattern, with a circular inscription band between them. The inscription can be translated as "See the light of the sun, the world is bright", and the characters are decorated with ℮ patterns and ❖ patterns between them. Plain wide margin.

# 21. 连弧纹日光镜

## 21. Sunlight mirror with linked arcs design

汉

2009 年涉案移交

直径 7 厘米，厚 0.15 厘米

Han Dynasty

It was transferred in the case in 2009

Diameter: 7cm. Thickness: 0.15cm

  圆形，圆钮，圆钮座，外环一周内向八连弧纹。主纹区为一圈铭文圈带，铭文"见日之光，天下大明"，铭文间以 ꙮ 纹和 ◈ 纹间隔，两侧各以一周栉齿纹为廓。宽素缘。

Round, round button, round button seat, surrounded by eight inward consecutive arc patterns on the outside. The main pattern area is a circle of inscriptions, with the inscription "See the light of the sun, the world is bright". The inscriptions are separated by ꙮ and ◈ patterns and each side is outlined by a band of fine-toothed pattern. Wide margin.

## 22. 连弧纹日光镜

汉

*2009 年涉案移交*

*直径 8.4 厘米，厚 0.3 厘米*

　　圆形，圆钮，圆钮座，外环一周内向八连弧纹，与钮座间隔短弧线和短直线纹。主纹区为一圈铭文圈带，铭文"见日之光，天下大明"，铭文间以 ℃ 纹间隔，两侧各以一周栉齿纹为廓。宽平缘。

## 22. Sunlight mirror with linked arcs design

Han Dynasty

It was transferred in the case in 2009

Diameter: 8.4cm. Thickness: 0.3cm

Circular, circular button, circular button seat, surrounded by eight inward consecutive arc patterns on the outside, short arc lines and short straight lines separated from the button seat. The main pattern area is a circle of inscriptions, with the inscription "See the light of the sun, the world is bright". The inscriptions are separated by ℃ patterns, and each side is outlined by a band of fine-toothed pattern. Wide flat edge.

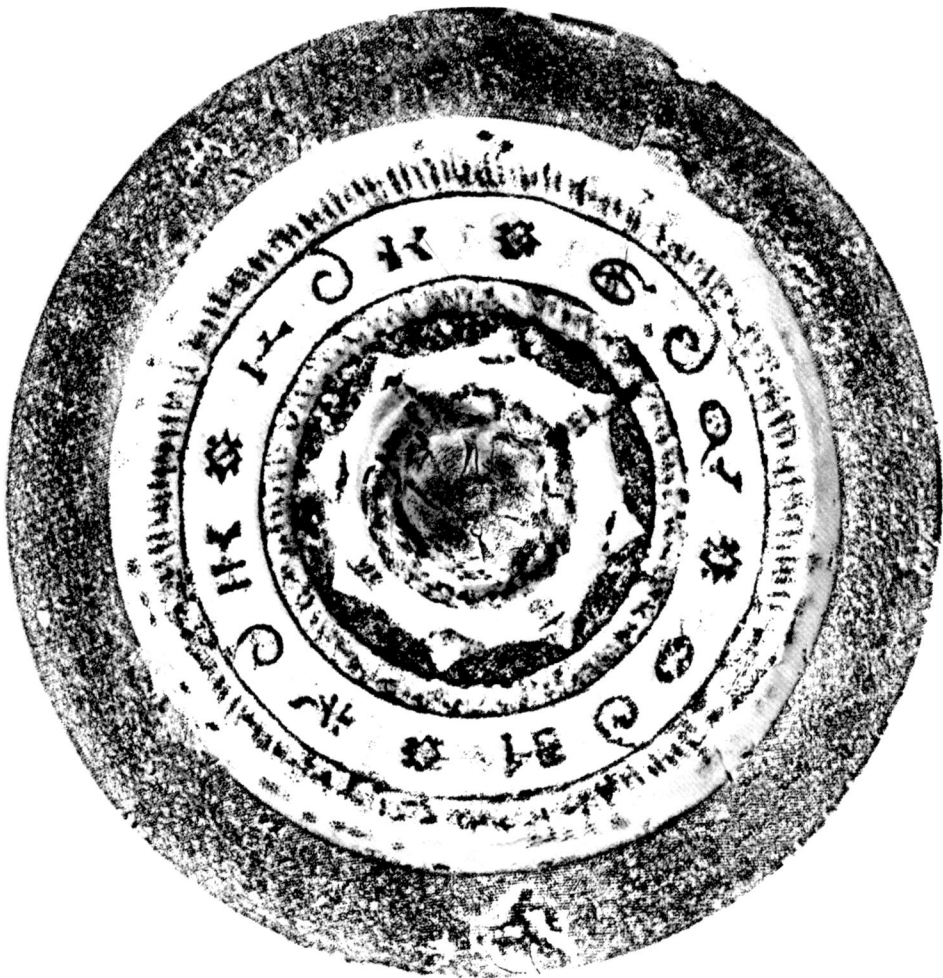

## 23. 连弧纹日光镜

汉

2009 年涉案移交

直径 6.3 厘米，厚 0.3 厘米

　　圆形，圆钮，圆钮座，钮座等距向外延伸四条短线纹，与内向八连弧纹圈相对。主纹区以两周栉齿纹为廓，内饰铭文一圈，铭文"见日之光，天下大明"，字铭间以 ℮ 纹和 ◈ 纹间隔。素缘。

## 23. Sunlight mirror with linked arcs design

Han Dynasty

It was transferred in the case in 2009

Diameter: 6.3cm. Thickness: 0.3cm

Circular, circular button, circular button seat, button seat extends four short lines equally outward, opposite to the inward eight continuous arc pattern. The main pattern area is outlined by two bands of fine-toothed pattern, with a circle of inscriptions "See the light of the sun, the world is bright". The inscriptions are separated by ℮ patterns and ◈ patterns. Plain margin.

# 24. 连弧纹日光镜

汉

2009 年涉案移交

直径 7.1 厘米，厚 0.4 厘米

　　圆形，半球钮，圆钮座。钮座外环饰一周内向八连弧纹，与钮座间饰若干短弧线纹。主纹区以两周栉齿纹为廓，内饰铭文一圈，铭文"见日之光，天下大明"，字铭间以 ℃ 纹和 ◈ 纹间隔，斜素缘。

# 24. Sunlight mirror with linked arcs design

Han Dynasty

It was transferred in the case in 2009

Diameter: 7.1cm. Thickness: 0.4cm

Circular, hemispherical button, circular button seat, surrounded by eight inward consecutive arc patterns on the outside, and several short arc patterns are decorated between the button seat. The main pattern area is outlined by two bands of fine-toothed pattern, with a circle of inscriptions "See the light of the sun, the world is bright". The inscriptions are separated by ℃ and ◈ patterns, slanted edges.

## 25. 连弧纹日光镜

汉

2009 年涉案移交

直径 7 厘米，厚 0.2 厘米

　　圆形，圆钮，圆钮座。钮座外环饰一周内向八连弧纹。主纹区以两周栉齿纹为廓，内饰铭文一圈，铭文"见日之光，天下大明"，字铭间以 ↻ 纹和 ◈ 纹间隔。宽素平缘。局部镜缘锈蚀严重，附着绿色锈蚀物。

## 25. Sunlight mirror with linked arcs design

Han Dynasty

It was transferred in the case in 2009

Diameter: 7cm. Thickness: 0.2cm

Round, round button, round button seat, surrounded by eight inward consecutive arc patterns on the outside. The main pattern area is outlined by two bands of fine-toothed pattern, with a circle of inscriptions "See the light of the sun, the world is bright". The inscriptions are separated by ↻ patterns and ◈ patterns. Wide plain edge. Local mirror edges are severely corroded, with green rust adhering.

## 26. 连弧纹日光镜

汉
2009 年涉案移交
直径 7.7 厘米，厚 0.3 厘米

　　圆形，圆钮，圆钮座，钮座外环饰一周内向八连弧纹圈，与钮座间饰若干短线纹。主区纹饰以两周栉齿纹为廓，内饰铭文一圈，铭文"见日之光，天下大明"，字铭间以 ↻ 纹和 ◈ 纹间隔。宽素平缘。

## 26. Sunlight mirror with linked arcs design

Han Dynasty
It was transferred in the case in 2009
Diameter: 7.7cm. Thickness: 0.3cm

Round, round button, round button seat, surrounded by eight inward consecutive arc patterns on the outside, and several short line patterns are decorated between the button seat. The main area is decorated with two bands of fine-toothed pattern as the outline, and the interior is the inscription "See the light of the sun, the world is bright", and the inscriptions are separated by ↻ patterns and ◈ patterns. Wide plain edge.

## 27. 连弧纹日光镜

汉

2009 年涉案移交

直径 8 厘米，厚 0.3 厘米

　　圆形，圆钮，圆钮座。钮座外环饰一周内向八连弧纹，与钮座间以短弧线纹间隔。主纹区以两周栉齿纹为廓，内饰铭文一圈，铭文"见日之光，天下大明"，字铭间以 ℃ 纹和 ◈ 纹间隔。宽素平缘，镜缘上有绿色锈蚀物。

## 27. Sunlight mirror with linked arcs design

Han Dynasty

It was transferred in the case in 2009

Diameter: 8cm. Thickness: 0.3cm

Round, round button, round button seat, surrounded by eight inward consecutive arc patterns on the outside, separated by a short arc pattern from the button seat. The main pattern area is outlined by two bands of fine-toothed pattern, with a circle of inscriptions "See the light of the sun, the world is bright". The inscriptions are separated by ℃ patterns and ◈ patterns. Wide plain edge with green rust on the mirror edge.

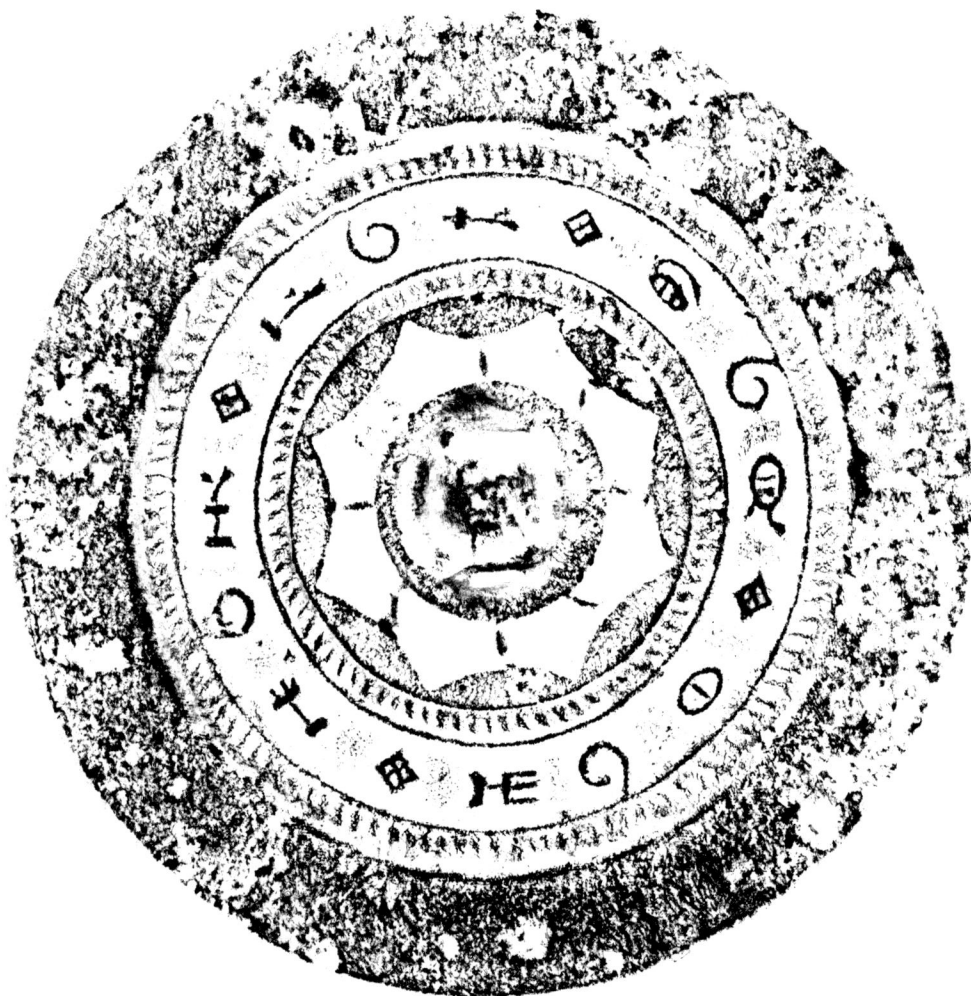

## 28. 连弧纹日光镜

汉
2009 年涉案移交
直径 7.5 厘米，厚 0.4 厘米

　　圆形，圆钮，圆钮座，钮座外环一周内向八连弧纹，与钮座间隔装饰双弧线纹和变形山字纹。主纹区为一圈铭文圈带，铭文"见日之光，长不相忘"，字铭间以 ◒ 纹和 ◈ 纹交替间隔，两侧以一周栉齿纹为廓。宽素平缘。

## 28. Sunlight mirror with linked arcs design

Han Dynasty
It was transferred in the case in 2009
Diameter: 7.5cm. Thickness: 0.4cm

Circular, round button, round button seat, surrounded by eight inward consecutive arc patterns on the outside, decorated with double arc patterns and deformed mountain shaped patterns at intervals from the button seat. The main pattern area is a circle of inscriptions "See the light of the sun, never forget each other". The inscriptions are alternated between ◒ and ◈ patterns, with a band of fine-toothed pattern on both sides as the outline. Wide plain edge.

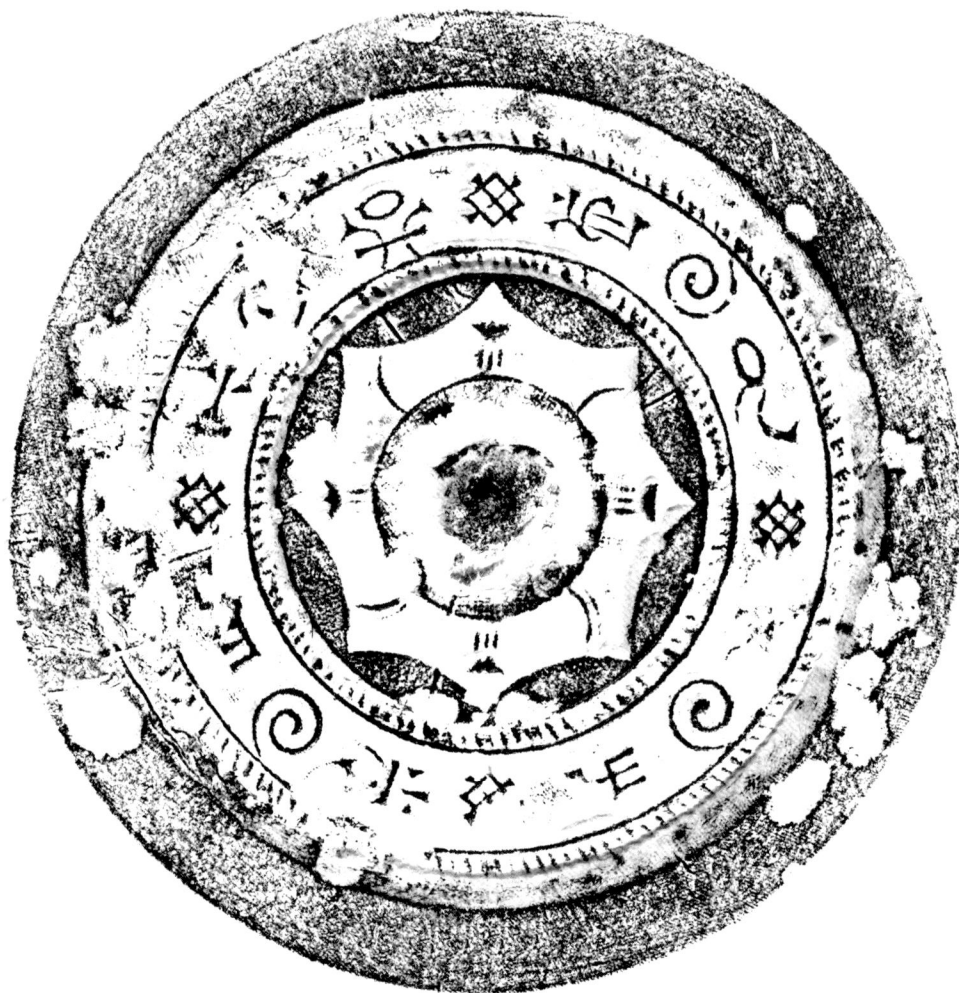

## 29. 铭文镜

汉

2009年涉案移交

直径6.9厘米，厚0.3厘米

　　圆形，圆钮，圆钮座，外环一周凸弦纹，与钮座间隔短直线纹。主纹区为一圈铭文圈带，两侧各以一周栉齿纹为栏，窄缘。

## 29. Mirror with design of inscription

Han Dynasty

It was transferred in the case in 2009

Diameter: 6.9cm. Thickness: 0.3cm

Round, round button, round button seat, with a convex string pattern around outside the seat, and a short straight line pattern spaced between the button seat. The main pattern area is a circle of inscriptions, with a band of fine-toothed pattern on both sides as a column, with a narrow edge.

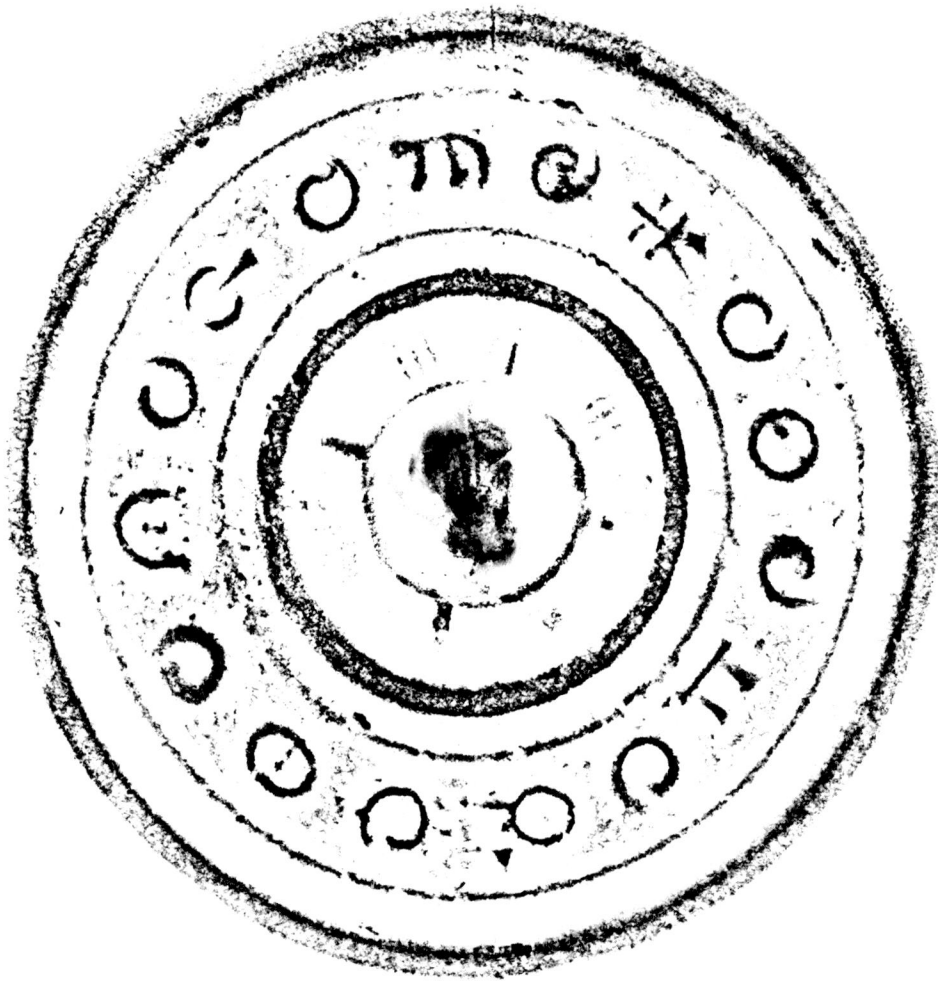

## 30. 铭文镜

汉
2009 年涉案移交
直径 6.6 厘米，厚 0.5 厘米

　　圆形，圆钮，圆钮座。钮座外环一周内向八
连弧纹，与钮座之间饰若干短线纹。主纹区以两周
栉齿纹为廓，内饰铭文一圈，字铭间以 乚 纹相隔。
素缘。

## 30. Mirror with design of inscription

Han Dynasty
It was transferred in the case in 2009
Diameter: 6.6cm. Thickness: 0.5cm

Round, round button, round button seat, surrounded by eight
inward consecutive arc patterns on the outside, and several short
lines are decorated between it and the button seat. The main
pattern area is outlined by two band of fine-toothed pattern,
with a circle of inscription. The inscriptions are separated by 乚
patterns. Plain margin.

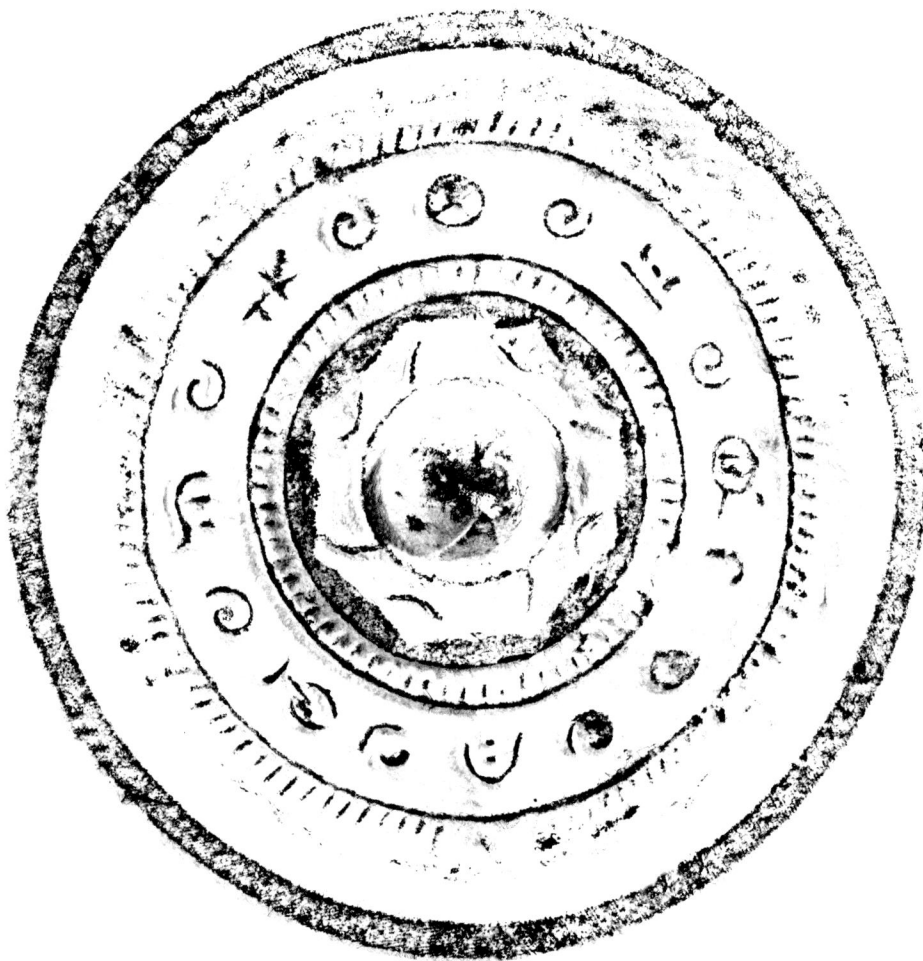

# 31. 铭文镜

## 31. Mirror with design of inscription

———

汉

2009 年涉案移交

直径 7.7 厘米，厚 0.3 厘米

Han Dynasty

It was transferred in the case in 2009

Diameter: 7.7cm. Thickness: 0.3cm

　　圆形，半球钮，圆钮座。此镜为日光镜，字体简化畸变较多。钮座外饰两周细弦纹，外围一周宽弦纹。宽弦纹圈与细弦纹圈之间饰短直线纹。主纹区为一圈铭文，字铭之间以 ⌒ 纹相隔。窄缘。

Circular, hemispherical button, circular button seat. This is a kind of sunlight mirror, the fonts are simplified and distorted. The button seat is adorned with two fine string patterns on the outside, and a wide string pattern on the outside. Decorate a short straight line pattern between the wide string pattern and the thin string pattern. The main pattern area is a circle of inscriptions. The inscriptions are separated by ⌒ patterns. Narrow edge.

## 32. 连弧纹昭明镜

汉

2009 年涉案移交

直径 8.9 厘米，厚 0.3 厘米

　　圆形，圆钮，圆钮座，外环一周内向十二连弧纹，与钮座间以短弧线和短直线纹间隔。主纹区为一圈铭文圈带，两侧各以一周栉齿纹为廓，宽素平缘。此镜为昭明镜，铭文漫漶且有错别，不能通读，仅可辨"内""光"等字，文字间多以"而"字间隔。昭明镜铭文前两句通常为："内清质以昭明，光象夫日月"。

## 32. Zhao-Ming mirror with linked arcs design

Han Dynasty

It was transferred in the case in 2009

Diameter: 8.9cm. Thickness: 0.3cm

Circular, circular button, circular button seat, surrounded by twelve inward consecutive arc patterns on the outside, separated by short arc lines and short straight lines between the button seat. The main pattern area is a circle of inscriptions, each side has a band of fine-toothed pattern as the outline, with a wide plain edge. This is the mirror with inscription of "Zhao Ming", the inscription is indistinguishable and has wrong,it can not read smoothly.Only the words "Nei" and "Guang" can be distinguished.The inscription is spaced by the word "Er". The first two lines of the inscription on Zhao Ming mirror are usually translated as "The quality is noble and clean and honest, and the loyalty is equal to the sun and moon".

.

## 33. 连弧纹昭明镜

汉

2009 年涉案移交

直径 6.4 厘米，厚 0.2 厘米

圆形，半球钮，圆钮座。钮座外饰一周内向八连弧纹，与钮座间饰若干短弧线纹。主纹区以两周栉齿纹为廓，内饰铭文一圈，铭文"内而清以昭明，光而象夫日"，素缘。

## 33. Zhao-Ming mirror with linked arcs design

Han Dynasty

It was transferred in the case in 2009

Diameter: 6.4cm. Thickness: 0.2cm

Circular, hemispherical button, circular button seat, surrounded by eight inward consecutive arc patterns on the outside, and several short arc patterns are decorated between it and the button seat. The main pattern area is outlined with two bands of fine-toothed pattern, and the interior is a circle of inscription. The inscription can be translated as "The quality is noble and clean and honest, and the loyalty is equal to the sun", with a plain margin.

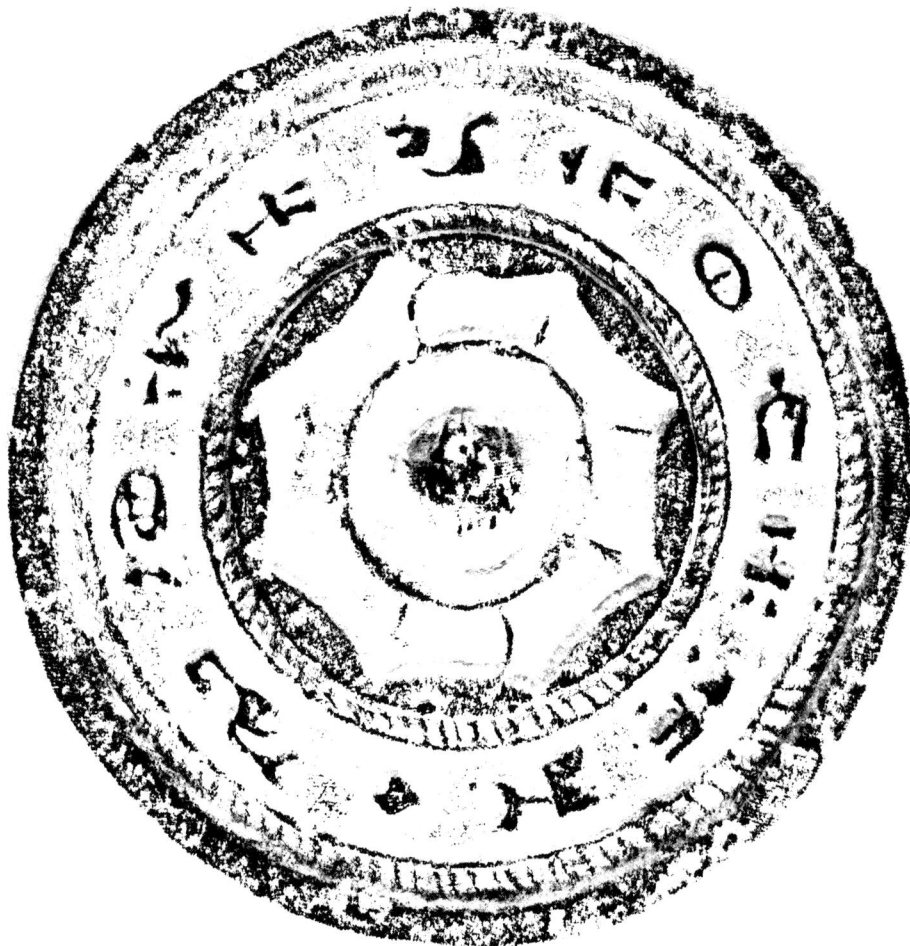

## 34. 连弧纹昭明镜

汉

2009 年涉案移交

直径 7.3 厘米

　　圆形，圆钮，圆钮座。钮座外环饰一周凸弦纹，一周内向八连弧纹。主区纹饰以两周栉齿纹为廓，内饰铭文一圈，铭文"内清以昭明，光象日月"，字铭间以"而"字间隔。卷缘。

## 34. Zhao-Ming mirror with linked arcs design

Han Dynasty

It was transferred in the case in 2009

Diameter: 7.3cm

Round, round button, round button seat. The outside of the button seat is decorated with a raised string pattern around it, and eight inward connected arc patterns around it. The main area is decorated with a two bands of fine-toothed pattern as the outline, and the interior has a circle of inscriptions "The quality is noble and clean and honest, and the loyalty is equal to the sun and moon" and the inscriptions are separated by the character "Er". Rolled-up edge.

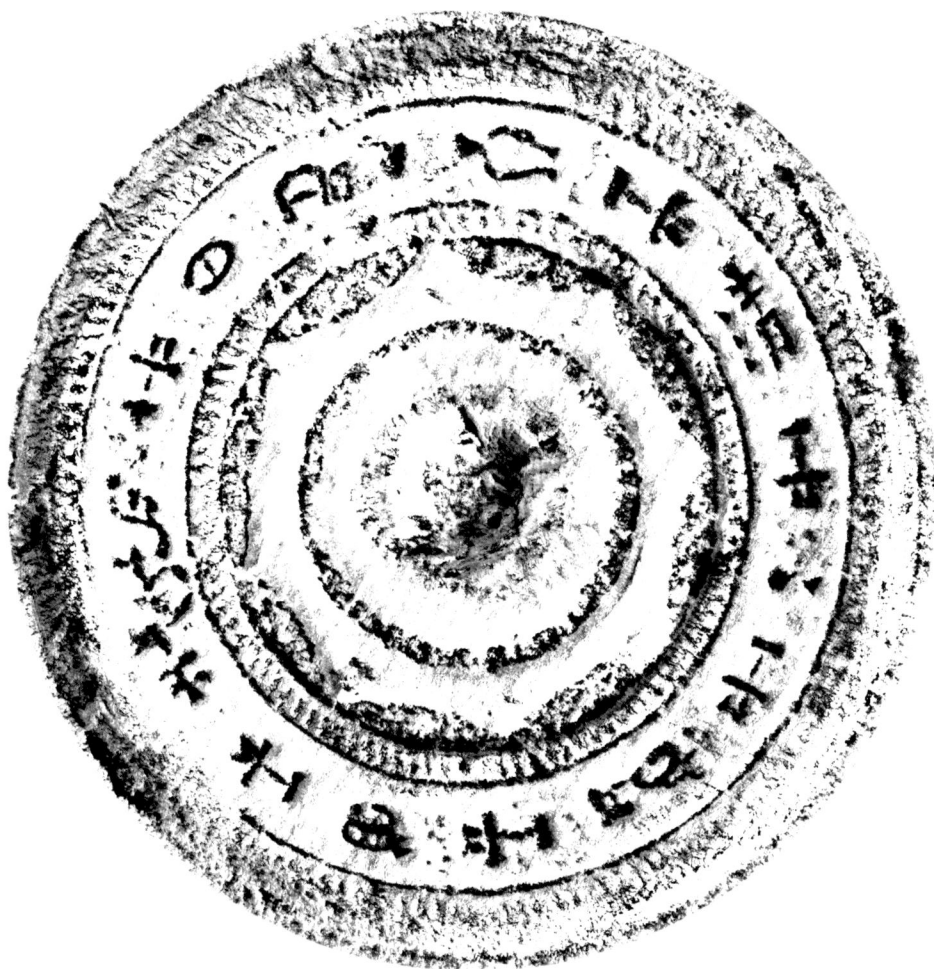

## 35. 连弧纹昭明镜

## 35. Zhao-Ming mirror with linked arcs design

汉

2009 年涉案移交

直径 6.6 厘米，厚 0.25 厘米

Han Dynasty

It was transferred in the case in 2009

Diameter: 6.6cm. Thickness: 0.25cm

　　圆形，拱形钮，圆钮座。钮座外环饰一周内向八连弧纹。主纹区以两周栉齿纹为廓，内饰铭文一圈，铭文"内清以昭明，光象日月"，字铭间以"而"字间隔。素缘。

Circular, arched button, circular button seat, surrounded by eight inward consecutive arc patterns on the outside. The main pattern area is outlined with two bands of fine-toothed pattern, and the interior is inscribed with a circle of inscription "The quality is noble and clean and honest, and the loyalty is equal to the sun and moon", and the inscriptions are separated by the character "Er". Plain margin.

## 37. 连弧纹昭明镜

汉

埇桥区出土

直径 10.5 厘米，厚 0.4 厘米

　　圆形，半球钮，圆钮座。钮座外有一周内向十二连弧纹，连弧纹与钮座间有若干短直线纹装饰。主纹区为一圈铭文圈带，铭文"内清质以昭明，光象夫日月不泄"，篆书，字体方正，每字间以"而"字相隔，铭文带两侧以栉齿纹为廓。宽素缘。

## 37. Zhao-Ming mirror with linked arcs design

Han Dynasty

It was collected in Yongqiao District

Diameter: 10.5cm. Thickness: 0.4cm

The mirror is round in shape. It has a half-sphere-shaped knob on a round base. Outside th base is adorned with twelve linked arcs design and short straight line patterns. The major motif is a band of inscription of "The quality is noble and clean and honest, and the loyalty is equal to the sun and moon", and the words are separated by "Er". Both sides of the inscription are decorated with a band of comb teeth pattern. The rim without design is broad and has a flat surface.

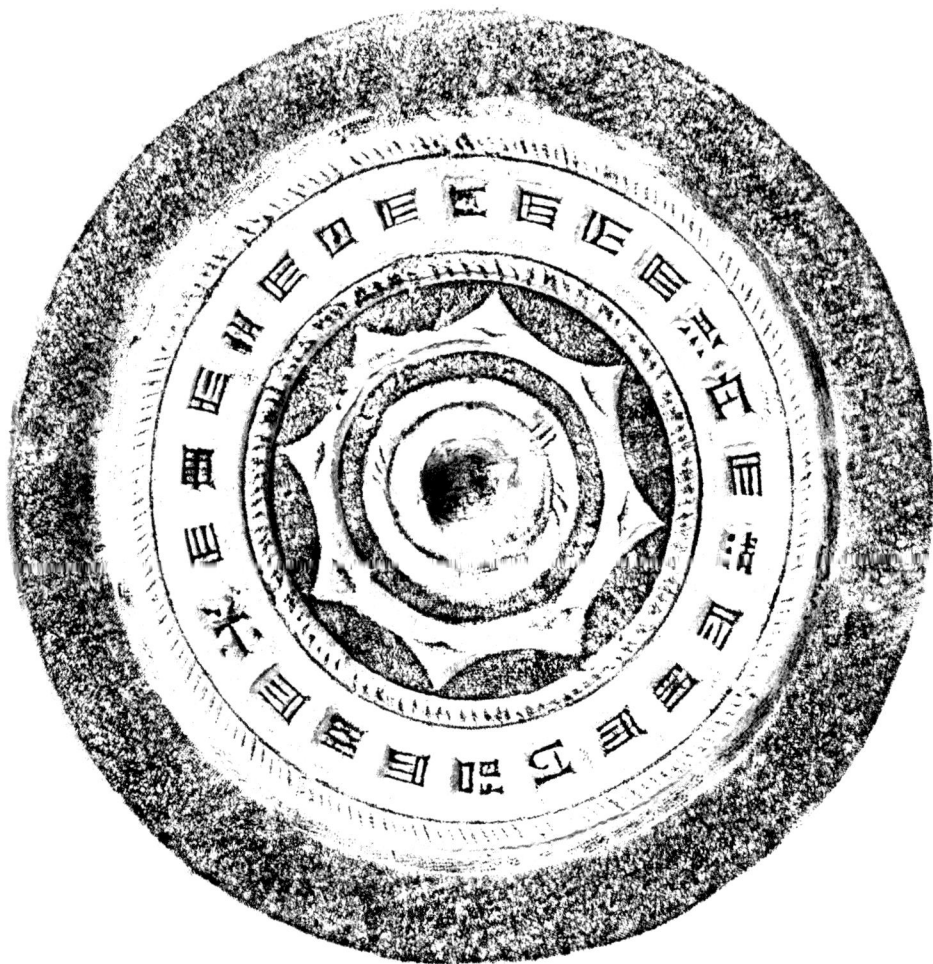

## 36. 连弧纹昭明镜

## 36. Zhao-Ming mirror with linked arcs design

汉

2009 年涉案移交

直径 7.6 厘米，缘厚 0.3 厘米

Han Dynasty

It was transferred in the case in 2009

Diameter: 7.6cm. Edge thickness: 0.3cm

　　圆形，圆钮，圆钮座，钮座外环一周宽弦纹带，一周内向八连弧纹。主纹区以两周栉齿纹为廓，内饰铭文一圈，铭文"内清以昭明，光象日月"。素缘。

Round, round button, round button seat, with a wide string pattern and eight continuous arc patterns around the outside of the button seat. The main pattern area is outlined with two bands of fine-toothed pattern, and the interior is inscribed with a circle of inscription "The quality is noble and clean and honest, and the loyalty is equal to the sun and moon". Plain margin.

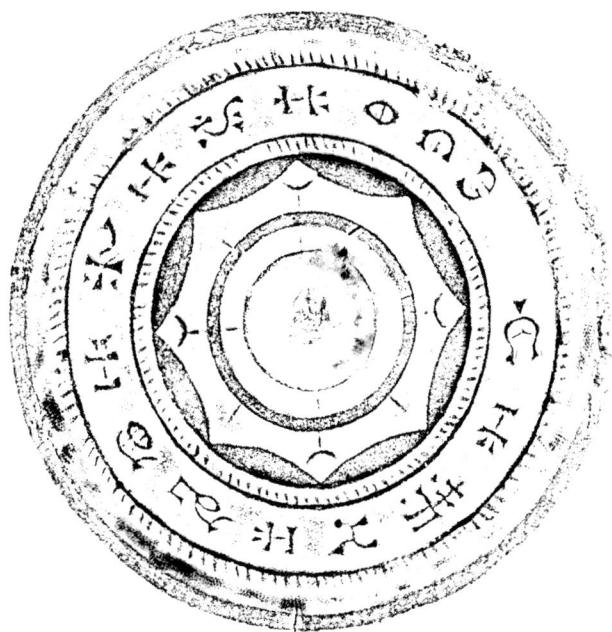

## 38. 连弧纹昭明镜

汉

埇桥区征集

直径 16.8, 缘厚 0.5 厘米

　　圆形, 圆钮, 并蒂十二连珠纹钮座, 外饰一周栉齿纹、一周凸圈带及八内向连弧纹。主纹饰区两周栉齿纹内为一周铭文圈带, 铭文 "内而青而以而昭明, 光而象夫而日之月兮, 而心忽忠扬兮不泄"。宽素平缘

## 38. Zhao-Ming mirror with linked arcs design

Han Dynasty

It was collected in Yongqiao District

Diameter: 16.8cm. Thickness: 0.5cm

The mirror is round in shape. It has a round knob on a base with twelve continuous beads. Outside the base are a band of eight inward linked arcs, a band of convex belt and fine-toothed pattern. The major motif is a band of inscription. The inscription can be translated as "The quality is noble and clean and honest, and the loyalty is equal to the sun and moon. The heart is loyal and cannot be released". The rim without design is broad and has a flat surface.

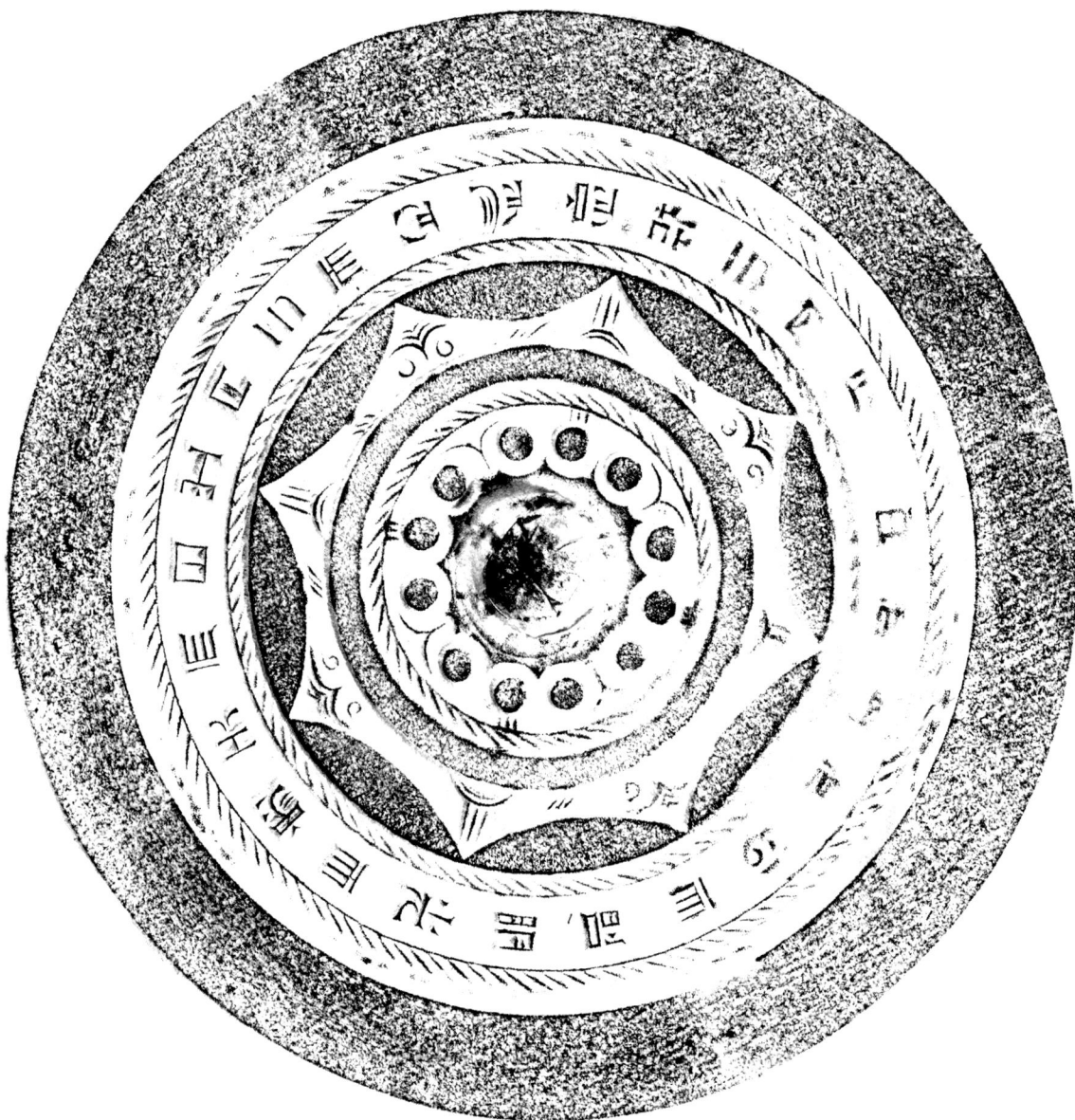

## 39. 连弧纹昭明镜

汉

2009 年涉案移交

直径 8.6 厘米，厚 0.3 厘米

　　圆形，半球钮，圆钮座。钮座外有一周内向十二连弧纹，连弧纹与钮座间有若干短直线纹装饰。主纹区为一圈铭文圈带，铭文"内清以昭明，光象日月"，篆书，字体方正，每字间以"而"字相隔，铭文圈带两侧以栉齿纹为廓。宽素缘。

　　昭明镜流行于西汉中后期，以西汉后期最盛行，是出土最多、流行范围最广的西汉铜镜之一。

## 39. Zhao-Ming mirror with linked arcs design

Han Dynasty

It was transferred in the case in 2009

Diameter: 8.6cm. Thickness: 0.3cm

Circular, hemispherical button, circular button seat. There are twelve continuous arc patterns on the outside of the button seat, with several short straight lines between the continuous arc patterns and the button seat for decoration. The main pattern area consists of a circle of inscriptions, which can be translated as "The quality is noble and clean and honest, and the loyalty is equal to the sun and moon". The seal script has a square and upright font, with each character separated by the character "Er". The two sides of the inscription circle are outlined with a band of fine-toothed pattern. Wide margin.

The Zhaoming Mirror was popular in the mid to late Western Han Dynasty, being the most popular in the late western Han Dynasty. It is one of the most unearthed and widely popular bronze mirrors of the Western Han Dynasty.

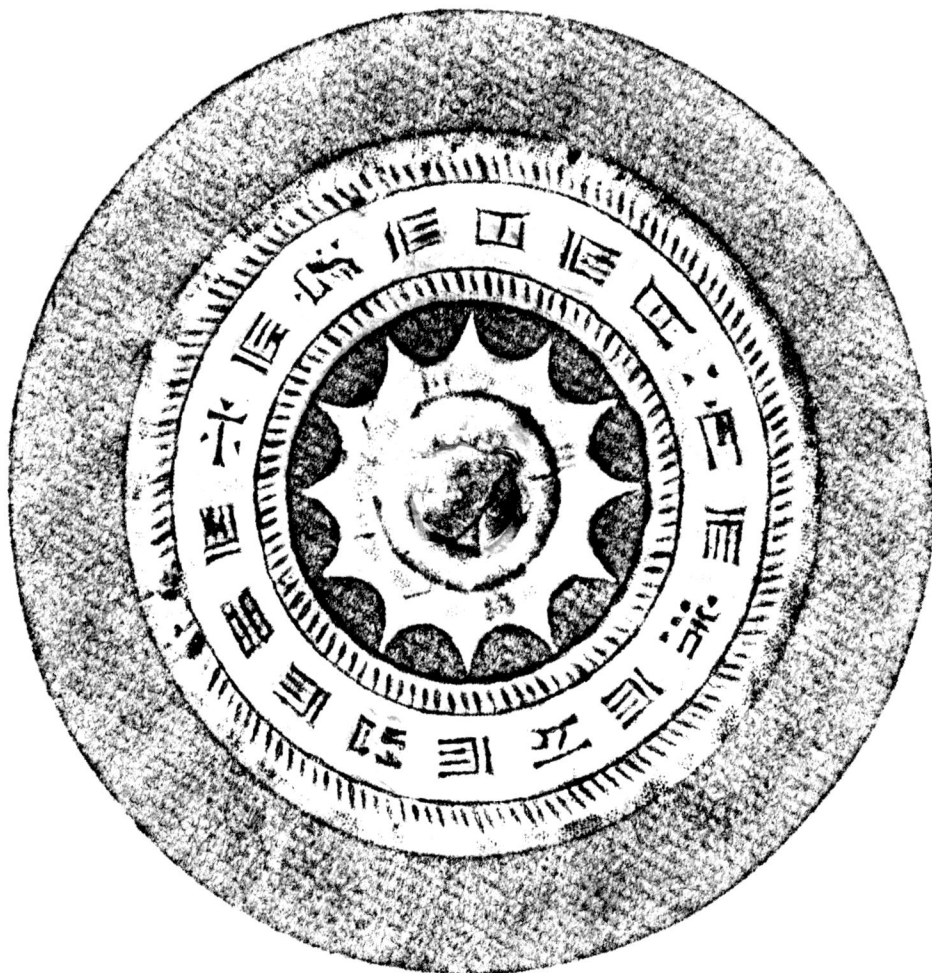

## 40. 连弧纹昭明镜

汉

2009 年涉案移交

直径 8.2 厘米，厚 0.3 厘米

　　圆形，半球钮，圆钮座，钮座外环一周内向
十二连弧纹。主纹区为一圈铭文带，铭文"内清以
昭明，光象日月"铭文间以"而"字间隔，两侧以
栉齿纹为廓。宽素平缘。

## 40. Zhao-Ming mirror with linked arcs design

Han Dynasty

It was transferred in the case in 2009

Diameter: 8.2cm. Thickness: 0.3cm

Circular, hemispherical button, round button seat surrounded by
twelve inward consecutive arc patterns on the outside. The main
pattern area is a circle of inscriptions which can be translated
as "The quality is noble and clean and honest, and the loyalty is
equal to the sun and moon" separated by the character "Er", and
the two sides are outlined by a band of fine-toothed pattern. Wide
plain edge.

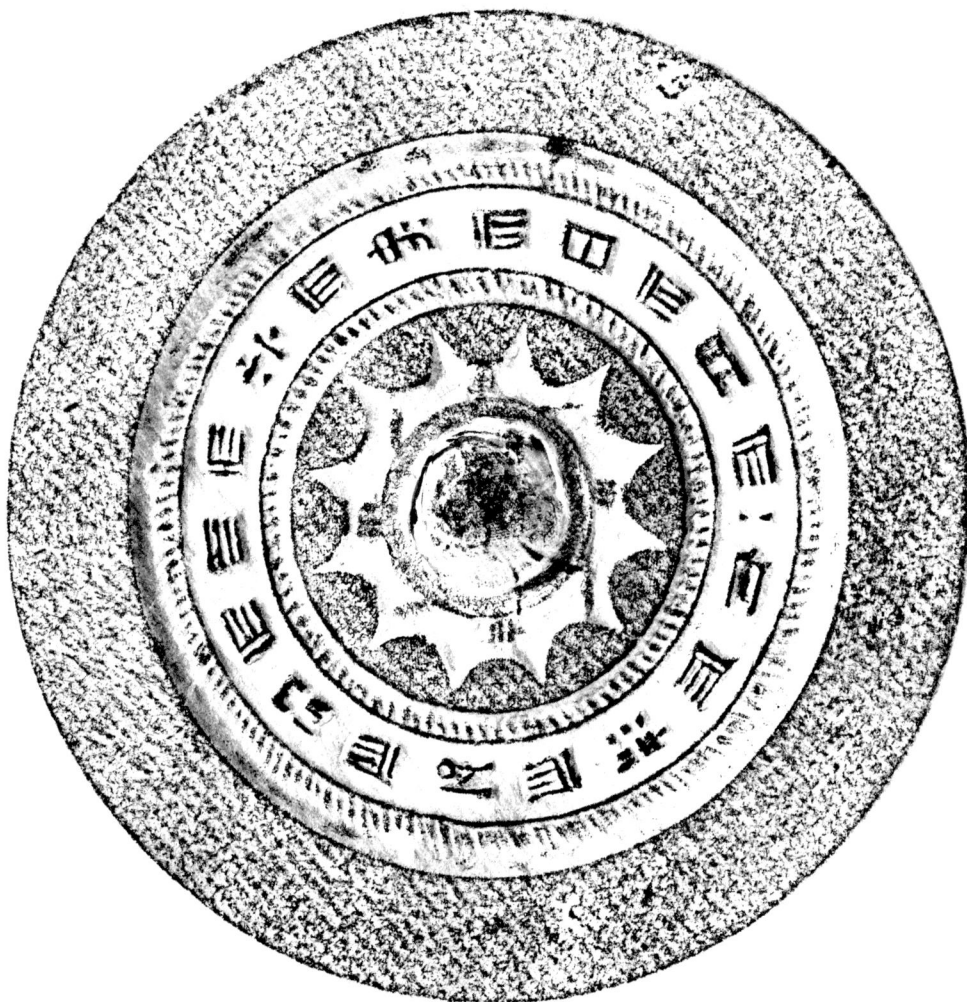

## 41. 连弧纹昭明镜

汉

2009 年涉案移交

直径 8 厘米，厚 0.2 厘米

　　圆形，圆钮，圆钮座。钮座外环一周内向十二连弧纹。主纹区以两周栉齿纹为廓，内置铭文一圈，铭文"内青（清）以明，光象日月"，字铭间以"而"字间隔、宽素平缘。

## 41. Zhao-Ming mirror with linked arcs design

Han Dynasty

It was transferred in the case in 2009

Diameter: 8cm. Thickness: 0.2cm

Round, round button, round button seat, surrounded by twelve inward consecutive arc patterns on the outside. The main pattern area is outlined by two bands of fine-toothed pattern, with inscription which can be translated as "The quality is noble and clean and honest, and the loyalty is equal to the sun and moon", and the characters are separated by the character "Er" with a wide plain edge.

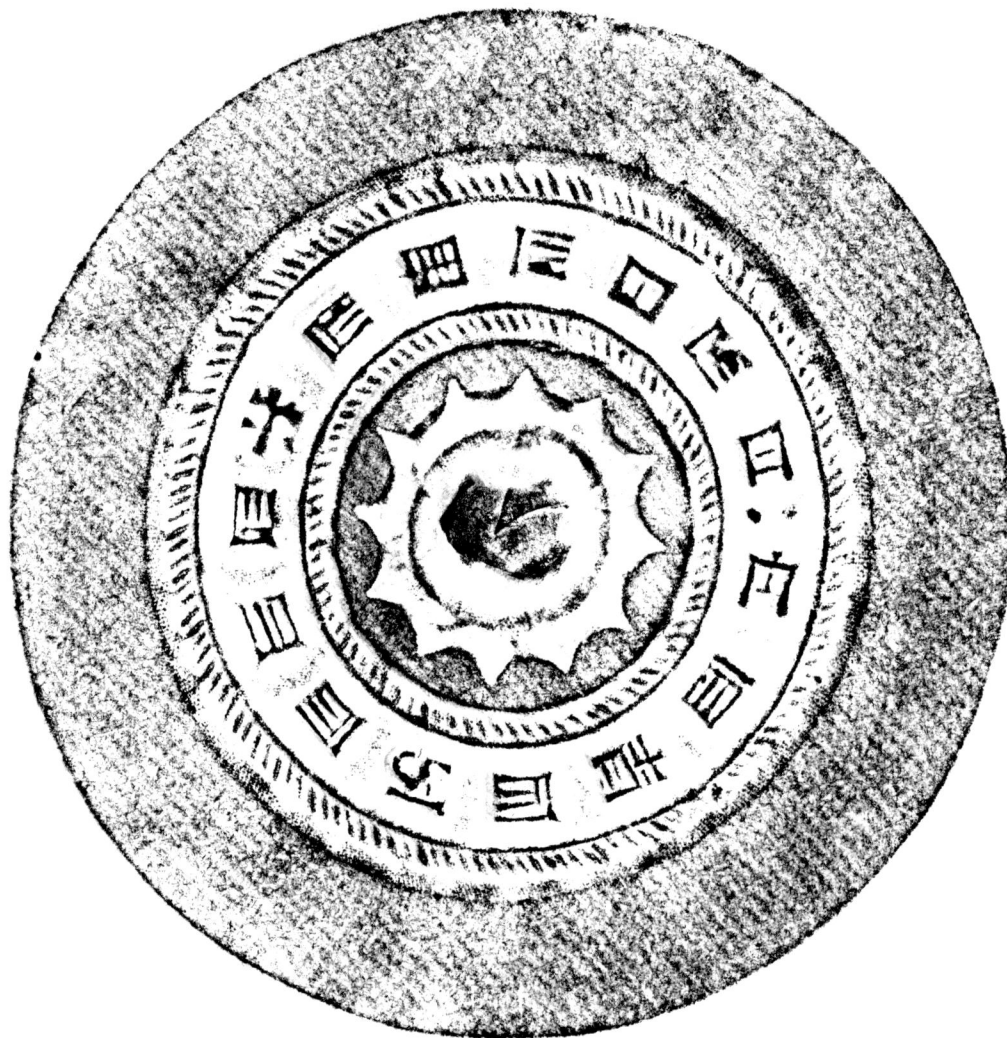

## 42. 连弧纹昭明镜

汉

埇桥区大泽乡出土

直径 13.5 厘米，厚 0.6 厘米

　　圆形，半球钮，柿蒂纹钮座。钮座外环一周宽弦纹带、一周内向八连弧纹，间饰短线纹。主纹区一圈铭文带，铭文"内清质以昭明，光象夫日月"，字铭间以"而"字间隔，两侧以一周栉齿纹为栏。宽素缘。

## 42. Zhao-Ming mirror with linked arcs design

Han Dynasty

Unearthed in Daze Township

Diameter: 13.5cm. Thickness: 0.6cm

Circular, hemispherical button, on a base with kaki calyx design. The outside of the button seat has a wide string pattern around it, eight inward arc patterns around it, and short line patterns between the decorations. The main pattern area is surrounded by an inscription belt, which means "The quality is noble and clean and honest, and the loyalty is equal to the sun and moon". The characters are separated by the character "Er", and there is a band of fine-toothed pattern on both sides as a column. Wide margin.

## 43. 连弧纹昭明镜
## 43. Zhao-Ming mirror with linked arcs design

汉

2009 年涉案移交

直径 8.8 厘米，厚 0.4 厘米

Han Dynasty

It was transferred in the case in 2009

Diameter: 8.8cm. Thickness: 0.4cm

　　圆形，圆钮，圆钮座。钮座外环一周宽弦纹带，与钮座以短线纹相连。主纹区以两周栉齿纹为廓，内饰铭文一圈，铭文"内青（清）以昭明，光象日月"，字铭间以"而"字间隔。宽素平缘。

Round, round button, round button seat with a wide string pattern around it, which is connected to the button seat with short line patterns. The main pattern area is outlined with two bands of fine-toothed pattern, and the interior is a circle of inscription which can be translated as "The quality is noble and clean and honest, and the loyalty is equal to the sun and moon", and the inscriptions are separated by the character "Er". Wide plain edge.

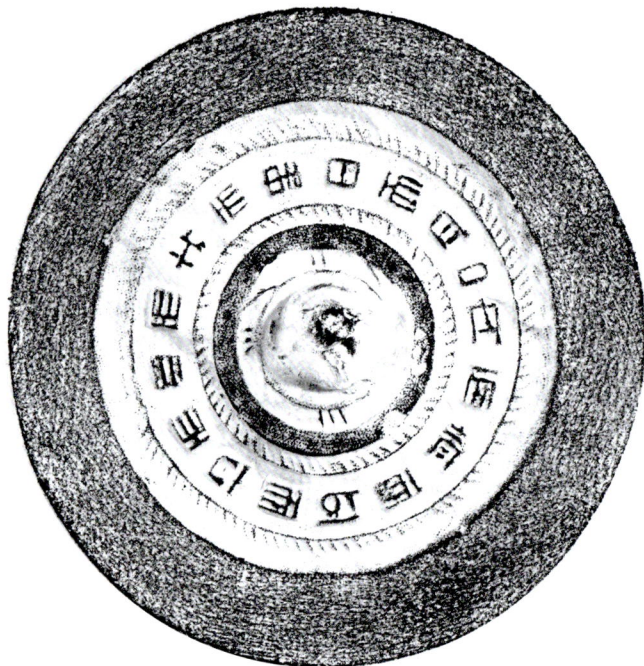

# 44. 连弧纹昭明镜

## 44. Zhao-Ming mirror with linked arcs design

汉

2009 年涉案移交

直径 8.3 厘米，厚 0.4 厘米

Han Dynasty

It was transferred in the case in 2009

Diameter: 8.3cm. Thickness: 0.4cm

　　圆形，圆钮，圆钮座。钮座外环饰一周内向八连弧纹，与钮座间饰若干短弧线纹。主纹区以两周栉齿纹为廓，内饰铭文一圈，铭文"内清以昭明，光日月"，字铭间以"而"字间隔。宽素平缘。

Round, round button, round button seat, surrounded by eight inward consecutive arc patterns on the outside, and several short arc patterns are decorated between the button seat. The main pattern area is outlined by two bands of fine-toothed pattern, with a circle of inscriptions, which can be translated as "The quality is noble and clean and honest, and the loyalty is equal to the sun and moon", and the inscriptions are separated by the character "Er". Wide plain edge.

## 45. 连弧纹昭明镜

汉

2001 年永安刘楼村征集

直径 10 厘米，厚 0.45 厘米

　　圆形，圆钮，圆钮座，钮座外环一周宽弦纹，一周内向八连弧纹。主纹区以两周栉齿纹为廓，内置一周铭文圈带，铭文"内清以昭明，光日月"，铭文间以"而"字间隔。宽平缘。

## 45. Zhao-Ming mirror with linked arcs design

Han Dynasty

It was solicited in Liulou Village , Yong'an town

Diameter: 10cm. Thickness: 0.45cm

Round, round button, round button seat, with a wide string pattern and eight consecutive arc patterns around the outside of the button seat. The main pattern area is outlined by two bands of fine-toothed pattern, with a circle of inscription band. The inscription can be translated as "The quality is noble and clean and honest, and the loyalty is equal to the sun and moon", and the inscriptions are separated by the character "Er". Wide flat edge.

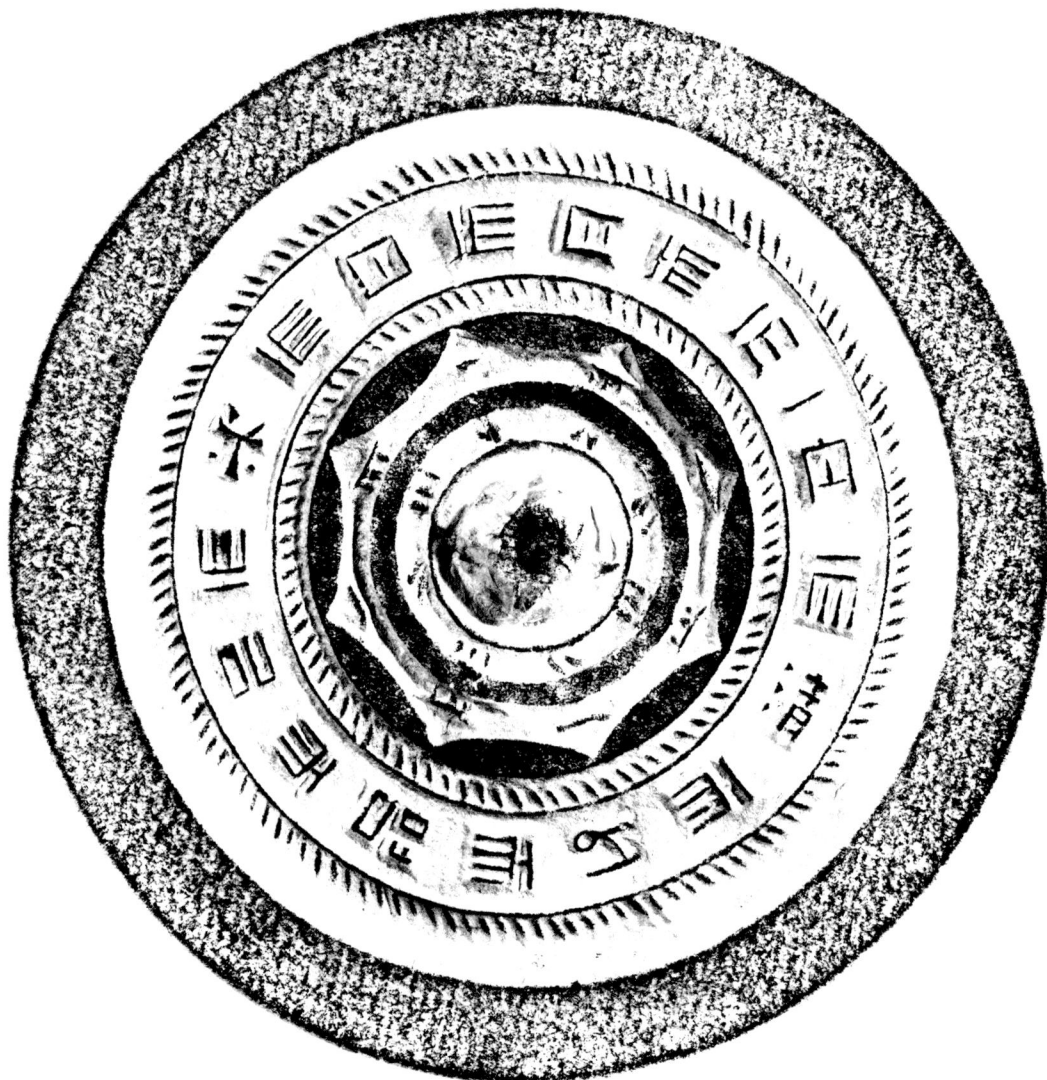

## 46. 连弧纹昭明镜
## 46. Zhao-Ming mirror with linked arcs design

汉

2009 年涉案移交

直径 8.4 厘米，厚 0.3 厘米

Han Dynasty

It was transferred in the case in 2009

Diameter: 8.4cm. Thickness: 0.3cm

　　圆形，圆钮，圆钮座，钮座外环一周内向十二连弧纹，与钮座间饰若干短线纹。主纹区以两周栉齿纹为廓，内饰铭文一圈，铭文"内清以昭明，光象日月"，字铭间以"而"字间隔。宽素平缘。

Round, round button, round button seat, with twelve consecutive arc patterns on the outside of the button seat, and several short line patterns decorated between the button seat. The main pattern area is outlined with two bands of fine-toothed pattern, and the interior is inscribed with a circle of inscription which can be translated as "The quality is noble and clean and honest, and the loyalty is equal to the sun and moon", and the inscriptions are separated by the character "Er". Wide plain edge.

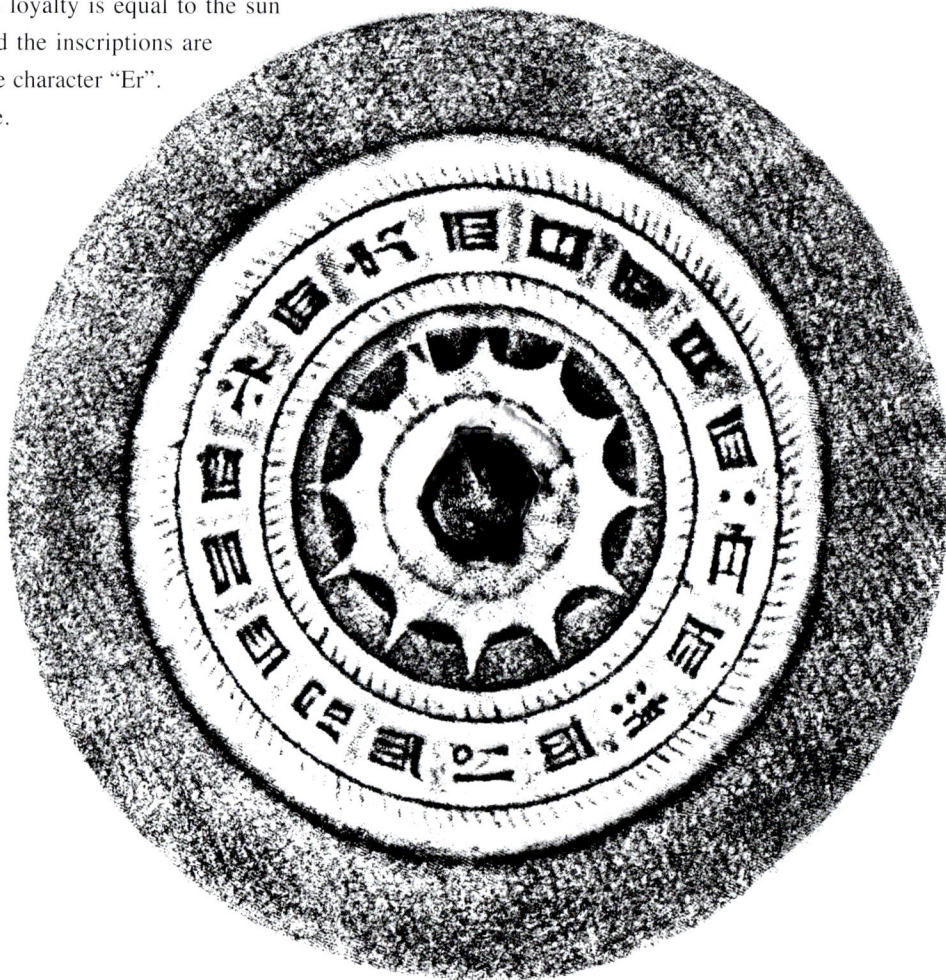

## 47. 连弧纹昭明镜

汉

萧县紫金花苑出土

直径 9.8 厘米，缘厚 0.5 厘米

　　圆形，半球钮，圆钮座。钮座外有一周内向十二连弧纹，连弧纹与钮座间有若干短直线纹装饰。主纹区为一圈铭文圈带，铭文"内清以昭明，光日月"，篆书，字体方正，每字间以"而"字相隔，铭文带两侧以栉齿纹为廓。宽素缘。

## 47. Zhao-Ming mirror with linked arcs design

Han

It was unearthed in Xiaoxian County

Diameter: 9.8cm. Thickness: 0.5cm

The mirror is round in shape. It has a half-sphere-shaped knob on a round base. Outside the base is a band of twelve inward linked arcs patterns, between the arcs and the base are serval short lines. The major motif is a band of inscription which can be translated as "The quality is noble and clean and honest, and the loyalty is equal to the sun and moon", in seal script which is spaced with Er-character-shaped pattern. Both side of the major motif are decorated with a band of fine-toothed pattern. The broad rim is without design.

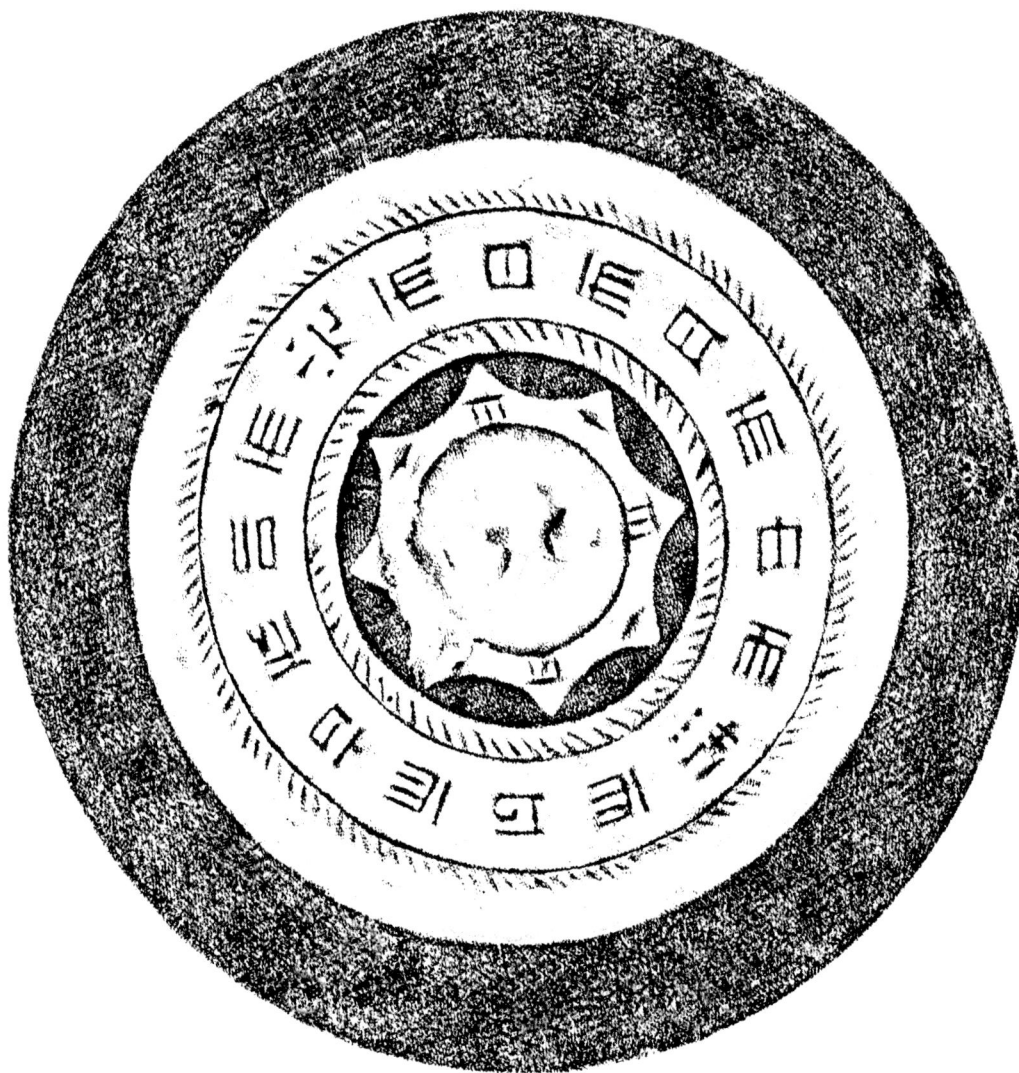

## 48. 铭文镜

汉

旧藏

直径 15.6 厘米，厚 0.5 厘米

　　圆形，圆钮，连珠纹钮座。两周凸宽弦纹将镜背分为内外两区，内区以两周栉齿纹为廓，内饰一圈铭文，"长相思，毋见日之光，天下大多明者富贵番昌"，外区以两周栉齿纹为廓，内饰一圈铭文，"君有行，妾有忧，行有日，反（返）无期。愿君强饭多勉之，印（仰）天大息，长相思，毋久"。宽素缘。

## 48. Mirror with design of inscription

Han Dynasty

Old collection

Diameter: 15.6cm. Thickness: 0.5cm

Circular, round button, continuous bead pattern button seat. The two circular convex wide string patterns divides the mirror back into two areas, the inner area is outlined by two bands of fine-toothed pattern, and the interior is surrounded by inscriptions, which can be translated as "Often miss, can not see the daylight. Most sensible people in the world are rich and prosperous". The outer area is outlined by two bands of fine-toothed pattern, and the interior is surrounded by inscriptions, which can be translated as "My husband is going out. l am very worried. l don't know when he will come back. l hope he can eat well. l look at the sky and sigh, hope he can think of me often and don't stay too long". Wide margin.

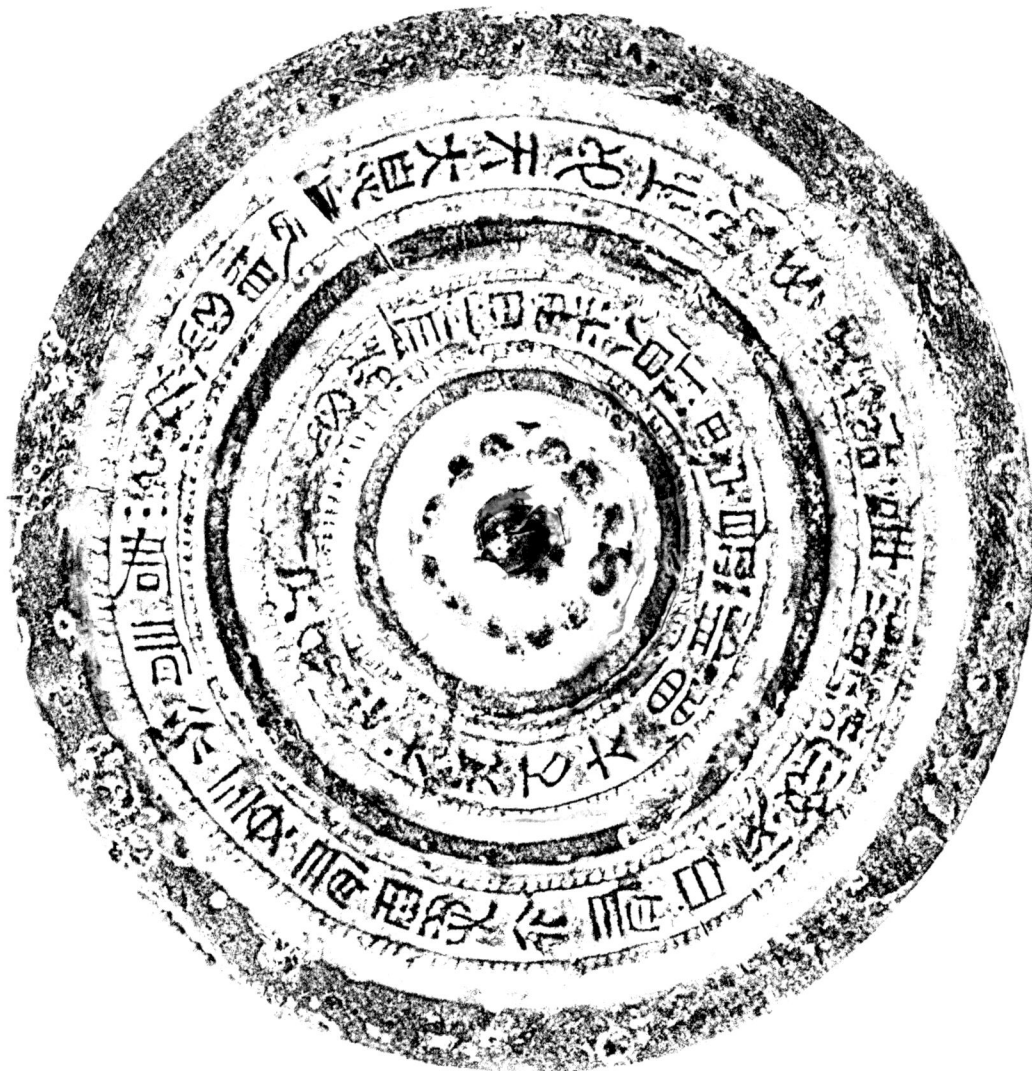

## 49. 四乳席纹镜

汉

2009 年涉案移交

直径 11 厘米，厚 0.3 厘米

圆形，圆钮，柿蒂纹座。钮座外环一周凹面宽带纹。主纹区遍布席纹，四个圆座乳钉等距分布。卷缘。

## 49. Mirror with design of four nipples and mat

Han Dynasty

It was transferred in the case in 2009

Diameter: 11cm. Thickness: 0.3cm

Round, round button, with kaki calyx design on the base. The outer ring of the button seat has a concave wide band pattern around it. The main pattern area is covered with mat patterns, with four circular breast nails evenly spaced. Rolled-up edge.

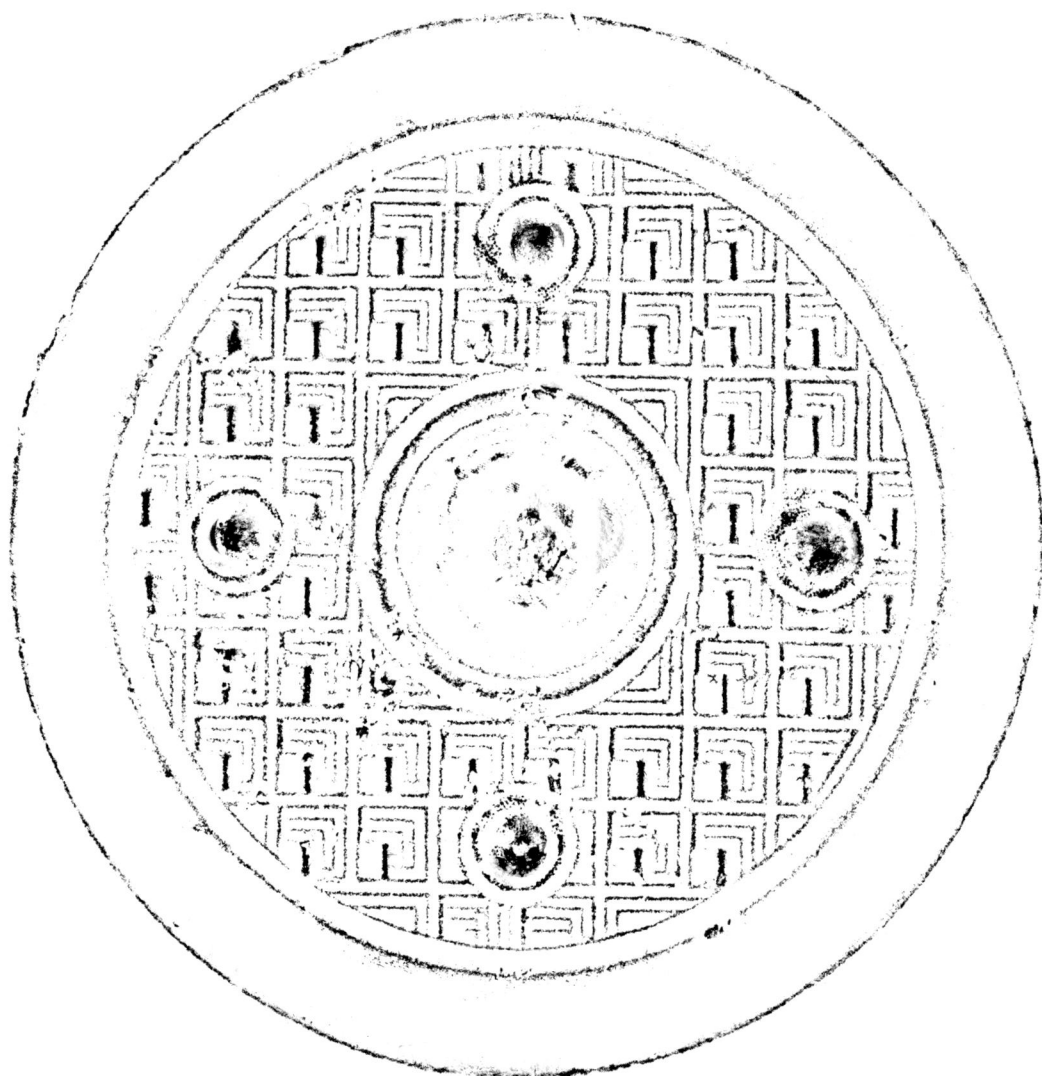

## 50. 席纹镜

汉

2009 年涉案移交

直径 11 厘米，厚 0.35 厘米

圆形，圆钮，柿蒂纹钮座。主纹区以两周双线弦纹圈为廓，其内满铺席纹。素卷缘。

## 50. Mirror with design of mat

Han Dynasty

It was transferred in the case in 2009

Diameter: 11cm. Thickness: 0.35cm

Circular, round button, with kaki calyx design on the base. The main pattern area is outlined by two circular double line string patterns, and covered with mat patterns. Plain rolled-up edge.

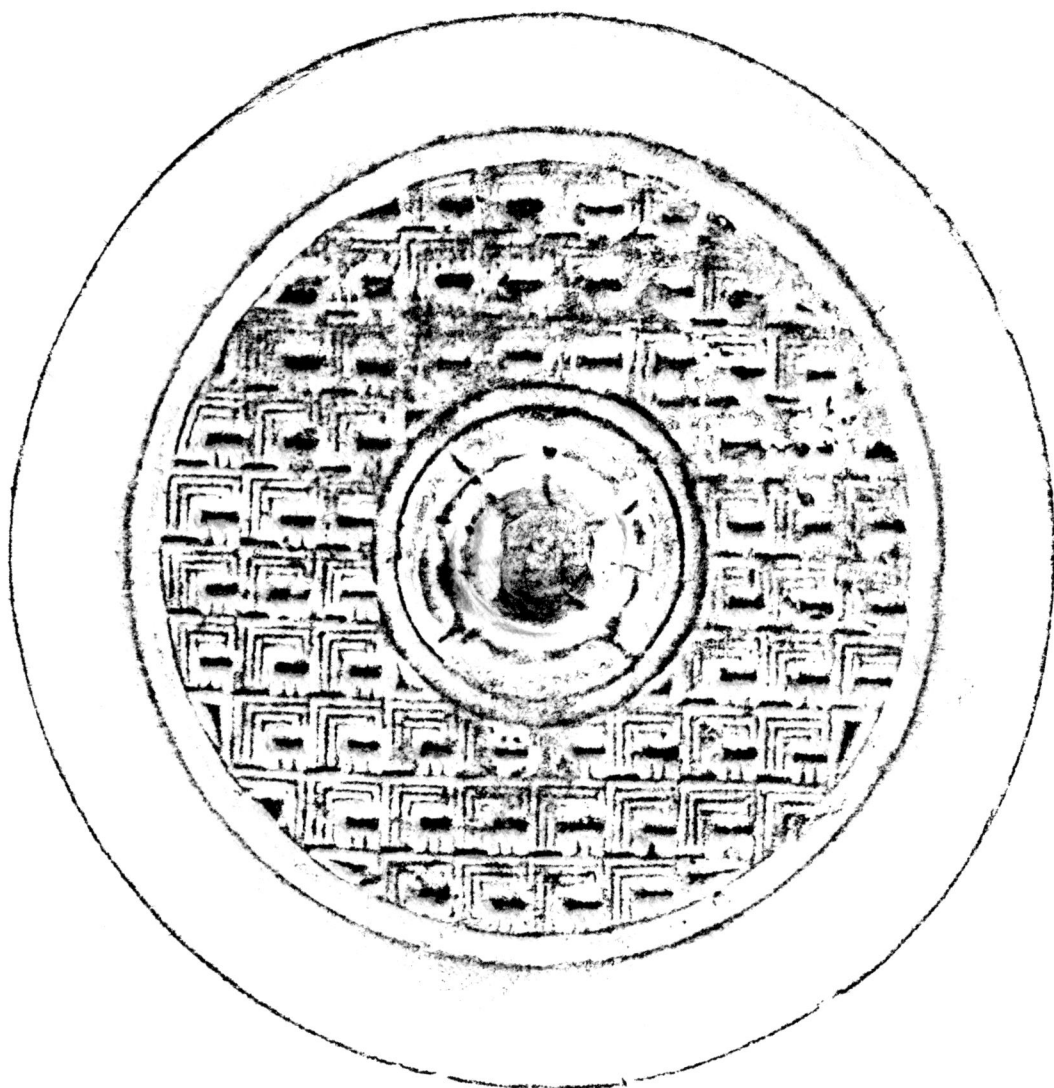

## 51. 四乳四虺纹镜

汉

1982 年夹沟出土

直径 10.2 厘米，缘厚 0.4 厘米

圆形，圆钮，圆钮座。钮座外饰一周宽凸弦纹，与钮座间饰交替排列的单弧线和双弧线一周。主纹区以两周栉齿纹为廓，四圆座乳钉将主纹区等分为四区，每区内置一虺形纹。虺纹躯体呈"S"形，头、尾各饰一站立鸟纹。素宽缘。

## 51. Mirror with design of four nipples and four serpents

Han Dynasty

It was unearthed in Jiagou in 1982

Diameter: 10.2cm. Edge thickness: 0.4cm

Round, round button, round button seat. The outer decoration of the button seat features a wide convex string pattern, with alternating single and double arcs arranged around the button seat. The main pattern area is divided into four areas by the two bands of fine-toothed pattern, and the four circular breast nails divide the main pattern area into four areas, with each area containing a serpent shaped pattern. The body of the serpent pattern is in an "S" shape, with a standing bird pattern on its head and tail. Plain wide margin.

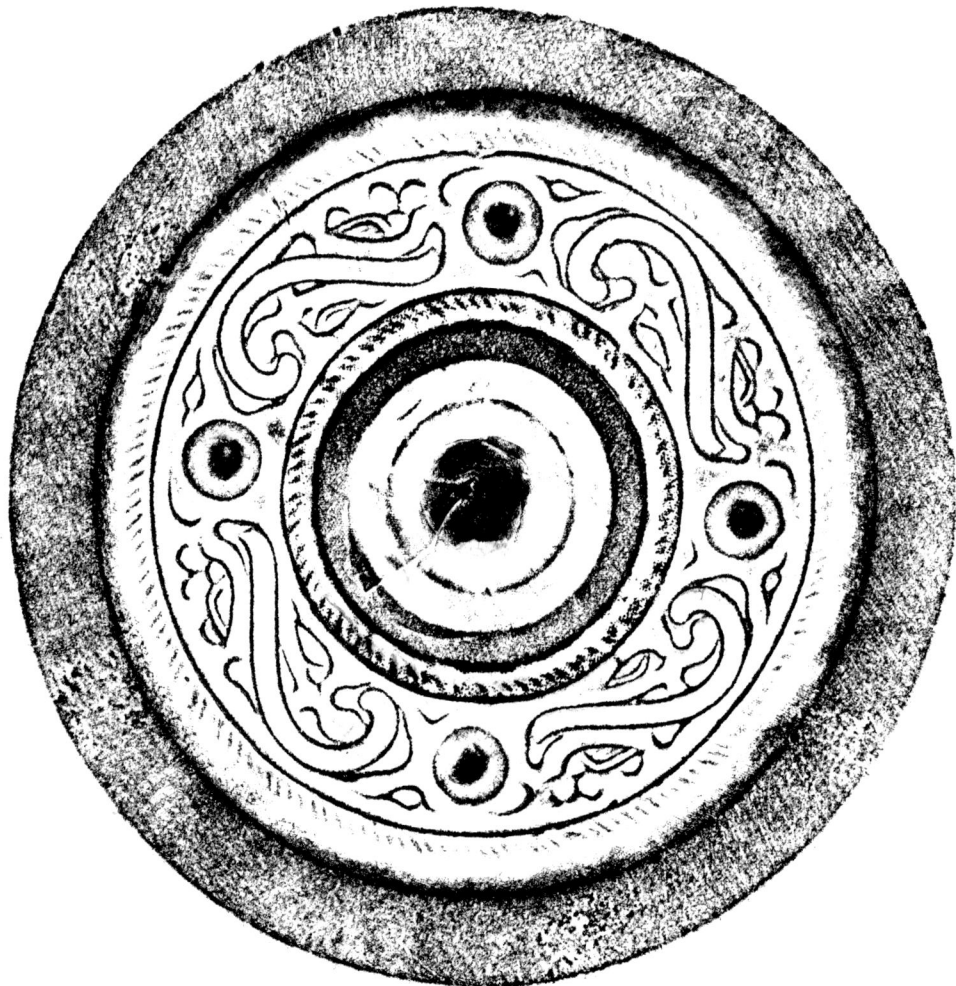

## 52. 四乳四虺纹镜

汉

1985 年宿县东关文化站征集

直径 11.6 厘米，缘厚 0.4 厘米

　　圆形，圆钮，圆钮座。钮座外饰一周宽凸弦纹，与钮座间饰短直线纹。主纹区以两周栉齿纹为廓，四圆座乳钉与四虺纹相间等距环绕，虺纹躯体呈 "S" 形，头、尾处各饰一鸟纹。素宽缘。

## 52. Mirror with design of four nipples and four serpents

Han Dynasty

It was collected in Suzhou dongguan Cultural Station

Diameter: 11.6cm. Edge thickness: 0.4cm

Round, round button, round button seat, surrounded by a wide convex string pattern, and short straight line patterns are adorned between it and the button seat. The main pattern area is outlined by two bands of fine-toothed pattern, surrounded by four circular breast nails and four serpent patterns at equal intervals. The serpent pattern body is in an "S" shape, and the head and tail are decorated with a bird pattern. Plain wide margin.

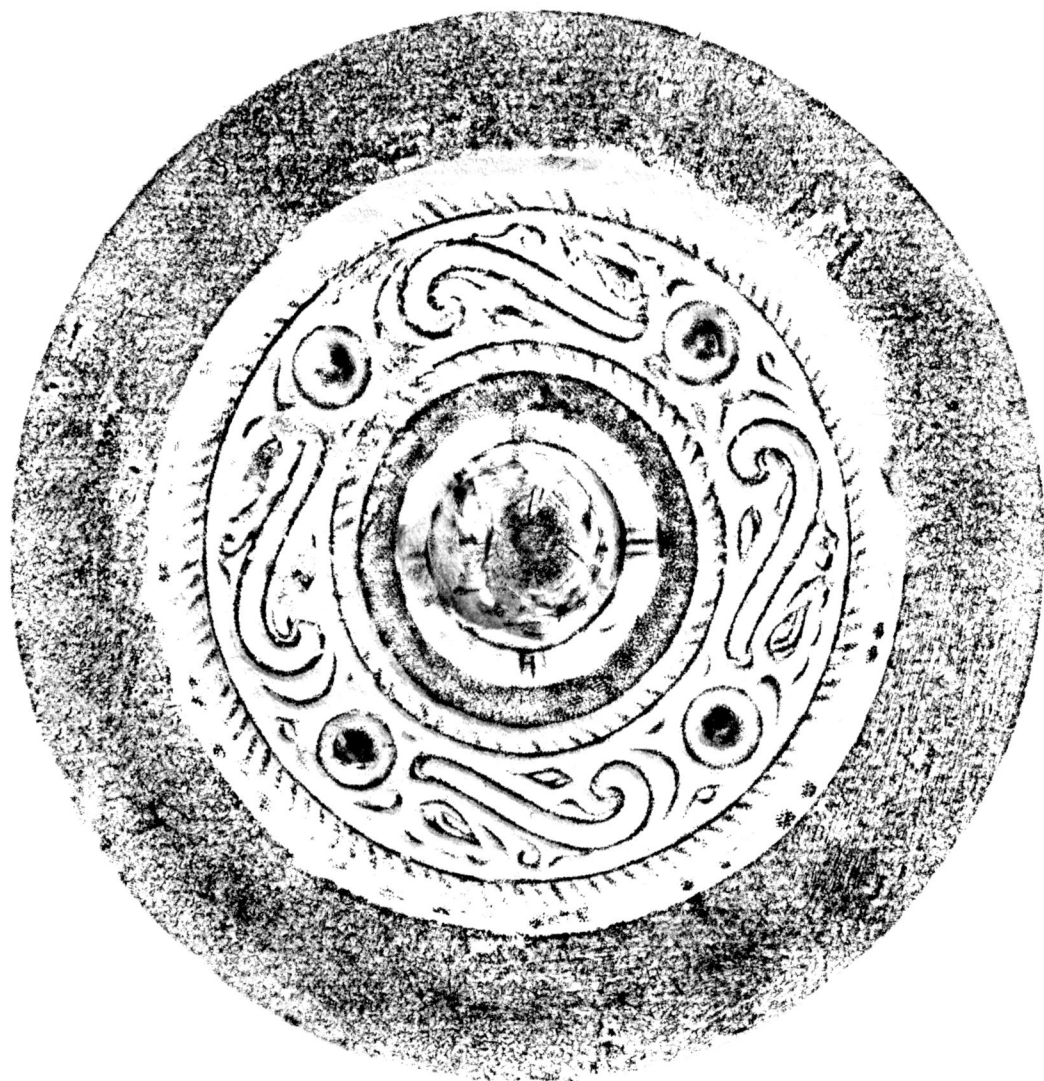

## 53. 四乳四虺纹镜

汉

1985 年大店昌圩中学征集

直径 10.3 厘米，厚 0.5 厘米

　　圆形，半球钮，圆钮座。座外环一周凸起的宽弦纹带，与钮座之间的空白处填以若干斜线纹作简单装饰。主纹为四乳四虺，乳钉下有圆形座，简化变形的虺呈 "S" 形，两侧点缀禽鸟纹饰。主纹区两侧以两周栉齿纹为廓。宽素平缘。

## 53. Mirror with design of four nipples and four serpents

Han Dynasty

It was collected from Changwei Middle School in Dadian in 1985

Diameter: 10.3cm. Thickness: 0.5cm

Circular, hemispherical button, circular button seat, surrounded by a wide convex string pattern, and the blank space between it and the button seat is filled with several diagonal lines for simple decoration. The main pattern is four breasts and four serpents, with a circular seat under the breast nail. The simplified and deformed serpents are in an "S" shape, and are adorned with bird patterns on both sides. On both sides of the main pattern area, there are two bands of fine-toothed pattern as the outline. Wide plain edge.

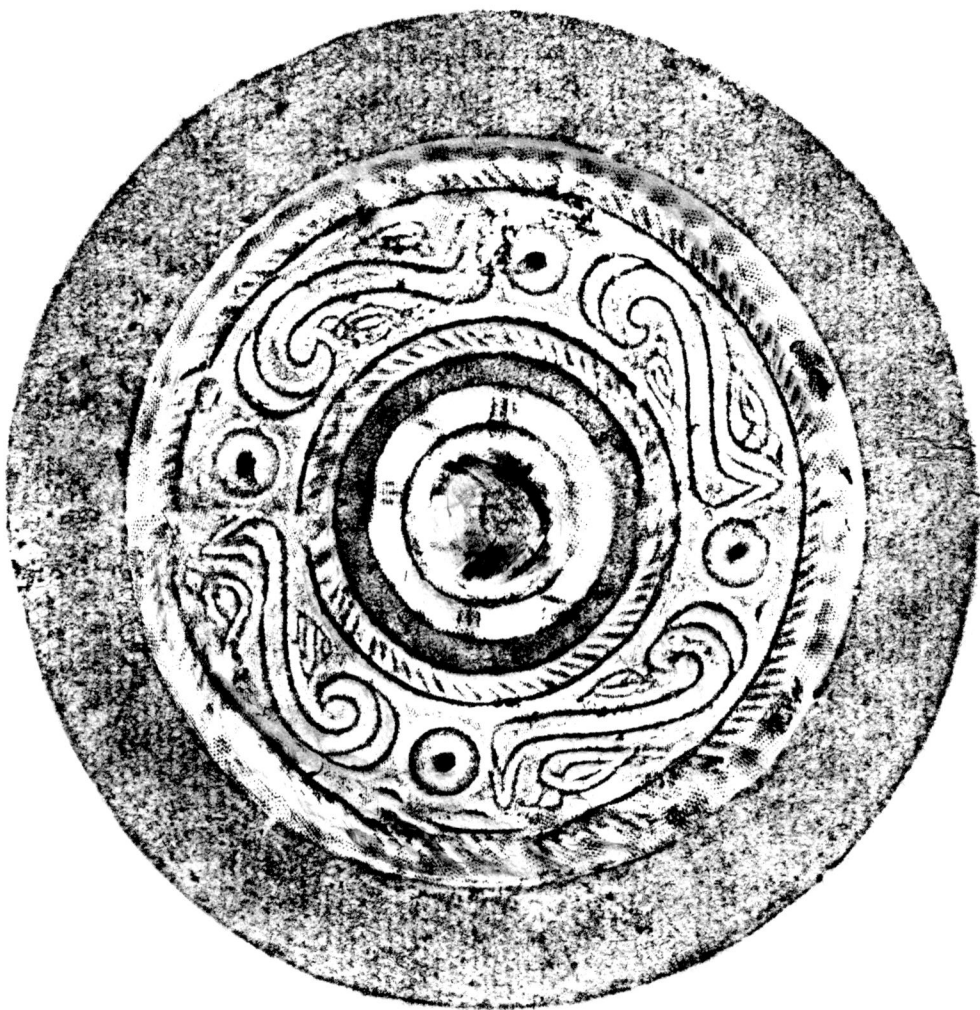

## 54. 四乳四虺纹镜

汉

埇桥区征集

直径 9.8 厘米，厚 0.5 厘米

圆形，半球钮，圆钮座。主纹区以两周栉齿纹为廓，其内四个圆座乳钉等距分布，将主纹区分为四区，每区内各饰一卷曲虺纹，虺纹两侧各饰一禽鸟纹。宽素平缘。

虺在中国古代传说中是一种毒蛇。铜镜中的虺纹常理解为是一种抽象的龙纹雏形。

## 54. Mirror with design of four nipples and four serpents

Han Dynasty

It was collected in Yongqiao District

Diameter: 9.8cm. Thickness: 0.5cm

Circular, hemispherical button, circular button seat. The main pattern area is outlined by two bands of fine-toothed pattern, with four circular breast nails evenly distributed within it. The main pattern is divided into four areas, each decorated with a curly serpent pattern and a bird pattern on both sides of the serpent pattern. Wide plain edge.

In ancient Chinese legend, the serpent is a venomous snake. The serpent pattern in bronze mirrors is often understood as an abstract prototype of dragon patterns.

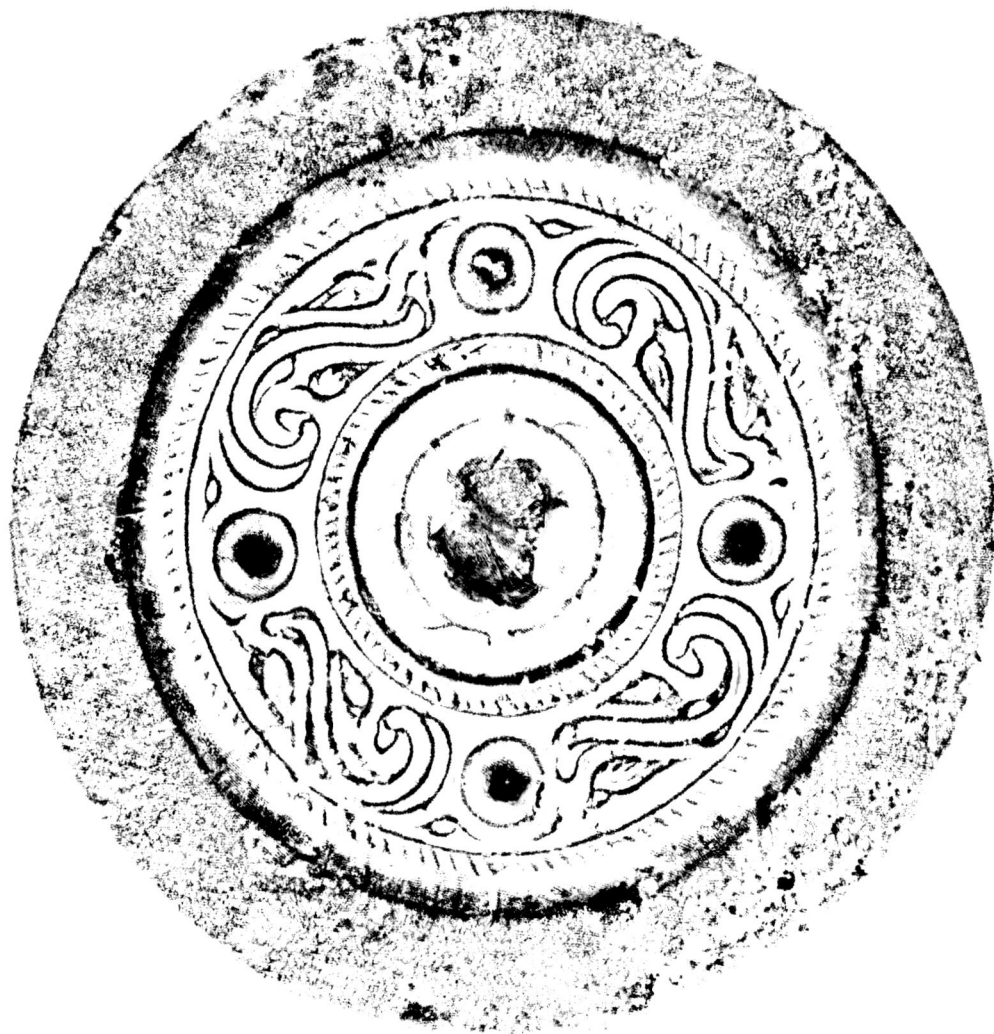

## 55. 四乳四虺纹镜

汉

埇桥区征集

直径7.4厘米，厚0.2厘米

　　圆形，圆钮，圆钮座。主区纹饰以两周栉齿纹为廓，四个圆座乳钉纹等距分布，将主纹区等分为四区，每区内各饰一个双线勾勒的虺纹。宽素平缘。

## 55. Mirror with design of four nipples and four serpents

Han Dynasty

It was collected in Yongqiao District

Diameter: 7.4cm. Thickness: 0.2cm

Round, round button, round button seat. The main area is decorated with two bands of fine-toothed pattern as the outline, and the four circular breast nail patterns are evenly distributed. The main pattern area is divided into four areas, and each area is decorated with a double line outlined serpent pattern. Wide plain edge.

## 56. 四乳四虺纹镜

汉

埇桥区征集

直径 8.4 厘米，缘厚 0.3 厘米

　　圆形，圆钮，圆钮座。钮座与内侧栉齿纹间饰若干短直线纹与弧线纹。主纹区以两周栉齿纹为廓，四个圆座乳钉等距分布，将主纹区分为四区，每区内置一个变形单线虺纹。宽素平缘。

## 56. Mirror with design of four nipples and four serpents

Han Dynasty

It was collected in Yongqiao District

Diameter: 8.4cm. Thickness: 0.3cm

Round, round button, round button seat. There are several short straight and curved lines between the button seat and the inner comb tooth pattern. The main pattern area is divided into four zones, with two bands of fine-toothed pattern as the outline and four circular breast nails evenly distributed. Each zone contains a deformed single line serpent pattern. Wide plain edge.

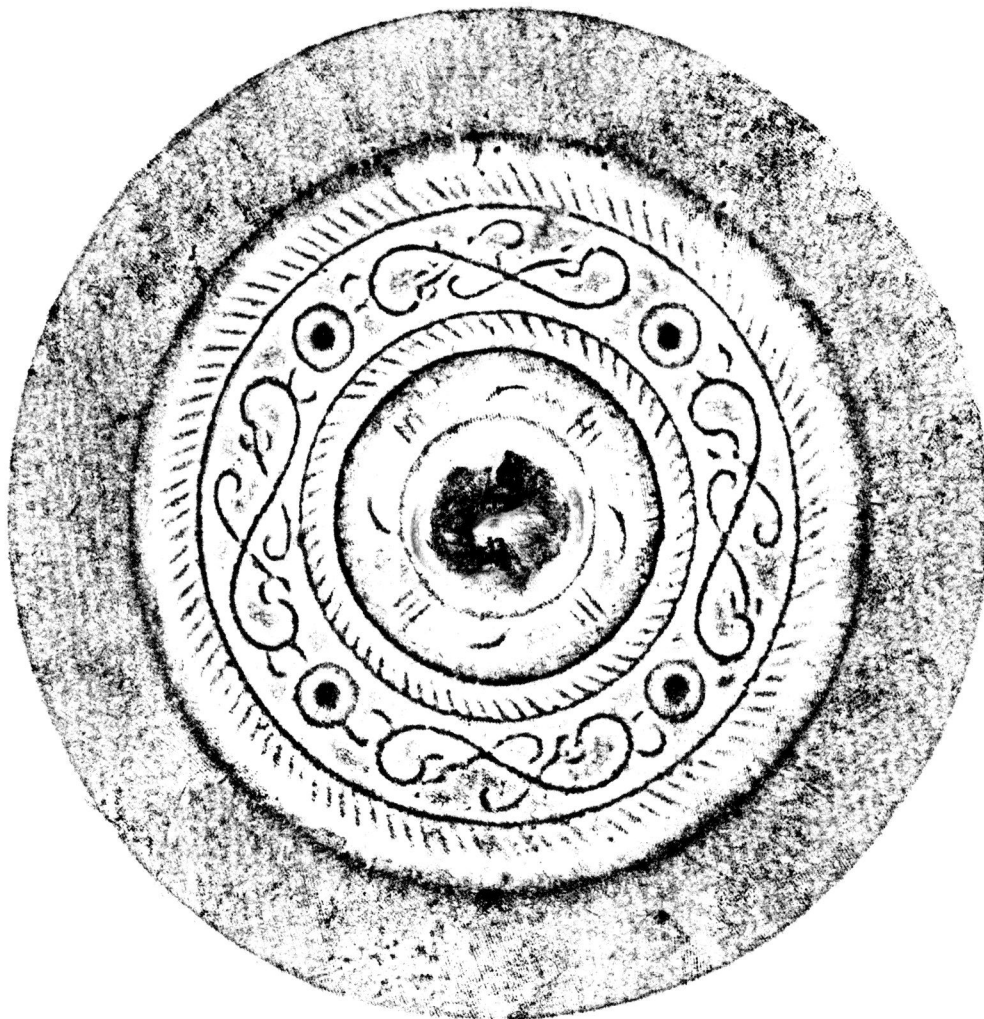

# 57. 四乳四虺纹镜

汉

1993年夹沟五柳尖山墓出土

直径 9.5 厘米，厚 0.35 厘米

　　圆形，半球钮，圆钮座，钮座外环一周弦纹，其外等间距分布四个圆座乳钉纹将主纹区分为四区，每区内各置一单线简易虺纹，虺纹两侧各置一点纹。近缘处环一周栉齿纹。宽缘，缘上一周三角锯齿纹。

# 57. Mirror with design of four nipples and four serpents

Han Dynasty

It was unearthed from the Wuliu Jian Mountain Tomb in Jiagou in 1993

Diameter: 9.5cm. Thickness: 0.35cm

Circular, hemispherical button, circular button seat, with a circumferential string pattern on the outside of the button seat. Four circular breast nail patterns are evenly spaced outside to distinguish the main pattern into four zones. Each zone is equipped with a single line simple pattern, and a dot pattern is placed on both sides of the serpent pattern. Near the edge, there is a band of fine-toothed pattern. Wide edge, with triangular serrations around the edge.

## 58. 四乳四兽纹镜

汉

1993 年夹沟五柳尖山墓出土

直径 13.7 厘米，缘厚 0.5 厘米

　　圆形，半球钮，圆钮座，外环一周连珠纹。主纹区四个乳钉将其分为四区，每区内饰一神兽纹。四乳四兽纹外环一周铭文圈，主纹区外环栉齿纹、锯齿纹、卷云纹各一周。镜缘内坡。

## 58. Mirror with design of four nipples and four animals

Han Dynasty

It was unearthed from the Wuliu Jian shan Tomb in Jiagou in 1993

Diameter: 13.7cm. Edge height: 0.5cm

Circular, hemispherical button, circular button seat, with a band of bead pattern around it. The main pattern area is divided into four areas by four breast nails, with one divine beast pattern on the interior of each area. Outside of the four breasts and four divine beast pattern is a band of inscription. Outside of the main pattern area is a band of fine-toothed pattern, serrated pattern and cirrus cloud pattern. Mirror edge inner slope.

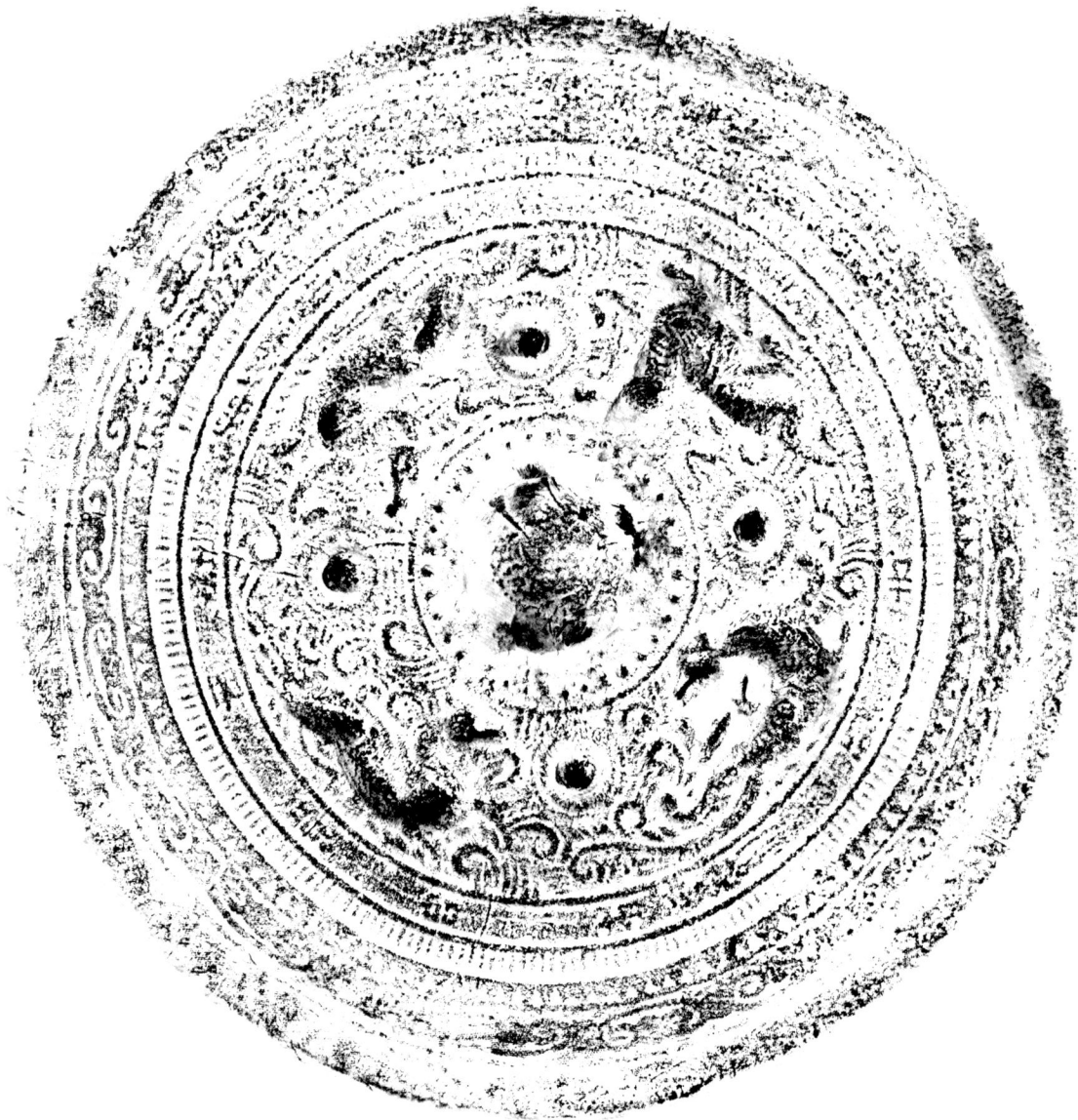

## 59. 四乳八鸟纹镜

## 59. Mirror with design of four nipples and eight birds

汉

2009 年涉案移交

直径 7.6 厘米，厚 0.4 厘米

Han Dynasty

It was transferred in the case in 2009

Diameter: 7.6cm. Thickness: 0.4cm

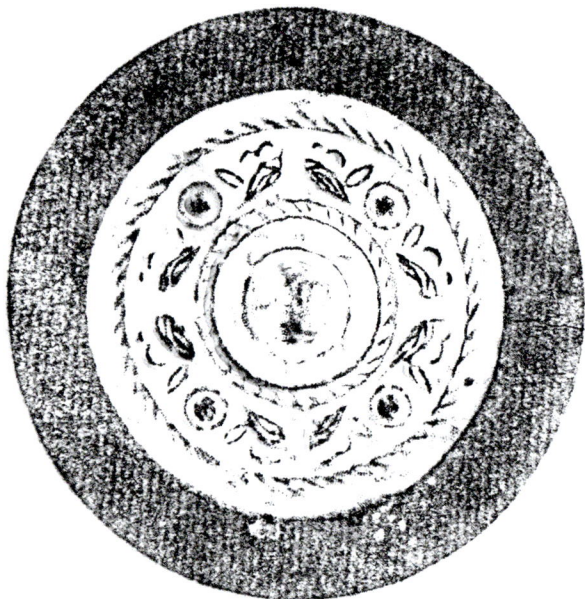

　　圆形，圆钮，圆钮座，钮座外一周弦纹带。主纹区内四个圆座乳钉等距分布，将其分为四区，每区内各饰一对禽鸟纹，两两相对，两侧以栉齿纹为廓。素宽缘。此镜鸟纹线条洗练，形态生动自然。

　　四乳八鸟纹镜流行于西汉晚期到东汉早期，纹饰布局采用了以四乳钉为基点组织主题纹饰的四分法，八鸟形象自然，生动活泼。

Round, round button, round button seat, with a string pattern around it. The four circular breast nails in the main pattern area are evenly distributed and divided into four zones. Each zone is decorated with a pair of bird patterns, opposite each other, with fine-toothed pattern on both sides as the outline. Plain wide margin. The bird pattern lines of this mirror are refined, and the form is vivid and natural.

The four nipples and eight birds patterned mirror was popular from the late Western Han Dynasty to the early Eastern Han Dynasty. The layout of the decoration adopted a four part method based on the four breast nails to organize the theme decoration. The eight bird image was natural and lively.

# 60. 四乳八鸟纹镜

## 60. Mirror with design of four nipples and eight birds

汉

2009 年涉案移交

直径 7.8 厘米，厚 0.2 厘米

Han Dynasty

It was transferred in the case in 2009

Diameter: 7.8cm. Thickness 0.2cm

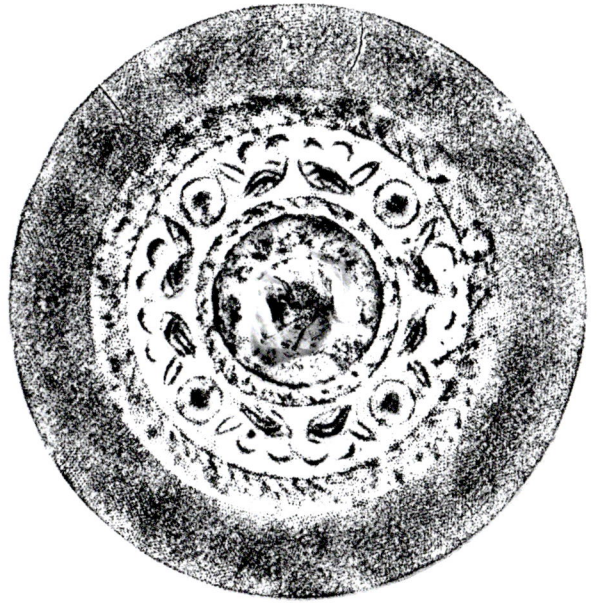

　　圆形，圆钮，圆钮座，钮座外环饰一周弦纹带。主区纹饰以两周栉齿纹为廓，四个圆座乳钉等距分布，将主纹区等分为四区，每区内饰一对相对立的禽鸟纹。素宽缘。此镜禽鸟刻画得生动细致，富有生活气息。

Round, round button, round button seat, with a string pattern outside of the button seat. The main area is decorated with two bands of fine-toothed pattern as the outline, and four circular breast nails are evenly distributed, dividing the main pattern area into four areas. Each area has a pair of opposite bird patterns in the interior. Plain wide margin. The vivid and meticulous depiction of birds in this mirror is full of vitality.

# 61. 四乳八鸟纹镜

汉

2009年涉案移交

直径8厘米，厚0.35厘米

　　圆形，圆钮，圆钮座。主纹区以两周栉齿纹为廓，四个圆座乳钉等距分布，将其分为四区，每区内各置一对禽鸟纹，二歧冠、覆羽翼、翘尾，两两相对。素宽缘。

# 61. Mirror with design of four nipples and eight birds

Han Dynasty

It was transferred in the case in 2009

Diameter: 8cm. Thickness 0.35cm

Round, round button, round button seat. The main pattern area is divided into four areas, with two bands of fine-toothed pattern as the outline and four circular breast nails evenly distributed. Each area is equipped with a pair of bird patterns, with a bifurcated crown, covered wings, and raised tail, facing each other. Plain wide margin.

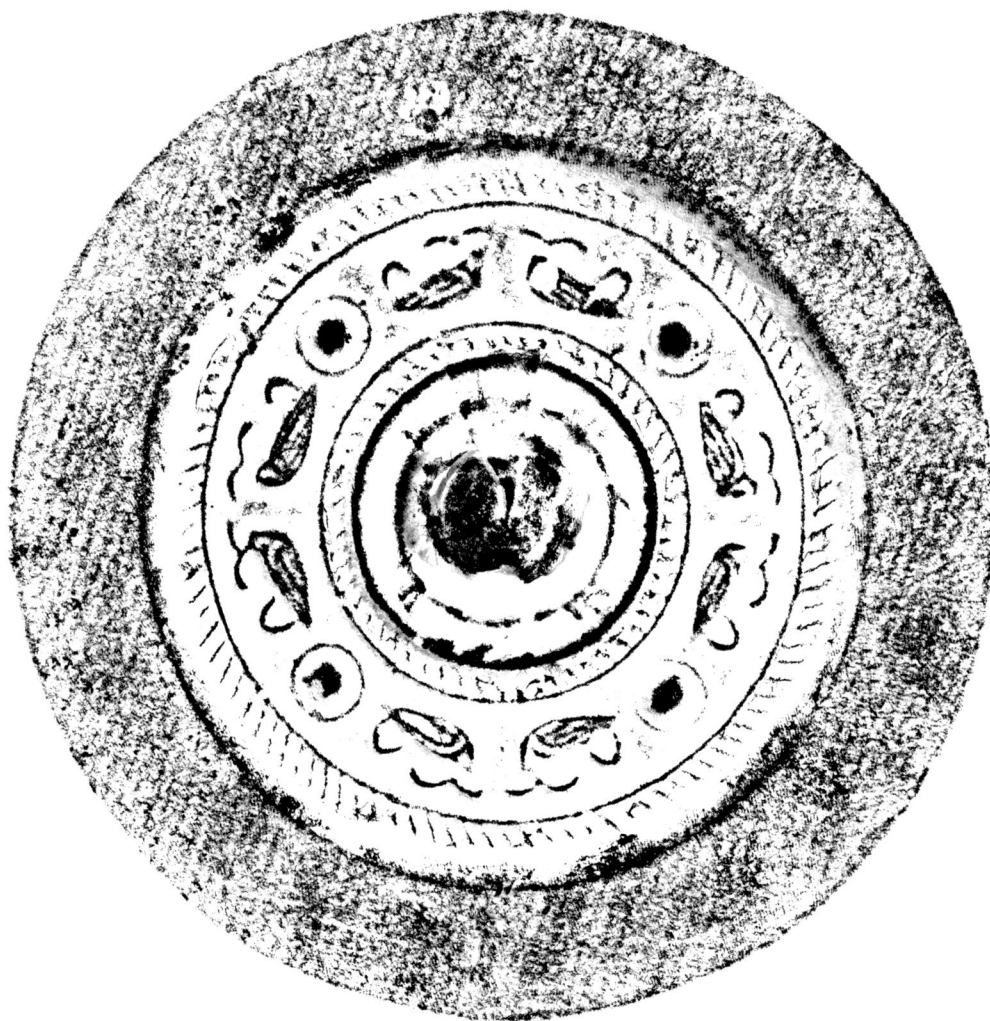

## 62. 四乳八鸟纹镜

汉

2009 年涉案移交

直径 9.1 厘米

　　圆形，圆钮，圆钮座。钮座外环饰一周宽弦
纹带，其间饰若干短斜线纹。主纹区以两周栉齿
纹为廓，四个圆座乳钉等距分布，将主纹区分为
四区，每区内饰一对站立禽鸟纹，两两相对。素
宽缘。

## 62. Mirror with design of four nipples and eight birds

Han Dynasty

It was transferred in the case in 2009

Diameter: 9.1cm

Round, round button, round button seat. Outside of the button seat is adorned with a wide string pattern band, with several short diagonal lines. The main pattern area is outlined by two bands of fine-toothed pattern, with four circular breast nails evenly distributed. The main pattern is divided into four areas, with one pair of standing bird patterns in each area, facing each other. Plain wide margin.

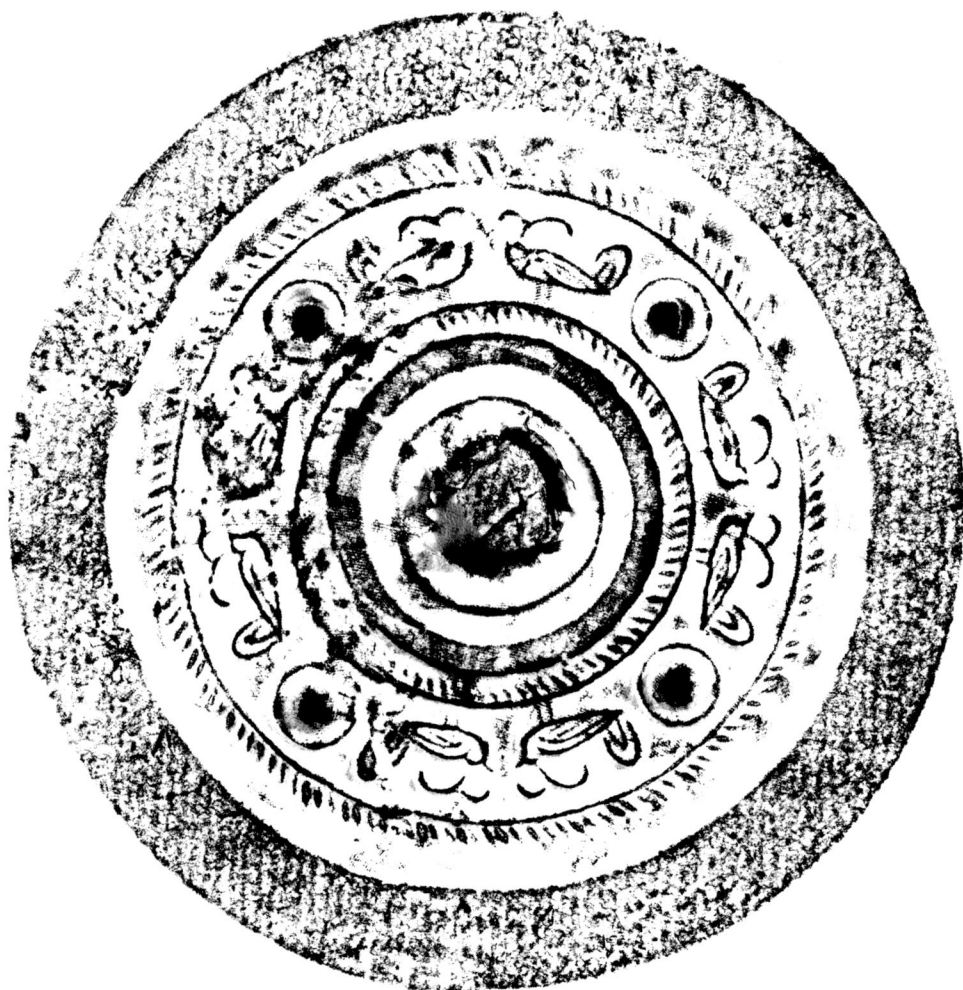

## 63. 四乳龙虎纹博局镜

汉

1991 年地区文化局移交

直径 10.2 厘米，厚 0.3 厘米

　　圆形，半球钮，柿蒂纹钮座。座外饰一双线方框，框外四角处各有一圆座乳钉与之相对。"TLV"博局纹将主纹区等分为四个区，每区内各置一神兽，神兽为龙虎，作奔走状，相间依次分布。主纹区外以一周栉齿纹为廓。宽缘，缘中饰一周双线波折纹。

　　博局镜，又称规矩镜，流行于西汉中晚期至东汉早期，其主要特征是镜背纹饰中有"T""L""V"三种符号纹饰。

## 63. Bo-Ju mirror with design of four nipples, dragon and tiger

Han Dynasty

It was transferred from the regional cultural bureau in 1991

Diameter: 10.2cm. Thickness: 0.3cm

Circular, hemispherical button, with kaki calyx design on the base. The exterior of the seat is decorated with a double line box, with a round breast nail at each corner opposite it. The "TLV" pattern (*Boju pattern*) divides the main pattern area into four zones, with each zone containing a divine beast. The divine beasts are dragon and tiger, in a running pattern, and distributed alternately. The main striation area is outlined by a band of fine-toothed pattern. Wide edge, with a double line ripple pattern around the edge.

Bo-Ju mirror, also known as GuiJu Mirror, was popular from the late Western Han Dynasty to the early Eastern Han Dynasty. Its main feature is the three symbol patterns of "T", "L", and "V" in the decorative patterns on the back of the mirror.

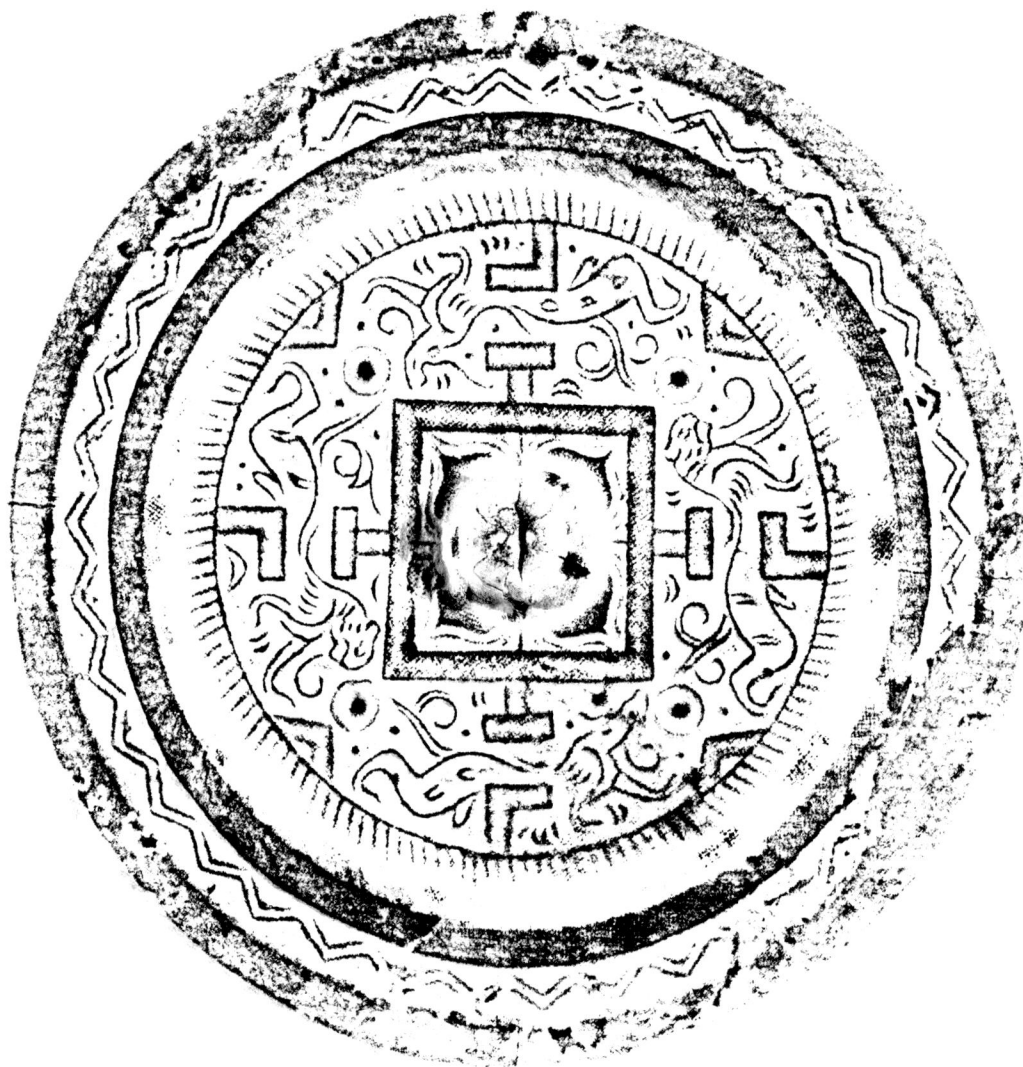

# 64. 八乳八鸟纹博局镜

汉

1979 年征集

直径 11.3 厘米，缘厚 0.4 厘米

　　圆形、半球形钮、柿蒂纹钮座，外围凹面形方格。一圈栉齿纹将铜镜分为内外两区。凹面形方格四边中间各向外延伸一个"T"字形纹，"T"字纹左右各置一圆座乳钉纹，"T"字纹与由栉齿纹圈带向内延伸出来的"L"字纹一一对应。栉齿纹向内延伸的四个"V"字纹与凹面形方格四角一一对应，"L"字纹与"V"字纹之间各饰一禽鸟纹。外区两周三角锯齿纹间夹一周双线波折纹。素窄缘。

# 64. Bo-Ju mirror with design of eight nipples and eight birds

Han Dynasty

It was collected in 1979

Diameter: 11.3cm. Edge thickness: 0.4cm

Circular, hemispherical button, on a base with kaki calyx design, surrounded by a concave square. A band of fine-toothed pattern divides the copper mirror into two zones: inner and outer. A T-shaped pattern extends outward from the middle of each of the four sides of the concave square grid, with a circular breast nail pattern placed on each side of the T-shaped pattern. The T-shaped pattern corresponds to the L-shaped pattern that extends inward from the fine-toothed pattern belt. The four V-shaped patterns extending inward correspond to the four corners of the concave square, with a bird pattern decorated between the L-shaped pattern and the V-shaped pattern. There is a double line ripple pattern between the two bands of triangular serrations pattern in the outer zone. Plain narrow margin.

64. Bo-Ju mirror with design of eight nipples and eight birds

# 65. 四乳四神博局镜

汉

1984年从祁县中学征集

直径 16.5 厘米，厚 0.6 厘米

　　圆形，半球钮，柿蒂纹钮座，座外环一双线方框，框外为主纹区，"TLV"形式的博局纹等距分布，"T"与"V"之间各置一四神纹饰，主纹区以祥云纹填充空白区域，外侧以一周栉齿纹为廓。宽平缘。

# 65. Bo-Ju mirror with design of four nipples and four deities

Han Dynasty

It was collected from Qixian Middle School in 1984

Diameter: 16.5cm. Thickness: 0.6cm

Circular, hemispherical button, with kaki calyx design on the base, with a double line box outside the seat. The main pattern area outside the box is evenly distributed in the form of "TLV", with four divine patterns placed between T-shaped pattern and V-shaped pattern. The main pattern area is filled with auspicious cloud patterns in the blank area, and the outer side is outlined with a band of fine-toothed pattern. Wide flat edge.

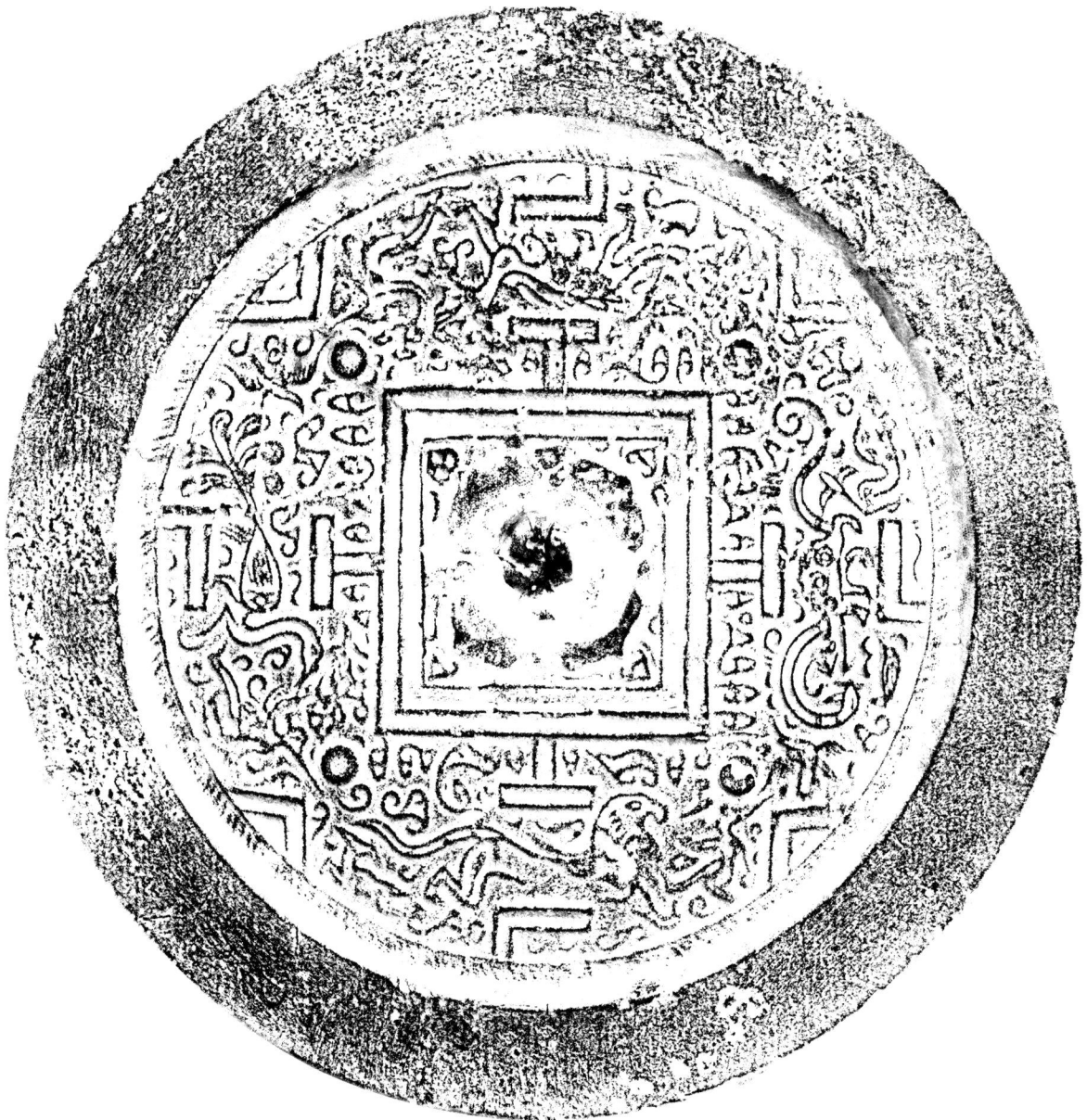

# 66. 四乳羽人神兽纹博局镜

汉

2009年涉案移交

直径 13.3 厘米，厚 0.5 厘米

　　圆形，圆钮，柿蒂纹钮座。钮座外环饰一个方框纹。方框四边中间向外延伸一个"T"形博局纹，与"L"形博局纹相对。方框四角与"V"形博局纹间各饰一个圆座乳钉纹。主区纹饰分四区，每区内各饰一对神兽纹：青龙配羽人，玄武配羊，白虎配熊，朱雀配禽鸟。主纹区外侧一周栉齿纹为廓。宽缘，由内向外，依次饰锯齿三角纹一周，变形蟠螭纹一周。镜背锈蚀物较多，覆盖了部分纹饰。

# 66. Bo-Ju mirror with design of four nipples, deities and beasts

Han Dynasty

It was transferred in the case in 2009

Diameter: 13.3cm. Thickness: 0.5cm

Circular, round button, with kaki calyx design on the base, decorated with a square pattern outride of the seat. A T-shaped pattern extends outward from the middle of the four sides of the box, opposite to the L-shaped pattern. A circular breast nail pattern is decorated between the four corners of the box and the V-shaped pattern. The main area decoration is divided into four areas, with each area decorated with a pair of divine animal patterns. The outer side of the main striated area is lined with a band of fine-toothed pattern. Wide edges, from the inside to the outside, are decorated with serrated triangular patterns, and deformed serpent patterns. There is a lot of rust on the back of the mirror, covering some of the decorative patterns.

## 67. 七鸟五铢纹博局镜

汉

2009 年涉案移交

直径 10.8 厘米，厚 0.5 厘米

圆形，半球钮，圆钮座，钮座外置一双线方框，方框每边向外延伸一"T"形博局纹，方框四角各有一圆座乳钉，将主纹区分为四区，第一区内"T"形博局纹两侧各置一禽鸟纹，呈站立状，"T"形上方有一卷云纹；第二区"T"形纹一侧置一禽鸟纹，呈飞翔状，另一侧置一五铢铜钱纹；第三区"T"形纹两侧纹饰模糊不清；第四区"T"形纹两侧各置一禽鸟纹，呈飞翔状。主纹区外侧以一周栉齿纹为廓。宽缘，缘上饰一周云气纹。

此镜属于简化博局镜。简化博局镜，即博局镜纹三种符号不同时出现，只出现其中一种或两种。

## 67. Bo-Ju mirror with design of seven birds and Wuzhu coin

Han Dynasty

It was transferred in the case in 2009

Diameter: 10.8cm. Thickness: 0.5cm

Circular, hemispherical button, circular button seat, with a double line box outside the button seat. Each side of the box extends outward with a T-shaped pattern, and each corner of the box has a circular breast nail to distinguish the main pattern into four areas. In the first area, there are bird patterns on both sides of the T-shaped pattern, in a standing shape. A roll of cloud pattern over the T-shaped pattern; On one side of the T-shaped pattern in the second area, there is a bird pattern in a flying shape, and on the other side, there is a Wuzhu coin pattern; The T-shaped pattern on both sides of the third zone is blurred; The fourth area has a bird pattern on both sides of the T-shaped pattern, resembling a flying pattern. The outside of the main area is outlined by a band of fine-toothed pattern. The wide edge is adorned with cloud pattern.

This mirror belongs to the simplified Bo-Ju mirror, that is, three symbols of the Bo-Ju pattern do not appear at the same time, only one or two of them appear.

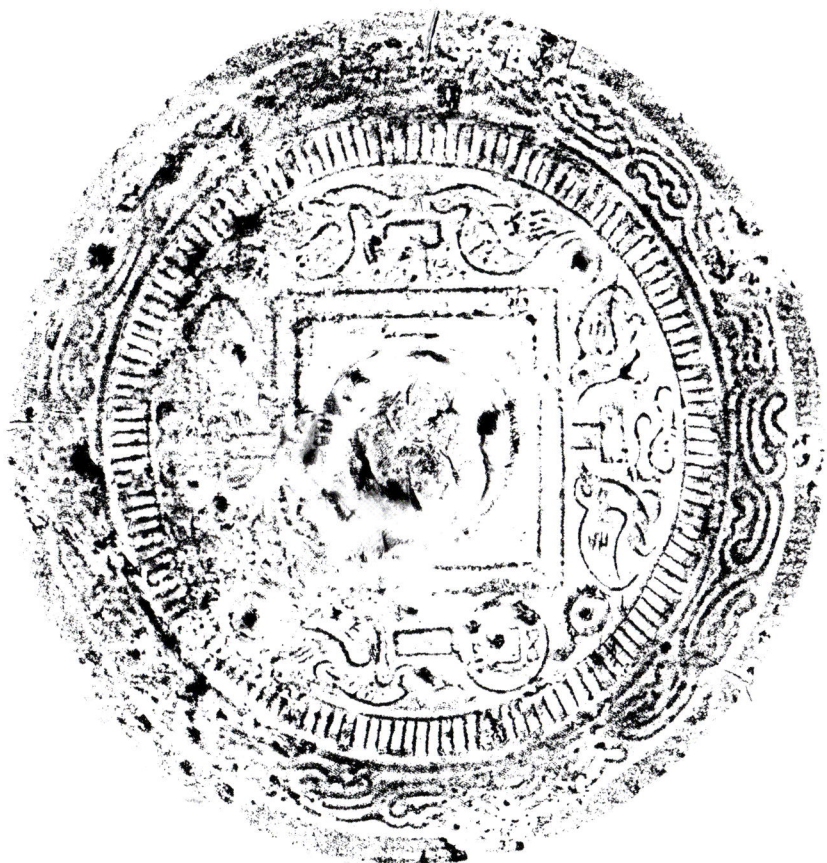

# 68. 七鸟纹博局镜

汉

2009 年涉案移交

直径 8.4 厘米，厚 0.4 厘米

圆形，圆钮，圆钮座。钮座外环饰一周双线方框纹。方框四边中间各向外延伸一个"T"形博局纹，其中三个"T"形纹两侧各饰一个禽鸟纹，第四个"T"形纹左侧饰一个圆座乳钉纹，右侧饰一个禽鸟纹。主区纹饰外侧以一周栉齿纹为廓。宽缘，缘上是一周三角锯齿纹，一周单线波折纹。

# 68. Bo-Ju mirror with design of seven birds

Han Dynasty

It was transferred in the case in 2009

Diameter: 8.4cm. Thickness: 0.4cm

Round, round button, round button seat. The outside of the button seat is decorated with a double line square pattern. A T-shaped pattern extends outward from the center of each of the four sides of the box, with three T-shaped patterns adorned with a bird pattern on each side. The fourth T-shaped pattern is adorned with a round breast nail pattern on the left side and a bird pattern on the right side. The outside of the main decoration area is outlined by a band of fine-toothed pattern. Wide edge, with a triangular serrated pattern and a single line wavy pattern around the edge.

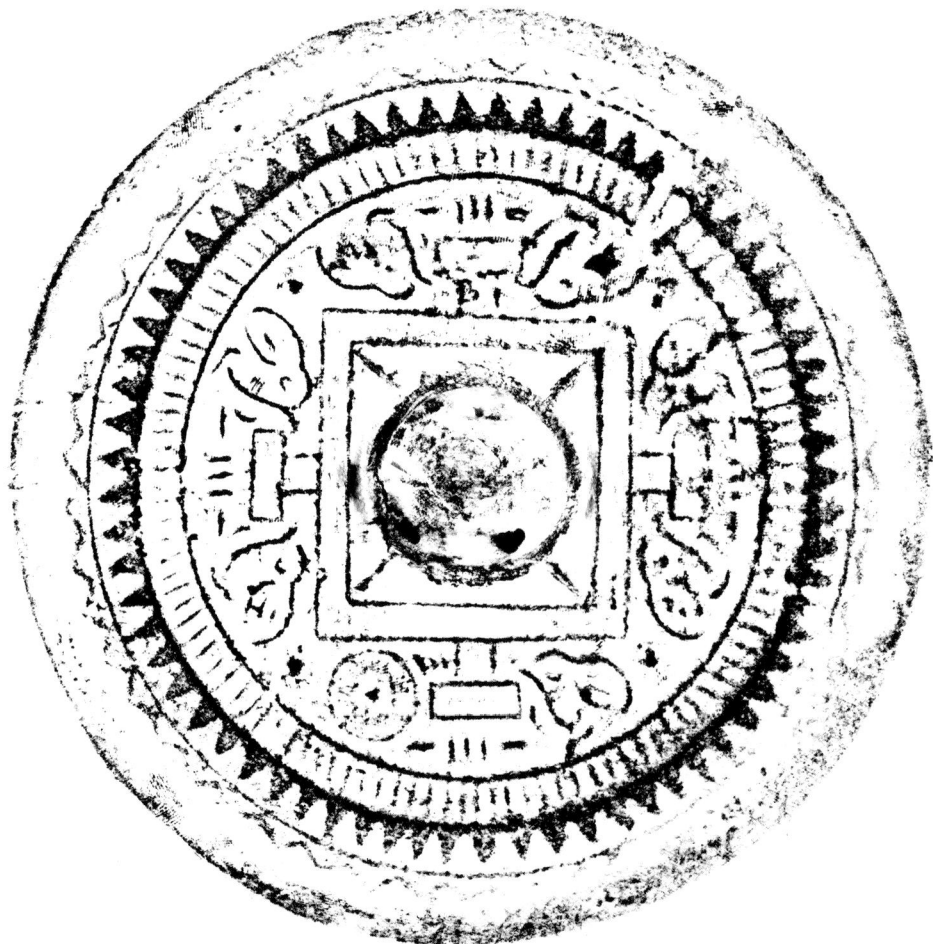

# 69. 四神博局镜

汉

2019 年泗县吴孟庄汉墓出土

直径 17.9 厘米，缘厚 0.4 厘米

　　圆形，圆钮，柿蒂纹钮座。内方内十二乳与十二地支相间分布。博局纹将内区分为四方八极，配置八乳、四神等纹饰，分别为：青龙配禽鸟、白虎配瑞兽、朱雀配羊、玄武配羽人，羽人作导引形态。外区铭文："白氏作镜真大好，上有仙人不知老，食□玉泉□□。"外饰一周栉齿纹、一周锯齿纹。云气纹缘。

# 69. Bo-Ju mirror with design of four deities

Han Dynasty

It was unearthed from the Han Tomb in Wumengzhuang, Sixian County

Diameter:17.9cm. Thickness:0.4cm

Round.Round button, with kaki calyx design on the base. The twelve breasts in the inner side are distributed alternately with the twelve earthly branches. The Bo Ju pattern distinguishes the interior into four directions and eight poles, equipped with patterns such as eight breasts and four deities. They are: Azure Dragon paired with birds, White Tiger paired with auspicious beasts, Vermilion Bird paired with sheep, Black Tortoise paired with feathered people, and feathered people used as guiding form. The inscription in outer region can be translated as "The mirror made by BaiShi is really great, with immortals who don't know how old they are, eating jade springs", and adorned with a band of fine-toothed pattern and a band of serrated pattern on the outside. Cloud pattern edge.

# 70. 四神博局镜

# 70. Bo-Ju mirror with design of four deities

汉

2020 年灵璧县山南村汉墓出土

直径 11.6 厘米，缘厚 0.4 厘米

Han Dynasty

It was unearthed from Han tomb in Shannan Village, Lingbi County in 2020

Diameter:11.6cm. Thickness:0.4cm

　　圆形，圆钮。博局纹划分的四方八极内均匀分布羽人神兽纹，两两一组，分别为青龙与羽人、玄武与瑞兽、白虎与羊、朱雀与禽鸟相对而立。主纹区外饰一周栉齿纹。双线波折纹缘。

Round in shape. Round button. Within the four directions and eight poles separated by the Bo-Ju pattern, there are evenly distributed patterns of feathered humans and divine beasts, separated in pairs, Azure Dragon and feathered humans, Black Tortoise and auspicious beasts, White tiger and sheep, and two birds standing opposite each other. The main pattern area is adorned with a band of fine-toothed pattern. Double corrugated lines edge.

## 71. 四神博局镜

汉

2020 年灵璧县山南村汉墓出土

直径 17 厘米，缘厚 0.5 厘米

圆形，圆钮，四瓣花钮座。内方内十二乳与十二地支相间分布。博局纹将内区分为四方八极，配置八乳、四神、瑞兽纹饰。外区铭文："上大山，见神人，驾交龙，乘浮云，食玉英，朱雀玄武顺阴阳。"云气纹缘。

## 71. Bo-Ju mirror with design of four deities

Han Dynasty

It was unearthed from Han tomb in Shannan Village, Lingbi County in 2020

Diameter:17cm. Thickness:0.5cm

Round in shape. Round button, four-petal flower button seat. The twelve breasts in the inner side are distributed alternately with the twelve earthly branches. The Bo-Ju pattern divides the interior into four directions and eight poles, equipped with patterns of eight breasts, four deities, and auspicious beasts. The inscription in the outer region can be translated as: "Climb the mountains, see immortal, drive the dragon, ride the floating cloud, eat the elite of jade, Rosefinch and Black Tortoise control the laws of change in nature." Cloud pattern edge.

## 72. 尚方铭四神博局镜

汉

2020年灵璧县山南村汉墓出土

直径16.2厘米，缘厚0.5厘米

　　圆形，圆钮，柿蒂纹钮座，博局纹将内区划
分为四方八极，配置八乳、四神禽兽，分别为：白
虎配独角兽、朱雀配羊、青龙配凤鸟、玄武配持草
羽人。外区铭文为："尚方作竞（镜）真大好，上
有山（仙）人不知老，渴饮玉泉饥食枣"。两周锯
齿纹夹一周双线波折纹。

## 72. Bo-Ju mirror with inscription of "Shang Fang" and the design of four deities

Han Dynasty

It was unearthed from Han tomb in Shannan Village, Lingbi County in 2020

Diameter: 16.2cm. Thickness: 0.5cm

Round in shape. Round button, with kaki calyx design on the base, Bo-Ju pattern divides the inner area into four directions and eight poles, equipped with eight breasts and four deities, White Tiger with unicorn, Rosefinch with sheep, Azure Dragon with phoenix, and Black Tortoise with grass feather person. The inscription in the outer region: The mirror made by Shangfang is really great, with immortals who don't know how old they are, drink jade spring when thirsty and eat jujube when hungry. Two bands of jagged patterns with one band of double line ripple pattern.

Collection of Bronze Mirrors in Suzhou Museum    193

## 73. 尚方铭四神博局镜

东汉
旧藏
直径 18 厘米，厚 0.4 厘米

　　圆形，圆钮，柿蒂纹钮座，外围双线方框中有十二圆座乳钉与十二辰铭相间。方框外八枚圆座乳钉与"TLV"博局纹将主纹区分为四方八极，四神与四瑞兽搭配均匀分布。主纹区外侧为一周铭文圈带，铭文"尚方作竟真大巧，上有仙人不知老，渴饮玉泉饥食枣。"主纹区外环一周栉齿纹。宽缘，缘上饰两周锯齿纹，间饰一周双线水波纹。

## 73. Bo-Ju mirror with inscription of "Shang Fang" and the design of four deities

Eastern Han Dynasty

Old collection

Diameter: 18cm. Thickness: 0.4cm

The mirror is round in shape. It has a round knob on a base with kaki calyx design. Outside the base is adorned with inscription and twelve nipples with round base. Outside the square is adorned with TLV-shaped patterns. The major motif has a band of inscription "The mirror made by Shangfang is really great, with immortals who don't know how old they are, drink jade spring when thirsty and eat jujube when hungry" and fine-toothed pattern surrounded. The broad rim is decorated with two bands of jagged pattern and a band of double line ripple pattern among them.

## 74. 四乳简化博局镜

汉

2009 年涉案移交

直径 9.7 厘米，厚 0.3 厘米

　　圆形，圆钮，圆钮座。主纹区以两周栉齿纹为栏，中间等距分布四个云纹，云纹是由一个圆座乳钉纹和两个涡纹组成，云纹之间间隔一个 "V" 形博局纹，"V" 形博局纹左右两侧各延伸出一个涡形纹。宽缘，缘上饰一周双线波折纹。

## 74. Simplified Bo-Ju mirror with design of four nipples

Han Dynasty

It was transferred in the case in 2009

Diameter: 9.7cm. Thickness: 0.3cm

Round, round button, round button seat. The main pattern area is divided by two bands of fine-toothed pattern, with four evenly spaced cloud patterns distributed in the middle. The cloud pattern is composed of a circular breast nail pattern and two vortex patterns, with a V-shaped Bo-Ju pattern extending between the cloud patterns, and a vortex pattern extending on both sides of the V-shaped Bo-Ju pattern. Wide edge, adorned with double line ripple pattern around the edge.

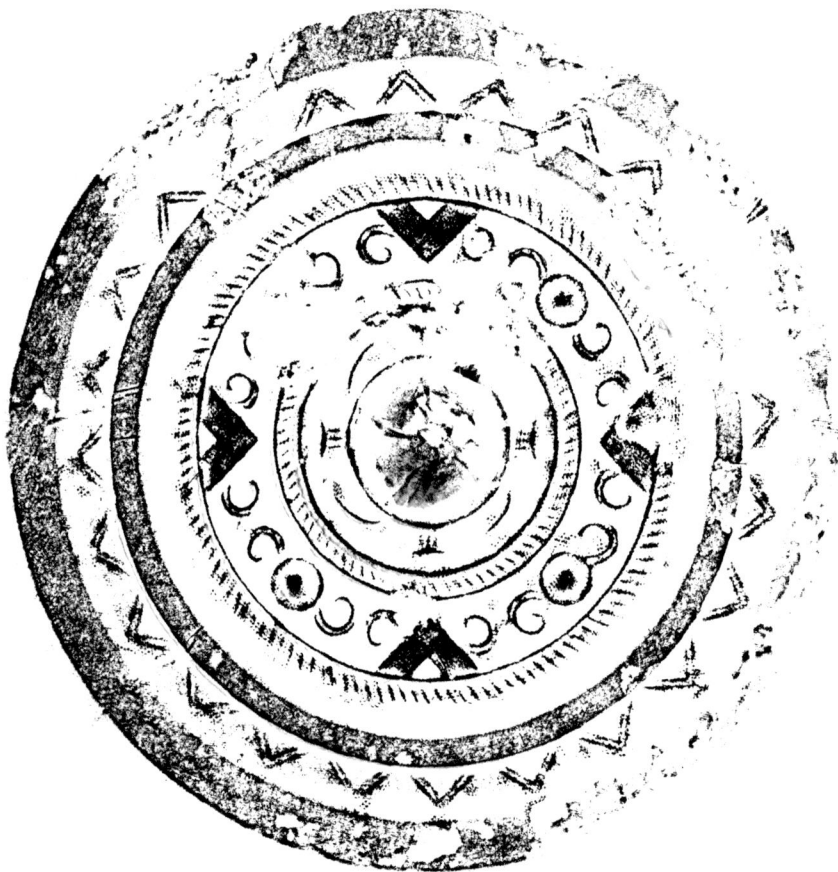

## 75. 四乳简化博局镜

汉

2009 年涉案移交

直径 8 厘米，厚 0.3 厘米

　　圆形，半球钮，圆钮座。钮座外两周栉齿纹间等距分布四组云纹，云纹由圆座乳钉和两个涡纹组成，云纹间各饰一双线 V 形博局纹。宽缘，缘上饰一周双线波折纹。

## 75. Simplified Bo-Ju mirror with design of four nipples

Han Dynasty

It was transferred in the case in 2009

Diameter: 8cm. Thickness: 0.3cm

Circular, hemispherical button, circular button seat. Four sets of cloud patterns are evenly distributed between the two bands of fine-toothed pattern on the outside of the button seat. The cloud pattern is composed of a circular breast nail and two vortex patterns, each decorated with a double line V-shaped pattern. Wide edge, adorned with double line ripple pattern around the edge.

## 76. 四乳简化博局镜

汉

2009 年涉案移交

直径 8.8 厘米，厚 0.2 厘米

　　圆形，圆钮，圆钮座。主纹区以两周栉齿纹为栏，等距分布的四个简化博局纹 V 形纹将其分为四区，每区内饰一个圆座乳钉纹和若干钩纹。宽缘，缘上饰一周双线波折纹。

## 76. Simplified Bo-Ju mirror with design of four nipples

Han Dynasty

It was transferred in the case in 2009

Diameter: 8.8cm. Thickness: 0.2cm

Round, round button, round button seat. The main pattern area outlined with two bands of fine-toothed pattern is divided into four zones by four equally spaced simplified regular V-shaped patterns, with a circular breast nail pattern and several hook patterns on the interior of each zone. Wide edge, adorned with double line ripple pattern around the edge.

# 77. 七乳兽纹镜

汉

大泽乡出土

直径 16.2 厘米，缘厚 0.5 厘米

　　圆形，半球钮，圆形钮座，外围一圈圆座乳钉纹。钮座外两圈栉齿纹间饰一圈 "S" 形云纹圈带。主纹区七个内向连弧纹座乳钉纹与四神、羽人、禽鸟纹相间分布，近缘处饰一圈栉齿纹。宽平缘内圈饰一周锯齿纹，外圈饰一周云气纹。

# 77. Mirror with design of seven nipples and animals

Han Dynasty

It was unearthed in Daze Township

Diameter: 16.2cm. Edge thickness: 0.5cm

Circular, hemispherical button, circular button seat, with a circular breast nail pattern on the periphery. An S-shaped cloud pattern band is adorned between the two bands of fine-toothed pattern on the outside of the button seat. In the main pattern area, there are seven inwardly connected arc-shaped breast nail patterns and four deities, winged figure and birds distributed alternately, with a band of fine-toothed pattern decorated near the edge. The inner circle of the wide flat edge is decorated with a band of jagged pattern, and the outside is decorated with cloud pattern.

# 78. 四神铭文镜

东汉

1993年夹沟五柳尖山墓出土

直径19厘米，缘厚0.6厘米

　　圆形，半球钮，圆钮座，钮座较小。纹饰分为内区、中区和外区。内区五个圆座乳钉与五个禽鸟纹相间排列，外围两周弦纹，弦纹间三弧线纹与"0"形纹相间分布。中区主要纹饰为神兽禽鸟纹，等距分布的六个圆座乳钉纹与朱雀、青龙、白虎、玄武、三只禽鸟及一神兽相间排列，外围一圈铭文圈，铭文"□□作镜大毋伤，上有朱雀仙人龙虎，中有七子利孙子，心者官吏士，富且受兮"，"受"为"寿"的别字。铭文圈外环绕一周栉齿纹。宽缘上内饰一周锯齿纹，外饰一周云气纹。

# 78. Mirror with inscription and design of four deities

Eastern Han Dynasty

It was transferred from the Wuliu Jian Shan Tomb in Jiagou Town in 1993

Diameter: 19cm. Edge thickness:0.6cm

Circular, hemispherical button, circular button seat, smaller button seat. The decoration is divided into inner zone, middle zone, and outer zone. The five circular breast nails in the inner area are arranged alternately with five bird patterns, and the two bands of chord pattern are distributed alternately with three curved lines patterns and 0-shaped patterns between the chord patterns. The main decoration in the central region is the divine beast and bird pattern, six evenly spaced circular breast nail patterns arranged in alternating with Vermilion Bird, Azure Dragon, White Tiger, Black Tortoise, three birds, and one divine beast. There is a circle of inscriptions around the periphery, with the inscription which can be translated as "The mirror is large and not broken, lt has Vermilion bird、immortal、dragon、tiger, and seven sons and grandchildren. A sincere man can become an official and will be prosperity and longevity." The word "Shou" is a byword for "Shou". The inscription is surrounded by a band of fine-toothed pattern. On the wide edge, there is a band of jagged pattern on the interior and cloud patterns on the exterior.

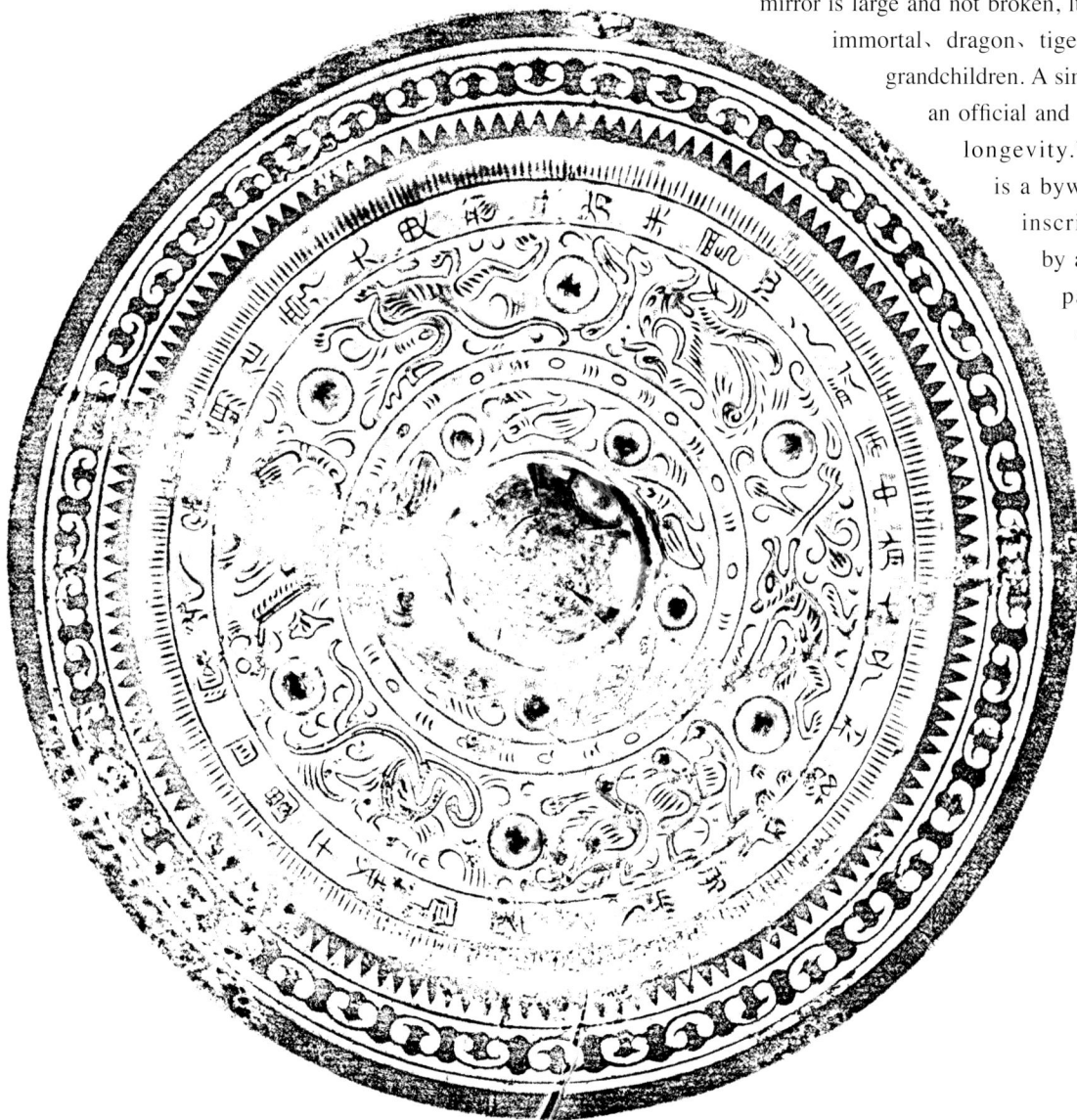

## 79. 神兽铭文镜

汉

泗县吴孟庄汉墓出土

直径 18.4 厘米，缘厚 0.4 厘米

　　圆形，圆钮，圆钮座。钮座外九个带座乳钉，间饰铭文与涡纹，铭文"宜子孙"，外环一周栉齿纹与两周宽弦纹，弦纹间饰若干三弧线纹与"0"形纹。主纹区六乳与举芝草跪拜羽人、白虎、朱雀、青龙、蟾蜍、鱼相间环列，外饰一周铭文圈带，铭文"尚方作镜真大巧，上有仙人不知老，渴饮玉"，文字简化较多，且镜铭最后一句不完整，完整铭文为："渴饮玉泉饥食枣"。铭文圈外饰一周栉齿纹、一周锯齿纹。云气纹缘。

## 79. Mirror with inscription and the design of mythical beasts

Han Dynasty

It was unearthed from the Han Tomb in Wumengzhuang, Sixian County

Diameter:18.4cm. Thickness:0.4cm

Round in shape. Round button, round button seat. There are nine breast nails with seats on the outside of the button seat, adorned with inscriptions and vortex patterns, with the inscription "Good for posterity". The seat is surrounded by a band of fine-toothed pattern and two bands of wide string pattern, with several three curved lines patterns and 0-shaped patterns between the string patterns. The six breasts in the main pattern area are arranged in alternating circles with the White Tiger, Vermilion Bird, Azure Dragon, toad, fish, feather man in kneeling and bowing posture. The outer decoration is adorned with a circle of inscriptions, with the inscription "The mirror made by Shangfang is really great, with immortals who don't know how old they are, drink jade spring when thirsty". The text is simplified and the last sentence of the inscription is incomplete,the full inscription should be "drink jade spring when thirsty and eat jujube when hungry". The outer decoration of the inscription circle includes a band of fine-toothed pattern and a band of serrated pattern. Cloud pattern edge.

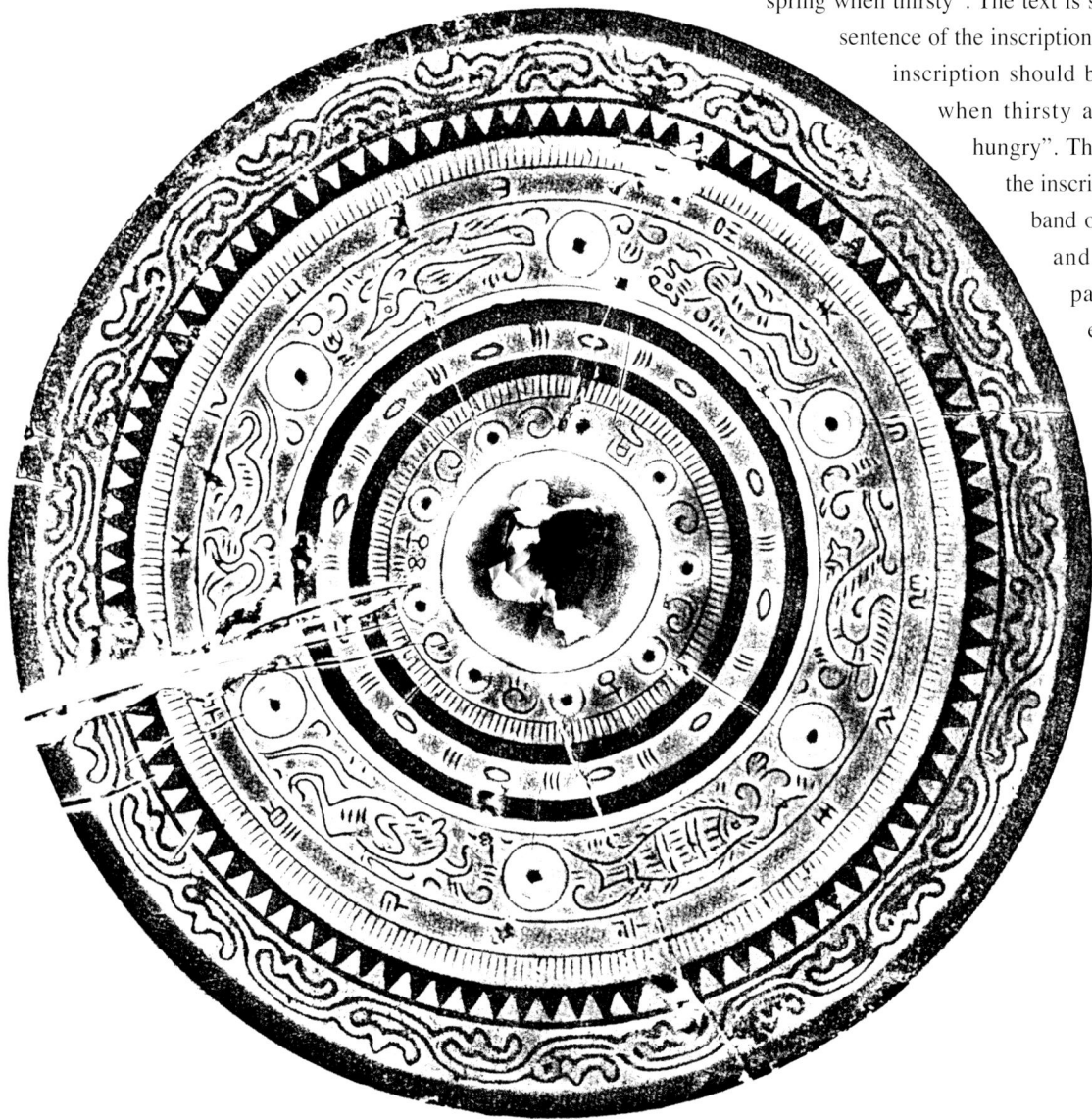

# 80. 神兽铭文镜

汉

灵璧师范学校出土

直径 17.7 厘米，缘厚 0.5 厘米

　　圆形，圆钮，圆钮座。钮座外九枚圆座乳钉与铭文相间排列，铭文"宜君王，乐未央，大富昌"，其外环一周铭文，铭文"涷治铜华清而明，以之为镜宜文章，左龙又虎主四彭，七子九孙治中央"。中区七枚八内向连弧纹座乳钉与两羽人、神兽相间分布。

# 80. Mirror with inscription and the design of mythical beasts

Han Dynasty

It was unearthed from Lingbi Normal School

Diameter: 17.7cm. Thickness: 0.5cm

Round in shape. Round button, round button seat. The nine round breast nails on the outside of the button seat are arranged alternately with the inscription "Beneficial to the monarch, always happy with abundance and prosperity". The outside band of inscription can be translated as "The copper of this mirror is refined and made of clean material, and the person who uses this mirror can write good article. The left dragon and the right tiger control the four star areas in the sky, seven sons and nine grandchildren are in the middle". Seven eight inward continuous arc shaped breast nails in the central area are distributed alternately with two feathered humans and divine beasts.

# 81. 云雷连弧纹镜

汉

2009 年涉案移交

直径 11 厘米

圆形，半球钮，圆钮座，钮座外环饰一周凸弦纹。主纹区饰内向八连弧纹一周，外环由八个涡纹及并行弧线组成的云雷纹一周，以栉齿纹为廓，斜缘，素面无纹。

连弧纹镜是汉代比较流行的镜型之一，它以内向连弧纹为主题纹饰，而铭文处于装饰从属地位。连弧纹镜始于战国晚期，流行于西汉至东汉中晚期。连弧纹镜一般分为云雷连弧纹镜、"长宜子孙"连弧纹镜和素连弧纹镜，云雷纹连弧纹镜流行于东汉中期，"长宜子孙"连弧纹镜盛行于东汉晚期。

云雷纹连弧纹镜，一般为圆钮座或四叶柿蒂纹钮座，内区为八连弧纹，外区云雷纹和弦纹。云雷纹一般是带圆心的小圆圈、带圆点的同心圆圈或涡纹与数目不等的斜线纹或弦纹相连而成。

# 81. Mirror with design of cloud and thunder and linked arcs

Han Dynasty

It was transferred in the case in 2009

Diameter: 11cm

Circular, hemispherical button, round button seat, with a raised string pattern on the outside of the button seat. The main pattern area is decorated with a band of eight inward linked arcs pattern, and the outside is composed of eight vortex patterns and parallel arcs, forming a cloud and thunder pattern around it. The outline is a band of fine-toothed pattern, with an oblique edge and no pattern on the plain surface.

The mirror with linked arcs pattern is one of the more popular mirror types in the Han Dynasty, with the inward linked arcs pattern as the theme decoration, while the inscription is in a subordinate position of decoration. The linked arcs pattern mirror began in the late Warring States period and was popular from the Western Han Dynasty to the middle and late Eastern Han Dynasty. The linked arcs mirror is generally divided into cloud thunder linked arcs mirror, "Good for posterity" linked arcs mirror, and plain linked arcs mirror. The cloud thunder linked arcs mirror was popular in the mid Eastern Han Dynasty, while the "Good for posterity" linked arcs mirror was popular in the late Eastern Han Dynasty.

The cloud and thunder linked arcs pattern mirror generally has a round button seat or a four leaf persimmon stem pattern button seat, with eight linked arcs patterns in the inner area and cloud and thunder patterns and string patterns in the outer area. Cloud and thunder patterns are generally formed by connecting small circles with centers, concentric circles with dots, or vortex patterns with varying numbers of diagonal or string patterns.

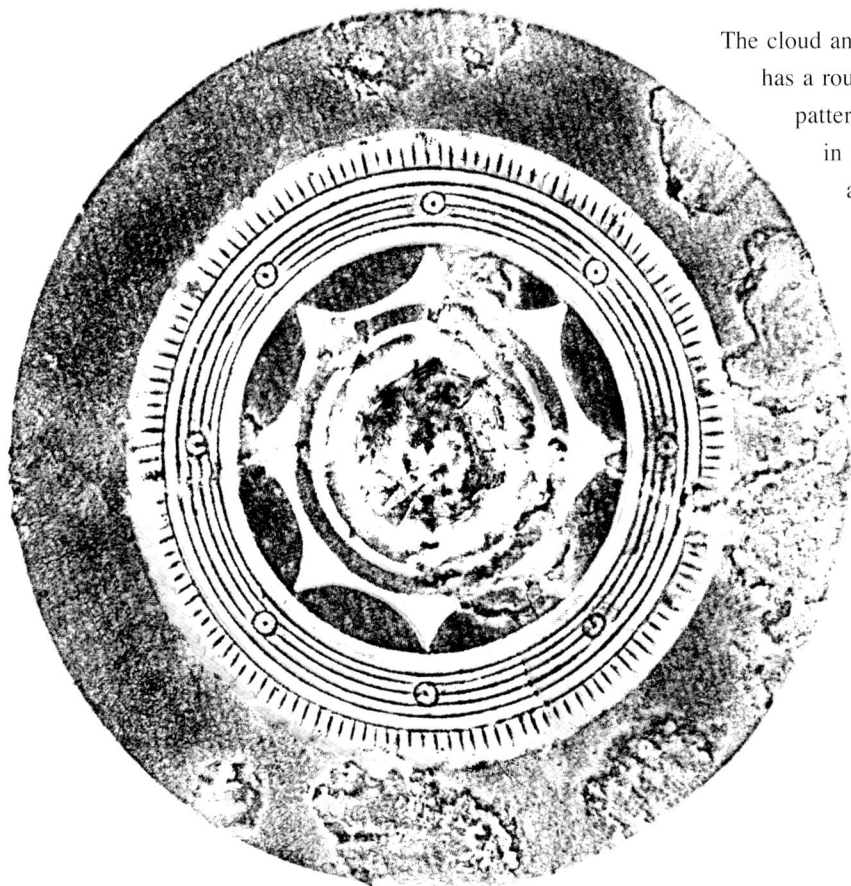

## 82. 云雷连弧纹镜

汉

灵璧师范学校出土

直径 7.1 厘米，缘厚 0.2 厘米

　　圆形，桥形钮，圆钮座，外环一周内向八连弧纹。外区饰两周栉齿纹，间饰一周由涡纹和弧线组成的云雷纹。素宽平缘。

## 82. Mirror with design of cloud and thunder and linked arcs

Han Dynasty

It was unearthed from Lingbi Normal School

Diameter:7.1cm. Thickness:0.2cm

Round in shape. Circular, bridge shaped button, circular button seat, with eight inward linked arcs patterns outside of it. The outer area is adorned with two bands of fine-toothed pattern, and the middle area is adorned with cloud and thunder pattern composed of vortex patterns and curved lines. Plain wide flat edge.

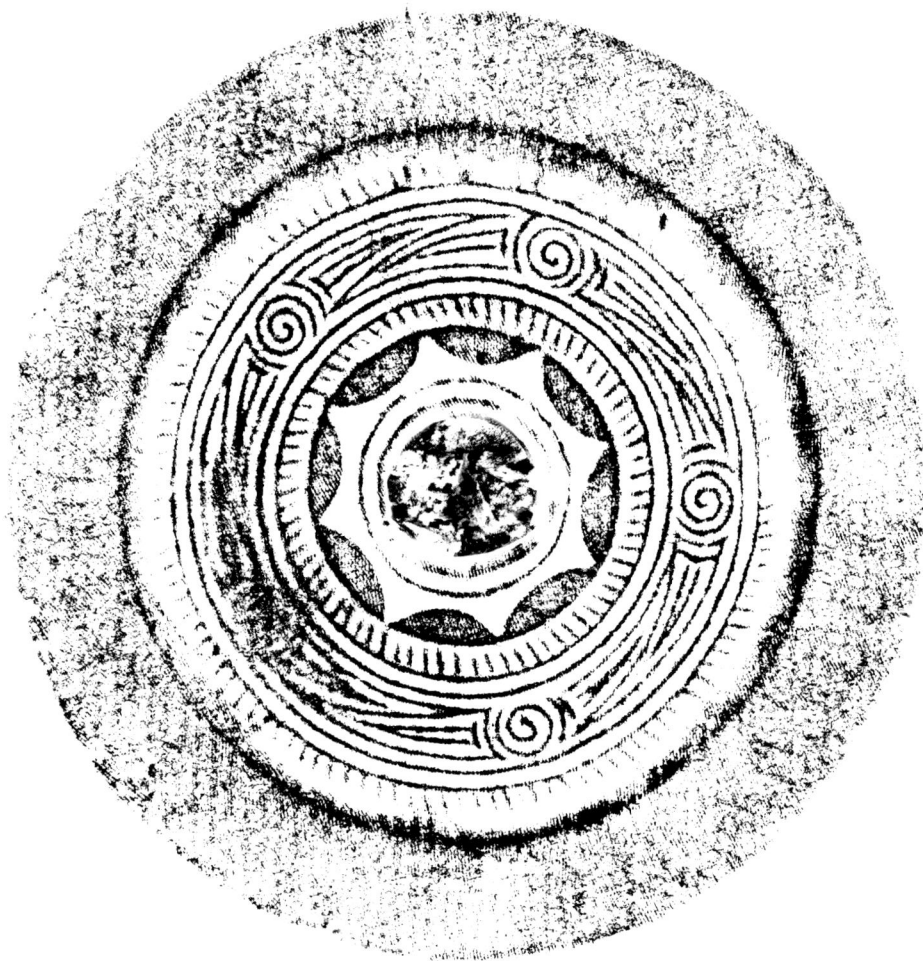

## 83. "长宜子孙"铭云雷连弧纹镜

汉

1996年曹村大山口汉墓出土

直径22厘米，缘厚0.3厘米

　　圆形，圆钮，柿蒂纹钮座，四柿叶间各一字铭，合为"长宜子孙"，外环一周栉齿纹、一周凸弦纹带。中区饰内向八连弧纹一周，连弧间有短线纹和小乳钉纹，象征着山川日月。外区饰两周栉齿纹，间饰一周由涡纹和弧线组成的云雷纹。素宽平缘。

## 83. Mirror with design of cloud and thunder and linked arcs and inscription of "Good for posterity"

Han Dynasty

It was unearthed from the Han Tomb at Dashankou in Caocun in 1996

Diameter: 22cm. Edge thickness: 0.3cm

Circular, round button, with kaki calyx design on the base, with one character inscription between the four persimmon leaves, collectively known as "Good for posterity". The seat is surrounded by a band of fine-toothed pattern and a convex string pattern belt. The central area is decorated with eight inward linked arcs pattern, with short lines and small breast nail patterns between the arcs, symbolizing the mountains, rivers, sun, and moon. The outer area is adorned with two bands of fine-toothed pattern, and the middle area is adorned with cloud and thunder pattern composed of vortex patterns and curved lines. Plain wide flat edge.

## 84. 云雷连弧纹镜

东汉
埇桥区征集
直径 13 厘米，厚 0.45 厘米

　　圆形，圆钮，柿蒂纹钮座，外环栉齿纹与凸弦纹带。中区饰内向八连弧纹一周。外区饰两周栉齿纹，间饰一周由涡纹和弧线组成的云雷纹。素宽平缘。

## 84. Mirror with design of cloud and thunder and linked arcs

Eastern Han Dynasty

It was collected in Yongqiao District

Diameter: 13cm. Thickness: 0.45cm

The mirror is round in shape. It has a round knob on a base with kaki calyx design, adorned with fine-toothed pattern and convex string pattern. Outside is a band of eight inward linked arcs, with a band of cloud and thunder design. The mirror has a broad rim without design.

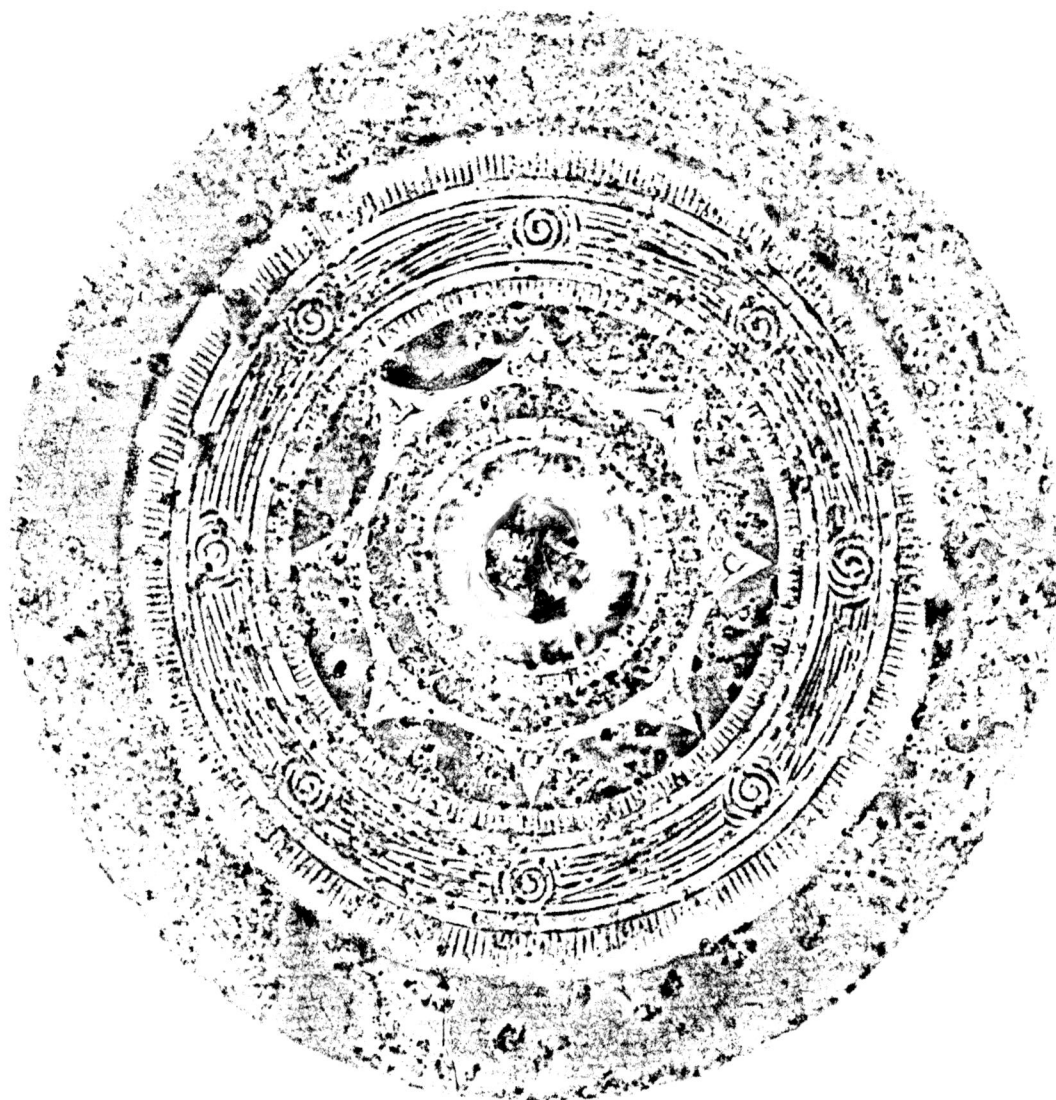

## 85. "长宜子孙" 连弧纹镜

汉

2013 年宿州市文物管理所拨交

直径 13.2 厘米，厚 0.3 厘米

　　圆形，圆钮，圆钮座，钮座向外延伸四叶纹，四叶纹之间以一字铭间隔，字铭"长宜子孙"，长脚花式篆，主纹区以一周内向八连弧纹为栏。宽素平缘。

　　"长宜子孙"连弧纹镜，绝大多数为四蝠形叶钮座，其外为八内向连弧纹组成的圈带。与云雷连弧纹镜不同的是其外区无云雷纹，一般为素宽缘。

## 85. Mirror with design of linked arcs and inscription of "Good for posterity"

Han Dynasty

It was allocated by Suzhou Heritage Management Institute in 2013

Diameter: 13.2cm. Thickness: 0.3cm

Round, round button, round button seat, button seat extending four leaf patterns outward, with a single character inscription between the four leaf patterns, with the inscription "Good for posterity". Long foot floral seal script, with the main pattern area surrounded by eight inward linked arcs patterns. Wide plain edge.

Most of the mirror with design of linked arcs and inscription of "Good for posterity" have four bat shaped leaf button seat which is surrounded by eight inward linked arcs patterns.Unlike the cloud and thunder linked arcs pattern mirror, there are no cloud and thunder patterns in its outer area, generally with a plain wide edge.

## 86. "长宜子孙"连弧纹镜

汉

2013 年宿州市文物管理所拨交

直径 21.4 厘米，厚 0.45 厘米

    圆形，圆钮，柿蒂纹钮座。一周宽带弦纹将纹饰分为内外两区，内区四叶纹与钮座相连，四叶之间饰一铭文，铭文"长宜子孙"，字体做长脚花式篆，十分秀丽；外区环饰一周内向八连弧纹，连弧纹之间以圆座乳钉与字铭依次排列，字铭"寿如山河"。宽素平缘。

    在连弧纹镜类型中，"长宜子孙"镜出土数量较多，流行较为广泛，盛行于东汉晚期。

## 86. Mirror with design of linked arcs and inscription of "Good for posterity"

Han Dynasty

It was allocated by Suzhou Heritage Management Institute in 2013

Diameter: 21.4cm.Thickness: 0.45cm

Circular, round button, persimmon stem pattern button seat. The wide band string pattern divides the decoration into two areas: the inner and outer. The four leaf pattern in the inner area is connected to the button seat, and an inscription is adorned between the four leaves, with the inscription "Good for posterity". The font is made of long foot floral seal, which is very beautiful; The outer area is adorned with eight inward linked arcs pattern, arranged in sequence with circular breast nails and inscriptions, with the inscription "Longevity is like mountains and rivers". Wide plain edge.

Among the types of linked arcs shaped mirrors, the mirror with inscription of "Good for posterity" has been unearthed in a large number and is widely popular, prevalent in the late Eastern Han Dynasty.

## 87. 神人龙虎纹画像镜

汉
1991 年地区文化局拨交
直径 13.8 厘米，缘厚 0.7 厘米

　　圆形，半球钮，圆钮座，外围一周连珠纹圈带。主纹区四个圆座乳钉将其分成四区，两组跪坐人物神兽纹和青龙、白虎纹相间分布于四区内，外环一周铭文圈，主纹区外以一周栉齿纹为廓。宽缘，缘上饰一周锯齿纹，一周云纹。

## 87. Mirror with design of immortal, dragon and tiger

Han Dynasty

It was appropriated by the Regional Cultural Bureau in 1991

Diameter: 13.8cm. Edge thickness: 0.7cm

Circular, hemispherical button, circular button seat, with a band of bead pattern around the periphery. The main pattern area is divided into four areas by four circular breast nails. Two groups of kneeling figures, divine beast patterns, Azure Dragon and White Tiger patterns are distributed alternately within the four areas. The outside is surrounded by a band of inscription, and the main pattern area is outlined by a band of fine-toothed pattern. Wide edge, adorned with a jagged pattern and a band of cloud pattern around the edge.

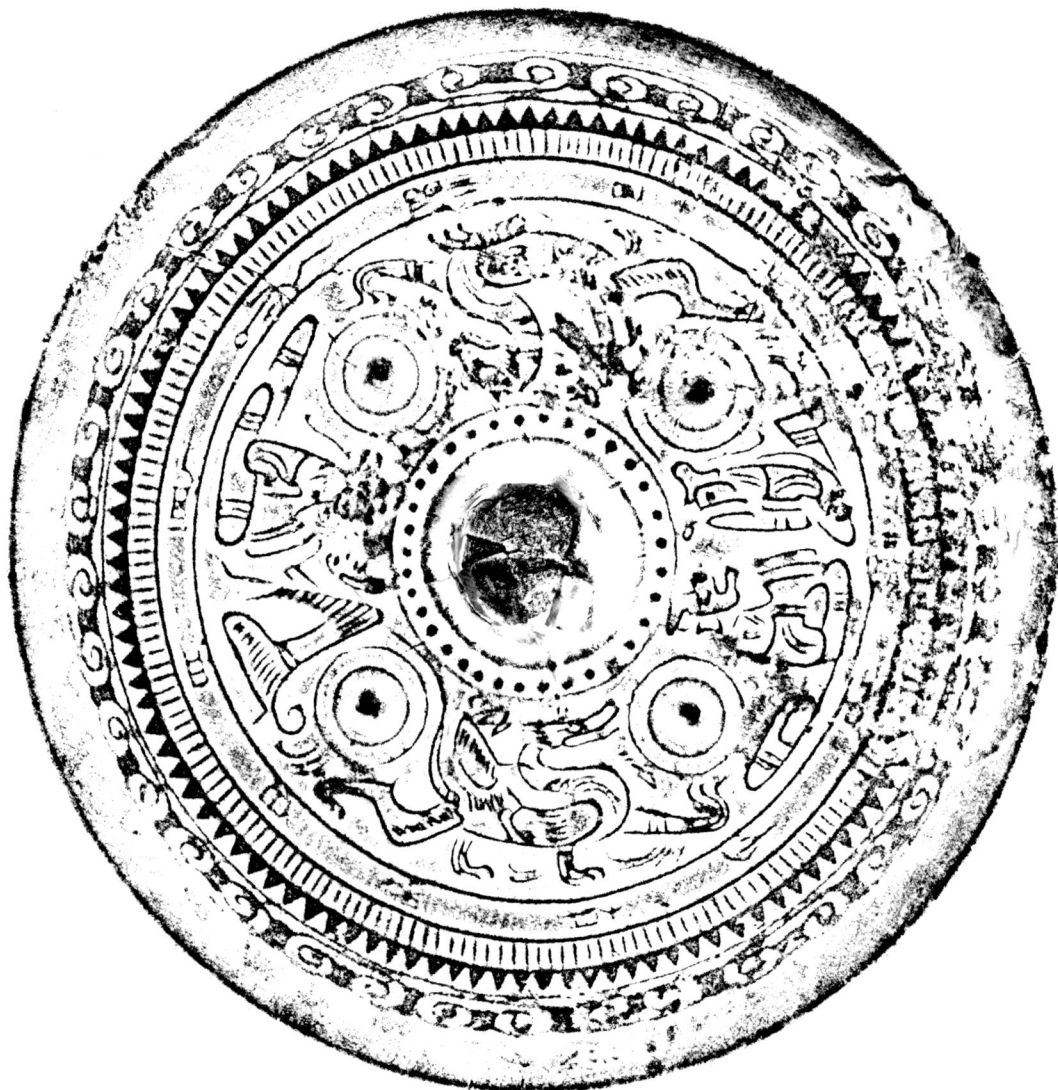

# 88. 四乳神兽画像镜

汉

桶桥区征集

直径 16.5 厘米，厚 0.7 厘米

　　圆形，圆钮，圆钮座，座外饰连珠纹。四个圆座乳钉将内区等分为四区，东王公、西王母与两神兽相间分布。外区一周铭文圈带，铭文为"□作明□□竟真大好，上有东王父西王母，富贵安乐长宜□□"，其外环栉齿纹、锯齿纹与"C"形连续云纹。

# 88. Mirror with design of four nipples and mythical beasts

Han Dynasty

It was collected in Yongqiao District

Diameter: 16.5cm. Thickness: 0.7cm

The mirror is round in shape. Round button, round button seat surrounded by a band of bead pattern. The major motif are gods and mythical creatures, spaced with four nipples. Outside is surrounded by a band of inscription "The mirror made by □ is really good. Above is the Eastern Prince and Western Queen Mother, riches and honour, peaceful and happy", decorated with fine-toothed pattern, triangle-shaped saw pattern and C-shape cloud pattern.

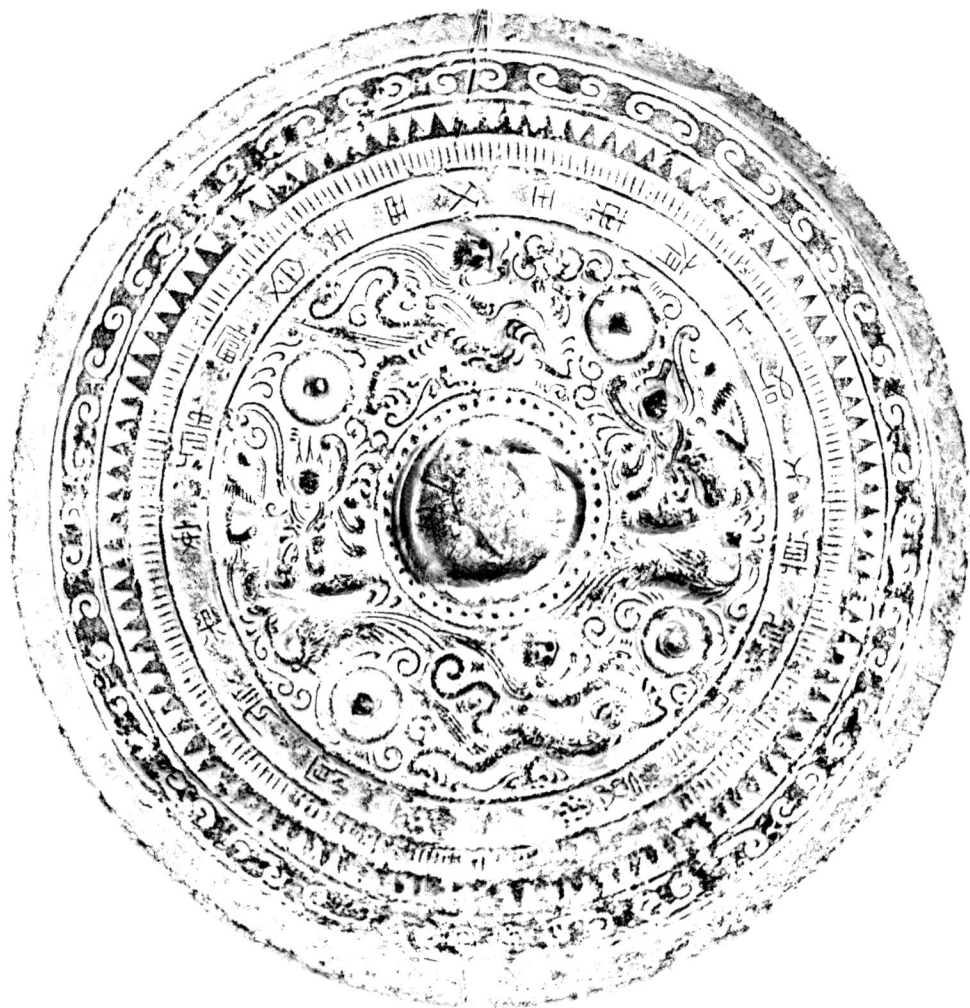

## 89. 三虎纹镜

## 89. Mirror with design of three tigers

汉

旧藏

直径 9.5 厘米，缘厚 0.4 厘米

Han Dynasty

Old collection

Diameter: 9.5cm. Thickness: 0.4cm

　　圆形，半球钮，圆钮座。绕座饰三虎纹，虎身均被钮座叠压。三虎顺时针排列，扭头侧转，形态相致。虎纹两侧各一弦纹圈。近缘处饰栉齿纹、锯齿纹、单线波折纹各一周。素缘。此镜虽采用浅浮雕线条式样，但纹饰立体感强，三虎造型栩栩如生。

The mirror is round in shape. It has a half-sphere-shaped knob on a round base. The base is surrounded with three tigers arranged clockwise. Outside the tigers design is adorned with fine-toothed pattern, single wavy line pattern and triangle-shaped saw pattern. The mirror has a rim without design. The tiger design on this mirror is carved with simple lines and has a vivid effect.

# 90. 四虎纹镜

## 90. Mirror with design of four tigers

汉

旧藏

直径 8.9 厘米，缘厚 0.4 厘米

Han Dynasty

Old collection

Diameter: 8.9cm. Edge thickness: 0.4cm

圆形，圆钮。钮座外均匀分布四虎，呈两虎对峙状，外环一周铭文圈带，铭文较模糊。近缘处，饰栉齿纹、锯齿纹与水波纹。素缘。

The mirror is round in shape with round knob, the four tigers are evenly distributed outside the knob base with a vague inscription band around the outside. Near the rim is decorated with fine-toothed pattern, triangle-shaped saw patter and water ripple pattern. The rim is without design.

# 91. 飞鸟纹镜
# 91. Mirror with design of bird

汉

埇桥区征集

直径 7.3 厘米，厚 0.2 厘米

Han Dynasty

It was collected in Yongqiao District

Diameter: 7.3cm. Thickness: 0.2cm

　　圆形，圆钮，圆钮座。一飞鸟叠压于钮下，首尾盘曲，双翼舒展。鸟身四周饰四枚圆座乳钉，近缘处饰栉齿纹、锯齿纹。

The mirror is round in shape, it has a roud knob with round base. Under the knob is a bird with outstretched wings, surrounded by four nipples with round base. Near the rim are decorated with fine-toothed pattern and triangle-shaped saw pattern.

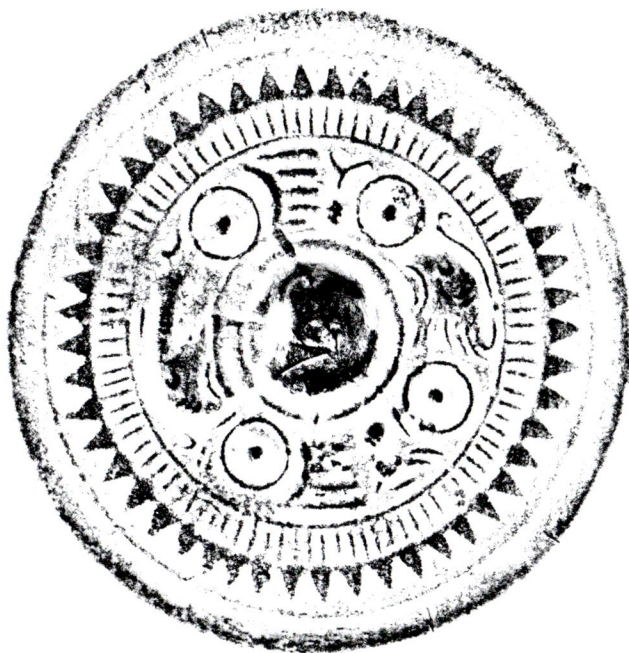

## 92. 飞鸟纹镜

汉

旧藏

直径 9 厘米，厚 0.45 厘米

　　圆形，圆钮，圆钮座。一飞鸟展翅飞翔，身躯部分叠压于钮下，间饰四个圆座乳钉。鸟首较小，体躯丰满，翅羽粗壮，强劲有力，双足外撑。近缘处饰栉齿纹与锯齿纹。

## 92. Mirror with design of bird

Han Dynasty

Old collection

Diameter: 9cm. Thickness: 0.45cm

The mirror is round in shape. It has a round knob on a round base. A bird spreads its wings with part of its body under the knob and four nipples with round base among them. It has strong wings and extends feet outward. Near the rim is adorned with fine-toothed pattern and triangle-shaped saw pattern.

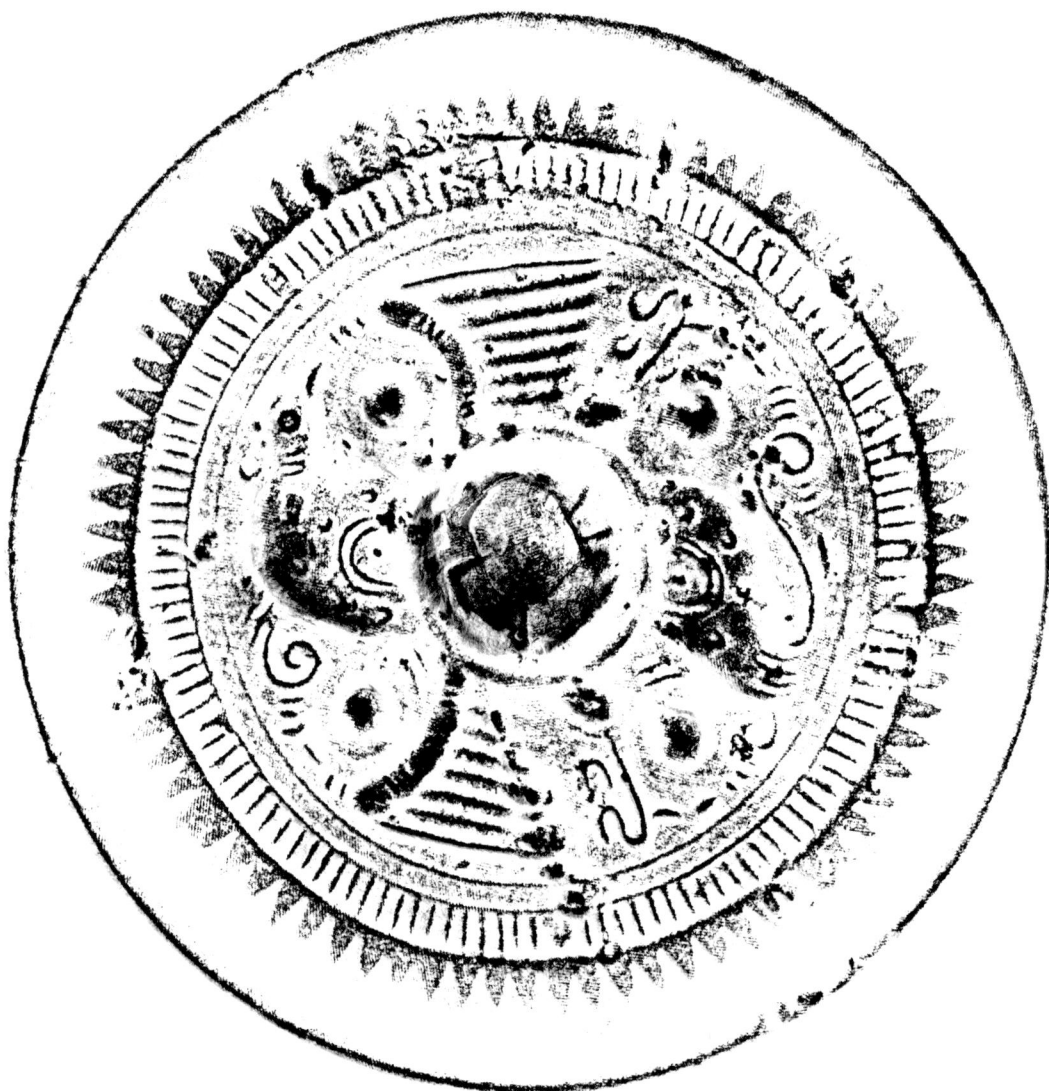

## 93. 变形四叶八凤纹镜

西晋
旧藏
直径 14.5 厘米，厚 0.25 厘米

　　圆形，连峰钮，斜窄缘，镜背内凹。钮座外向外等距延伸四叶纹，四叶间各饰一组形态秀丽且图案化的双凤纹。镜缘饰内向十六连弧纹。

## 93. Mirror with design of four leaves and eight phoenixes

Western Jin Dynasty

Old collection

Diameter: 14.5cm. Thickness: 0.25cm

The mirror is round in shape. It has a peak-shaped knob. The rim is narrow and slanting inside, adorned with linked arcs design. The outside of the knob base is adorned with leaf patterns and two phoenixes among them.

## 94. 龙虎对峙纹镜

隋

1979 年征集

直径 10.9 厘米，缘厚 0.9 厘米

　　圆形，半球钮，圆钮座。钮座外饰一龙一虎，呈对峙状，瞪目、张口、身体蜷曲。钮座下，饰一神兽，环钮而卧，身饰三乳钉纹。主纹区外饰两周弦纹。近缘处饰一周栉齿纹。宽平缘。

## 94. Mirror with design of the conflict between dragon and tiger

Sui Dynasty

It was collected in 1979

Diameter: 10.9cm. Edge thickness: 0.9cm

Circular, hemispherical button, circular button seat. The exterior of the button seat is decorated with a dragon and a tiger, in a confrontational shape, staring and opening mouth with a curled body. Under the button seat, adorned with a divine beast, lying with the button, adorned with three breast nail patterns. The main pattern area is adorned with two circumferential string patterns. A band of fine-toothed pattern near the edge. Wide flat edge.

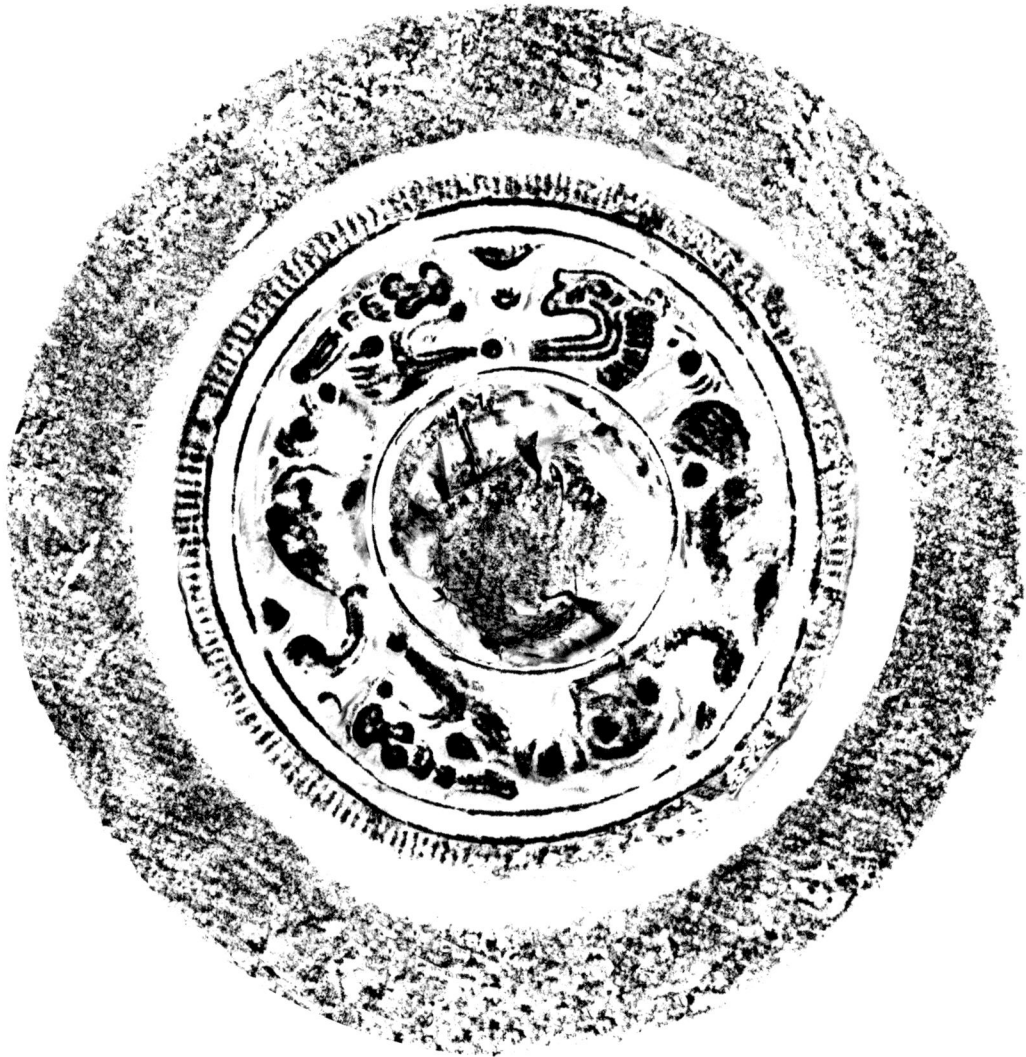

## 95. 瑞兽葡萄纹镜

唐
1979 年征集
直径 10 厘米，厚 0.9 厘米

  圆形，伏兽钮。由瑞兽和葡萄蔓枝构成主题纹饰。内区高浮雕四只瑞兽，呈伏卧状，首尾相连，其间饰以葡萄枝叶和果实。外区，葡萄枝叶、果实、鸟兽纹相间分布。窄缘，近缘处饰花草纹。

## 95. Mirror with design of auspicious animals and graps

Tang Dynasty

It was collected in 1979

Diameter: 10cm. Edge thickness: 0.9cm

Round, with a squatting beast-shaped knob. The theme decoration is composed of auspicious beasts and grape vines. In the inner area, there are four auspicious beasts in high relief, crouching, end to end, decorated with grape branches, leaves, and fruits. In the outer area, grape branches and leaves, fruits, and bird and beast patterns are distributed alternately. Narrow edge, decorated with floral patterns near the edge.

# 96. 雀绕花枝菱形镜

唐

1985 年征集

直径 10 厘米，缘厚 0.7 厘米

　　八瓣菱花形，歪圆钮，镜背以一圈凸弦纹为栏，分为内外两区。内区等距置四只禽鸟，分别为两雀两雁，雀展翅飞翔，雁曲颈俯首而立，间饰四花枝纹。外区菱花瓣内间饰蜂蝶与花枝纹，动静分明，妙趣横生。缘边沿凸起。

　　雀绕花枝镜是唐代比较流行的镜型，一般以菱形镜居多，内区纹饰常以四禽鸟同向绕钮排列，间饰花枝纹，禽鸟有鸳鸯、鹊、雀、雁等，有的嬉戏浮游，有的展翅飞翔，有的静静而立。花枝多为有叶有苞的小折枝花，一般形式一致，画面简洁清新。菱形镜的周边常配以蜂蝶花枝各四组，与内区相映成趣，形成一幅形象生动的花鸟小景。

# 96. Flower of water chestnut shaped mirror with design of sparrows flying around the flower branches

Tang Dynasty

It was collected in 1985

Diameter: 10cm. Thickness: 0.7cm

Eight-petal flower of water chestnut shaped, with crooked circular button, and a convex string pattern on the back of the mirror as a column, divided into two areas: inner and outer. Four birds are equidistant in the inner area, each consisting of two wild sparrows and two geese. The sparrows spread their wings and fly, with the wild geese bending their necks and bowing their heads, adorned with four flower branch patterns. The outer area is adorned with bee and butterfly patterns and flower branches on the inner petals, with distinct movements and interesting scenes. The edge is raised.

The mirror with design of sparrows winding flower branches is a popular mirror type in the Tang Dynasty, usually consisting of a flower of water chestnut shaped mirror. The decorative patterns in the inner area are often arranged with four birds winding around the buttons in the same direction, with flower branch patterns in between. Birds include mandarin ducks, magpies, sparrows, geese, etc. Some are playful and floating, some spread their wings and fly, and some stand quietly. The flower branches are mostly small folded flowers with leaves and buds, generally in the same form, and the picture is simple and fresh.

The periphery of flower of water chestnut shaped mirror is often paired with four groups of bees, butterflies, flowers, and branches, which complement the inner area to create a vivid and lively scenery of flowers and birds.

## 97. 双鸾双兽葵形镜

唐

1988 年朱仙庄河东村小新河出土

直径 16.6 厘米，缘厚 0.5 厘米

八出葵花形，圆钮，八瓣莲花纹钮座。钮座外等距间饰四瑞兽。钮座左右两边各置一鸾鸟、曲颈、振翅、卷尾，相对而立。钮座上方的瑞兽，头有独角，身有双翼，四肢作奔腾状。钮座下方的奔腾的瑞兽，头似狮子，身形矫健，其左右两边各置一花叶纹。

双鸾双兽镜始于唐代早中期，流行于唐代中晚期，镜背装饰趋于生动自然。

## 97. Mallow-shaped mirror with design of double phoenixes and double auspicious animals

Tang Dynasty

It was unearthed in Xiaoxinhe, Hedong Village, Zhuxianzhuang Town in 1988

Diameter: 16.6cm. Edge thickness: 0.5cm

The mirror is in shape of eight-petal mallow and has a round knob, eight petal lotus patterned button seat. Four auspicious beasts are adorned equidistant outside the button seat. On the left and right sides of the button seat, there is a phoenix bird with a curved neck, flapping wings, and curling tail, standing opposite each other. The auspicious beast above the button seat has a single horn on its head, two wings on its body, and its limbs are in a galloping shape. The galloping auspicious beast below the button seat, with its head resembling a lion and a robust body, adorned with flower leaf patterns on both sides.

The mirror with design of double phoenixes and double auspicious animals originated in the early and middle Tang Dynasty and became popular in the middle and late Tang Dynasty. The decoration on the back of the mirror tends to be vivid and natural.

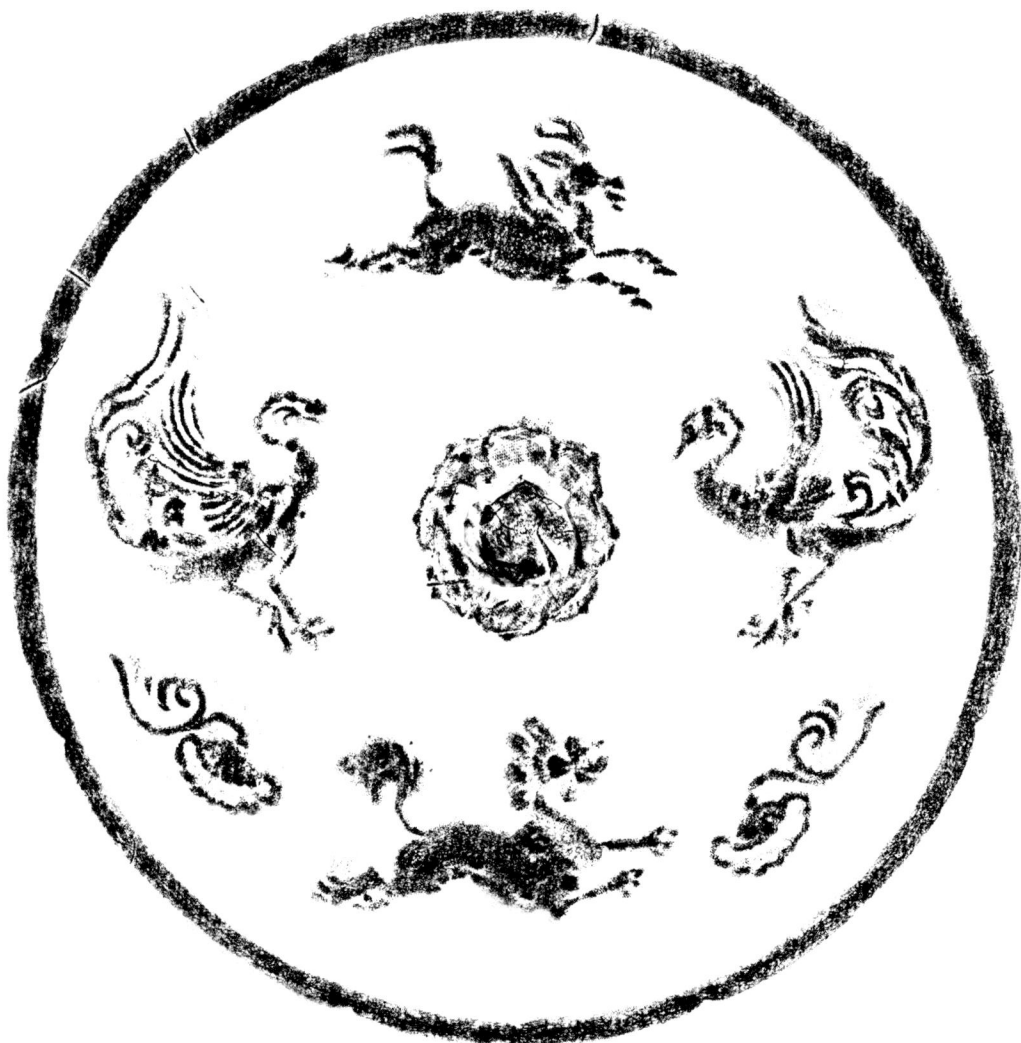

## 98. 双鸾双兽葵形镜

唐

2009 年涉案移交

直径 16.8 厘米，厚 0.5 厘米

　　八出葵花形，拱形钮，八瓣莲花纹钮座。镜背饰双鸾双瑞兽纹，双鸾体型大致相同，振翅、卷尾，口衔绶带。钮座上方瑞兽形如飞马状，有角和短羽，也有学者称之为独角兽，呈奔驰状。钮座下方瑞兽形如飞狮，左右各饰一花叶纹。镜纹简洁生动。

　　鸾是古代传说中的祥瑞之鸟，《山海经》中记载："其状如翟而五采文，名曰鸾鸟，见则天下安宁"。

## 98. Mallow-shaped mirror with design of double phoenixes and double auspicious animals

Tang Dynasty

It was transferred in the case in 2009

Diameter: 16.8cm. Thickness: 0.5cm

The mirror is in shape of eight-petal mallow and has a arched button, eight petal lotus patterned button seat. The back of the mirror is decorated with double phoenixes and double auspicious animals pattern, with roughly the same body shape, flapping wings and curling tails, and holding a ribbon in the mouth. The auspicious beast above the button seat is shaped like a flying horse, with horns and short feathers. Some scholars also refer to it as a unicorn, which is in a galloping shape. Under the button seat, the auspicious beast is shaped like a flying lion, adorned with flower leaf patterns on both sides. The mirror pattern is concise and vivid.

Phoenix is a bird of auspiciousness in ancient legends. According to the "Classic of Mountains and Seas", its shape is like Zhai with five colors, named phoenix. Seeing it, the world is peaceful".

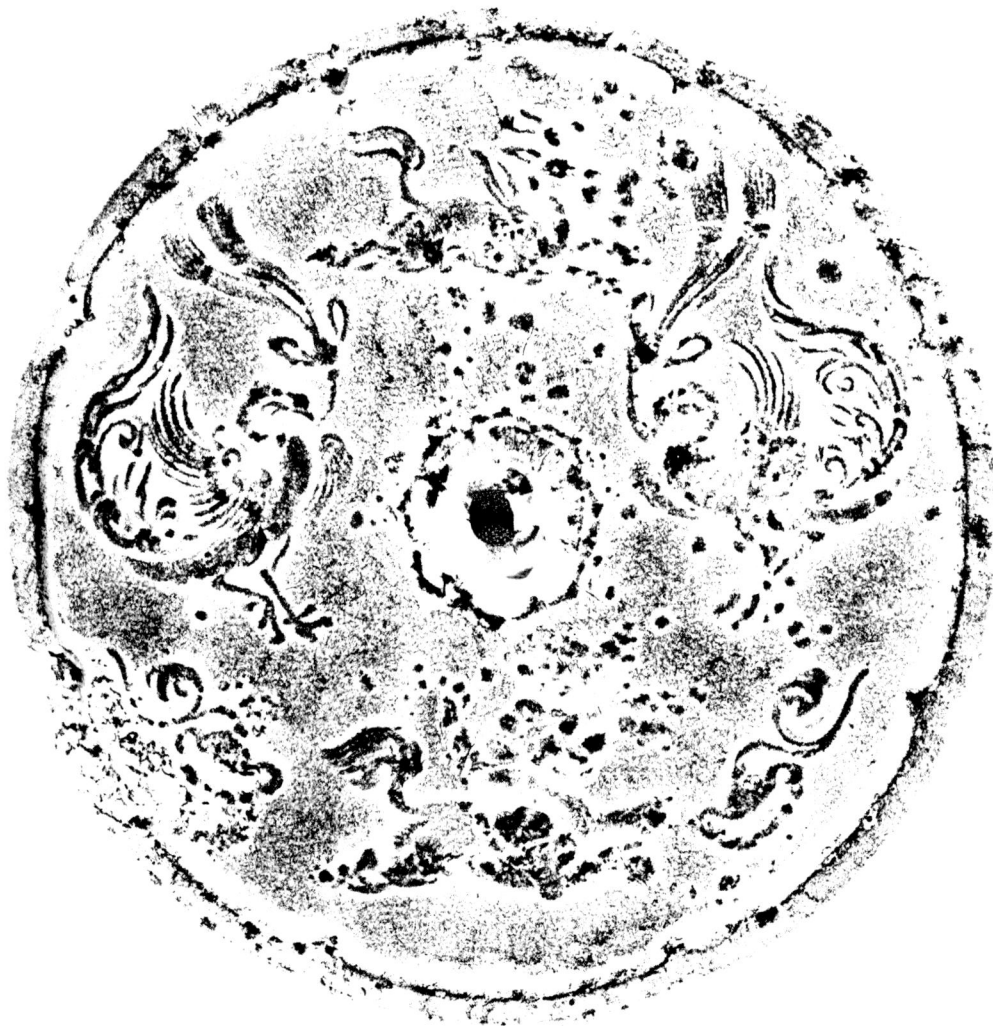

## 99. 双鸾双兽葵形镜

唐

1979 年征集

直径 17 厘米，缘厚 0.4 厘米

　　八出葵花形，圆钮，八瓣莲花钮座。钮座外等距分置四神兽，钮座左右各一口衔绶带的鸾鸟，鸾鸟展翅卷尾，身形优雅。绶带带一花结，带尾飘逸至近镜缘处。镜钮上方为一奔驰的瑞兽，头饰独角，身有双翼，有学者称之为"独角兽"。镜钮下方一奔驰的似马瑞兽，鬃毛细密，矫健奔放，其左右两侧各饰一花叶纹。素缘。

## 99. Mallow-shaped mirror with design of double phoenixes and double auspicious animals

Tang Dynasty

It was collected in 1979

Diameter: 17cm.Thickness: 0.4cm

The mirror is in shape of eight-petal mallow and has a round knob, eight petal lotus button seat. Four divine beasts are equidistant outside the button seat, with a phoenix carrying ribbons on each side of the button seat. The elegant phoenix spreads its wings and curls its tail. The ribbon has a flower knot, and the tail of the ribbon floats to the edge of the mirror. Above the mirror button is an auspicious beast with a single horn and wings, which some scholars refer to as a "unicorn". Below the mirror button is a galloping beast like horse with a fine and vigorous mane, adorned with flower leaf patterns on both sides. Plain margin.

## 100. 缠枝莲花葵形镜

唐
1979 年征集
直径 27.2 厘米，缘厚 0.6 厘米

　　八出葵形，圆钮，八瓣莲花钮座，围以连珠
纹圈带。其外蔓枝相连，蔓枝上生出花叶、花苞
及花瓣，四朵盛开的莲花瓣间饰四片宽大的叶纹。
素缘。

## 100. Mallow-shaped mirror with design of interlocking lotus

Tang Dynasty

It was collected in 1979
Diameter: 27.2cm. Thickness: 0.6cm

The mirror is in shape of eight-petal mallow. It has a round knob on an eight-petal base with a band of beads. The outer part is interlocking flowers, in the middle of the four lotus petals are four broad leaves. The mirror has a rim without design.

## 101. 宝相花葵形镜

唐

2009 年涉案移交

直径 16.2 厘米，厚 0.35 厘米

六出葵形，圆钮，花瓣纹钮座，外饰一圈凸弦纹。主纹为两种不同样式的花卉纹各三朵相间环绕。一组为六瓣莲花，花叶中置点状花蕊；另一组为旋转式六叶片组成的花瓣内心，外围三叶片及三弧形花瓣。素缘。

宝相花一般指的是将某些自然形态的花朵（主要是荷花）进行艺术处理，变成一种装饰化的花朵纹样。

## 101. Mallow-shaped mirror with design of Baoxiang flowers

Tang Dynasty

It was transferred in the case in 2009

Diameter: 16.2cm. Thickness: 0.35cm

The mirror is in shape of six-petal mallow and has a round knob, petal patterned button seat, with a convex string pattern on the exterior. The main pattern consists of two different styles of floral patterns, each surrounded by three alternating flowers. One group consists of six-petal lotus flowers with dotted stamens and pistils in the middle of the leaves; The other group consists of a rotating six-leaf petal surrounded by three leaves and three curved petals. Plain margin.

The composite flowers design generally refers to the artistic treatment of certain natural forms of flowers (mainly lotus flowers) into a decorative flower pattern.

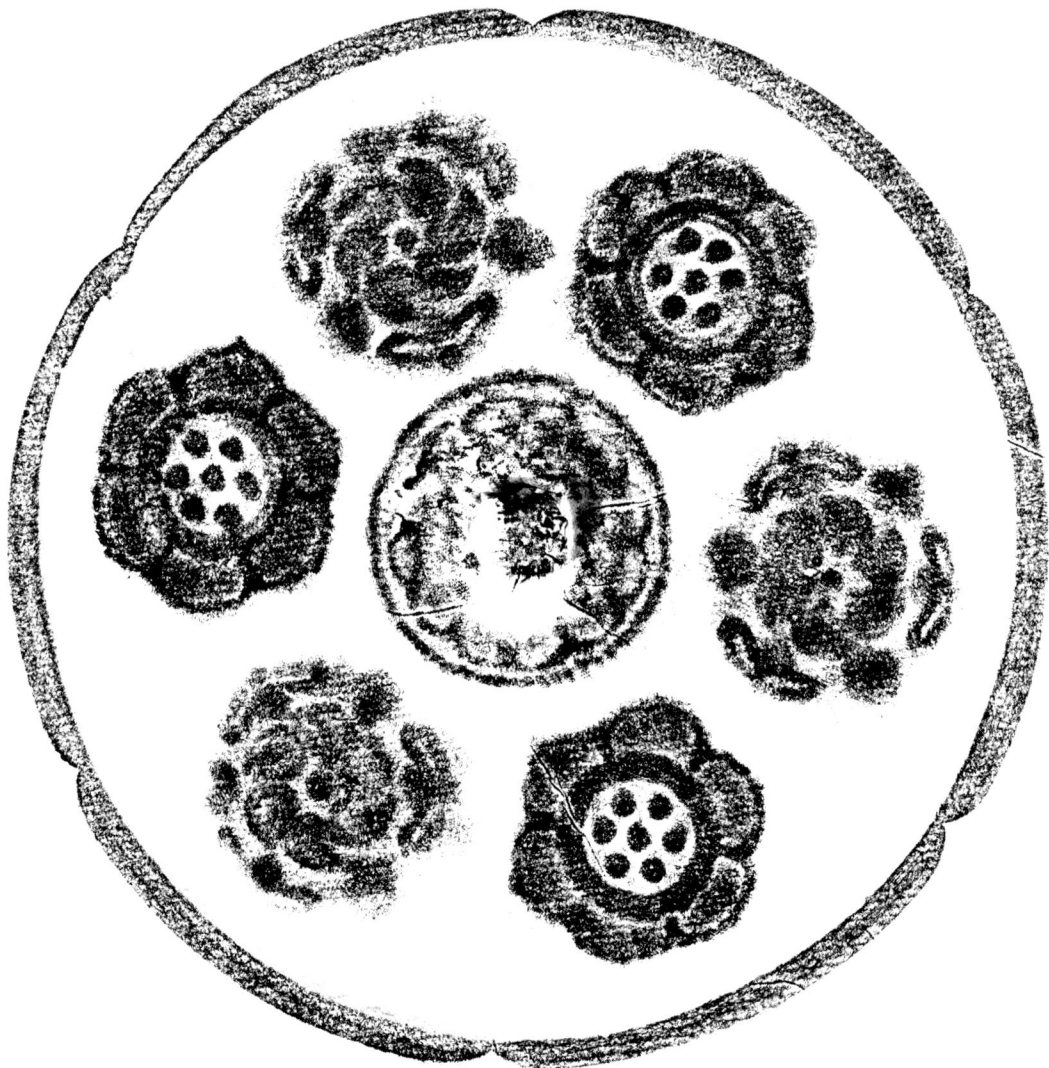

## 102. 缠枝花卉纹镜

唐
1985年宿县西寺坡区高口乡圩里村征集
直径11厘米，缘厚0.7厘米

　　八瓣菱花形，圆钮无座，绕钮饰以缠枝花卉
纹。镜面微弧，镜体浑厚，工艺良好。镜背内凹，
菱花形厚素宽缘，缘边沿凸起。

## 102. Mirror with design of interlocking flowers

Tang Dynasty

It was collected in Weili Village, Gaokou Township, Xisipo District, Su County in 1985

Diameter: 11cm. Edge thickness: 0.7cm

Eight petal of the flower of water chestnut shaped, with round button without seat, adorned with interlocking flowers. The mirror surface is slightly curved, and the mirror body is thick and well crafted. The mirror back is concave, with a flower of water chestnut shaped thick and wide plain edge with the outside is raised.

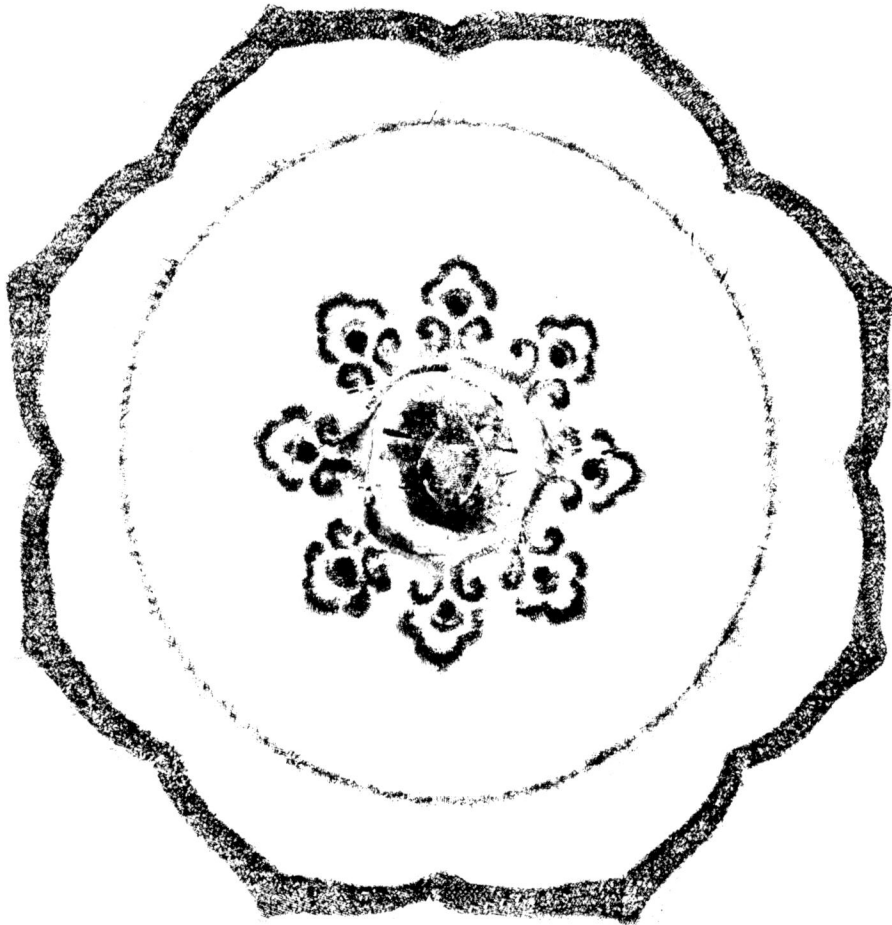

## 103. 花卉纹镜

宋

1987 年征集

直径 12.8 厘米，缘厚 0.3 厘米

　　圆形，圆钮，花纹钮座。主纹区六条宽带纹将镜背分为九个区，似"井"字形。井字形四角外侧各置一朵花卉纹，上方两朵花卉为细瓣花卉，似菊花；下方两朵花卉，花瓣比上侧的花卉略粗，似莲花。近缘处一周凸起弦纹为栏。素卷缘。

## 103. Mirror with design of flowers and plants

Song Dynasty

It was collected in 1987

Diameter: 12.8cm. Edge thickness: 0.3cm

The mirror is circular, with round button and flower patterned button seat. The six broad band patterns in the main pattern area divide the mirror back into nine areas, like the shape of the character "#". A flower pattern is placed on the outer side of each of the four corners of the "#" shaped pattern, and the two flowers above are thin petal flowers, resembling chrysanthemums; The two flowers below have slightly thicker petals than the flowers on the upper side, resembling lotus. The raised string pattern near the edge. Plain rolled-up edge.

# 104. 素面镜

宋

1984 年祁县邱园村征集

直径 12.8 厘米，厚 0.3 厘米

　　圆形，桥形钮。素背，镜背多处划痕。素缘，铸造比较粗糙，修边不规整。

# 104. Mirror without design

Song Dynasty

It was collected in Qiuyuan Village. Qixian Town

Diameter: 12.8cm. Thickness: 0.3cm

The mirror is circular and has a bridge shaped button. Plain back. There are multiple scratches on the mirror back. Plain edge, relatively rough casting, irregular trimming.

## 105. 弦纹镜

宋
1979 年征集
直径 14.2 厘米，厚 0.4 厘米

圆形，平顶圆钮。素镜背，近缘处环一周弦纹。卷缘。

## 105. Mirror with string design

Song Dynasty
It was collected in 1979
Diameter: 14.2cm. Thickness: 0.4cm

Circular, flat top circular button. On the back of the plain mirror, there is a circular string pattern near the edge. Rolled-up edge.

# 106. 四方委角镜

宋

1979 年拣选

直径 13 厘米，缘厚 0.2 厘米

　　镜为委角方形，桥形钮，镜体较薄。镜背素面无纹，四边缘微弧并凸起，四角外沿呈圆弧状，缘面内侧微凸。

# 106. Square mirror with curved angle

Song Dynasty

It was selected in 1979

Diameter: 13cm. Edge thickness: 0.2cm

The mirror is in the shape of square with curved angle, it has a bridge-shaped knob.The mirror is relatively thin. There is no decoration on the back of the mirror. Four edges slightly curved and raised, the outer edges of the four corners forming a circular arc, and the inner edge surface slightly convex.

## 107. 玉兔捣药纹镜

## 107. Mirror with pattern of fairy tale of Jade Rabbit Tamping Medicine

宋

1991 年宿县地区文化局拨交

直径 11.6 厘米，缘厚 0.6 厘米

Song Dynasty

It was allocated by the Cultural Bureau of Su County in 1991

Diameter: 11.6cm. Edge thickness: 0.6cm

镜为圆形，铜镜下方近缘处置两个半环形钮。主纹区内，一棵枝繁叶茂的月桂树下置一只兔子，兔子呈站立状，双耳向后直立，两只前爪紧握一臼杵，似捣药状。近缘处饰两周弦纹。卷缘。

The mirror is circular, with two half circular buttons disposed near the lower edge of the copper mirror. In the main pattern area, a rabbit is placed under a lush laurel tree. The rabbit is standing, with its ears standing back and two front claws tightly gripping a pestle, resembling in the state of pounding medicine. Decorate two circular string patterns near the edge. Rolled-up edge.

## 108. 四乳八鸟铭文镜

## 108. Mirror with design of four nipples, eight birds and inscription

宋

1991 年宿县地区文化局拨交

直径 9 厘米，缘厚 0.7 厘米

Song Dynasty

It was allocated by the Cultural Bureau of Su County in 1991

Diameter: 9cm. Edge thickness: 0.7cm

　　镜为圆形，圆钮，钮顶平，圆形钮座，钮座外一周宽弦纹带。印模仿制汉镜，铸造工艺粗糙，纹饰模糊。主纹区四个圆座乳钉将其分为四区，每区内饰有两只禽鸟，禽鸟两两相对，中间置一篆书铭文"家常贵富"。主纹区左右两侧各以一圈栉齿纹为栏。宽平缘。

The mirror is circular, with a round button and a flat top. The button seat is circular, and there is a wide string pattern around the outside of the button seat. The mold imitates Han mirrors, with rough casting process and blurred patterns. The main pattern area is divided into four areas by four circular breast nails. Each area has two birds in the interior, with birds facing each other in pairs and the inscription of "Homely riches and honour" placed in the middle. The main pattern area is surrounded by a band of fine-toothed pattern on both sides. Wide flat edge.

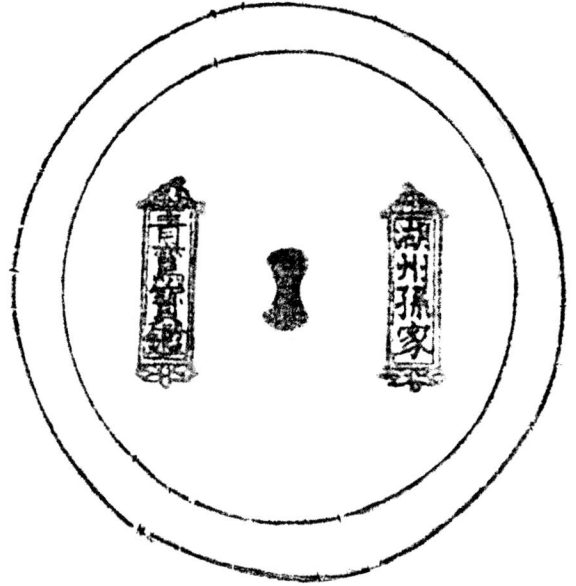

# 109. "湖州孙家"铭文镜

# 109. Mirror with inscription of "Hu Zhou Sun Jia"

宋

1979 年拣选

直径 8.2 厘米，缘厚 0.4 厘米

Song Dynasty

It was selected in 1979

Diameter: 8.2cm. Edge thickness: 0.4cm

　　圆形，银锭形钮，钮左右两侧各置一印戳式双线长方形框，框上下饰草叶纹，右侧方框内有一列铭文"湖州孙家"，应为铸造商家的商号，左侧方框内有一列铭文"青鸾宝鉴"，近缘处一圈凸弦纹。卷缘。

Circular, silver ingot shaped button, with a stamp-style double line rectangular frame on both sides of the button. The upper and lower parts of the frame are decorated with grass patterns. There is a column of inscriptions "Hu Zhou Sun Jia" in the right box, which should be the name of the foundry merchant. There is a column of inscriptions "Qing Luan Bao Jian" in the left box, and a convex string pattern near the edge. Rolled-up edge.

## 110. 葵花形湖州镜

## 110. Mallow-shaped mirror with inscription of "Hu Zhou"

宋

1985 年在宿县西寺坡大泽乡金湖村征集

直径 11 厘米，厚 0.3 厘米

Song Dynasty

It was collected in Jinhu Village, Daze Township, Xisipo, Suxian County in 1985

Diameter: 11cm. Thickness: 0.3cm

镜为六出葵花形，桥形钮，镜背素地无纹饰。钮右侧近缘处有两行铭文"湖州真石家　念二叔照子"，呈长方形印戳式，铭文部分损毁。钮左侧近缘处有笔划纤细的阴刻"徐州验记官"。缘微凸起呈弧面。镜体较薄，表面银灰色，含铅、锌成分明显偏多。

这面铜镜形制、工艺与江西鄱阳县的北宋大观三年（1109 年）墓出土的一面铜镜相同，与浙江诸暨市一座南宋嘉泰元年（1201 年）墓出土的一件六弧葵花镜完全相同。湖州镜主要流行于南宋时期。

The mirror is in shape of six-petal mallow, with a bridge shaped button and a plain back. No pattern decoration. There are two lines of inscriptions on the right edge of the button, "This is an authentic mirror made by the 22nd Uncle of the Shijia family in Huzhou", in a rectangular stamping style, with some of the inscriptions damaged. On the left side of the button, there is a slender engraved "Inspector of Xu Zhou". The edge is slightly raised and curved. The mirror body is relatively thin, with a silver gray surface and significantly more lead and zinc components.

This bronze mirror has the same shape and craftsmanship as the mirror unearthed from a tomb in the third year of the Daguan reign of the Northern Song Dynasty (1109 AD) in Boyang County, Jiangxi Province, and is identical to the mirror unearthed from a tomb in the first year of the Jiatai reign of the Southern Song Dynasty (1201 AD) in Zhuji County, Zhejiang Province. Huzhou mirrors were mainly popular during the Southern Song Dynasty.

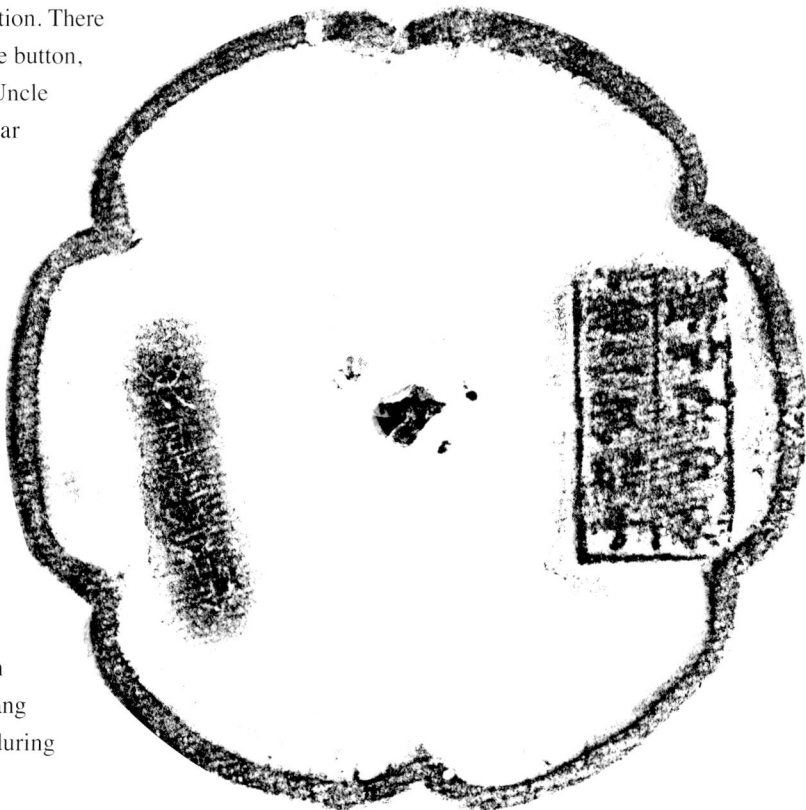

## 111. 飞凤纹桃形执镜

宋

1992年西寺坡家征集

连柄长 12.8 厘米，柄长 8 厘米，镜面直径 8.7～10.3 厘米，缘厚 0.4 厘米

桃形，带柄，素缘。天空流云钩月，一凤鸟昂首展翅飞腾，身形矫健。

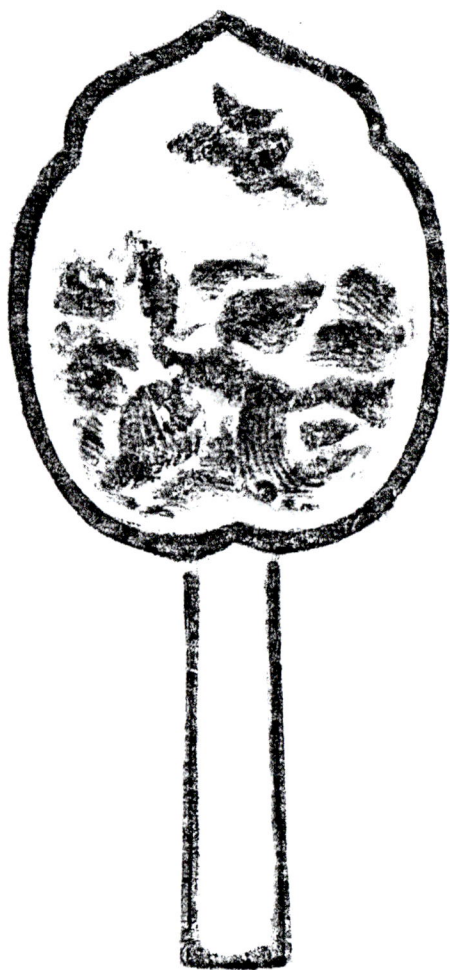

## 111. Peach-shaped mirror with pattern of flying phoenix

Song Dynasty

It was collected from Xisipo in 1992

The length including the handle: 12.8cm. The length of the handle: 8cm.

The mirror diameter: 8.7-10.3cm. Edge thickness: 0.4cm

Peach shaped, with handle, plain margin. The sky is full of flowing clouds and the moon is hooked, and phoenix is soaring with its head held high above the sea, with a robust physique.

## 112. 鱼化龙纹桃形执镜

辽

1979 年拣选

全长 21 厘米，镜面直径 10.5～11.5 厘米，柄长 9.5 厘米，柄宽 1.8～2.2 厘米，缘厚 0.6 厘米

　　镜为桃形，带柄，胎体厚重。柄内置莲花、荷叶纹，荷叶内卷。镜背天空云纹缭绕，一瑞兽盘曲于波涛起伏的海面上，龙头鱼尾双羽翼，张口瞠目，伸舌吐信，头生短角，鬣发飘卷，正展翅向上飞跃，其身下置波涛纹，汹涌澎湃。整个画面采用浅浮雕式的工艺技法，纹饰流畅，形象生动。素缘。

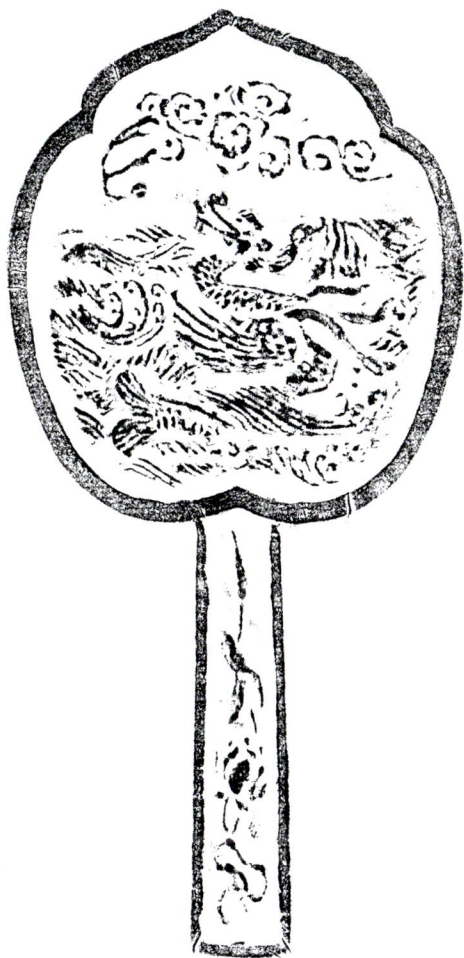

## 112. Peach-shaped mirror with pattern of fish becomes a dragon

Liao Dynasty

It was selected in 1979

Total length: 21cm.The mirror diameter: 10.5-11.5cm. The handle length: 9.5cm. The handle width: 1.8-2.2cm. The Thickness: 0.6cm

The mirror is peach shaped, with a handle and a thick and heavy body. The handle is equipped with lotus and lotus leaf patterns, and the lotus leaves are rolled inward. The sky in the mirror is shrouded in cloud patterns. A divine beast is coiled on the undulating sea surface, with a dragon head、 a fish tail and double wings. It opens its mouth and eyes, stretches out its tongue, has short horns on its head, and its hair is fluttering and curling. It is spreading its wings and soaring upwards, with wave patterns beneath its body, waves surging turbulently. The entire screen adopts a shallow relief style craftsmanship technique, with smooth patterns and vivid images. Plain margin.

## 113. 马小山造款铭文镜

## 113. Mirror with inscription of "Made by Ma Xiaoshan"

元

2009 年涉案移交

直径 12.8 厘米，厚 0.4 厘米

Yuan Dynasty

It was transferred in the case in 2009

Diameter: 12.8cm. Thickness: 0.4cm

　　镜为圆形，圆钮。钮上刻铭文"马小山造"，四字楷书款。镜背素面无纹。

The mirror is circular with round button. The button is inscribed with "Made by Ma Xiaoshan" in regular script. The mirror back has a plain surface without patterns.

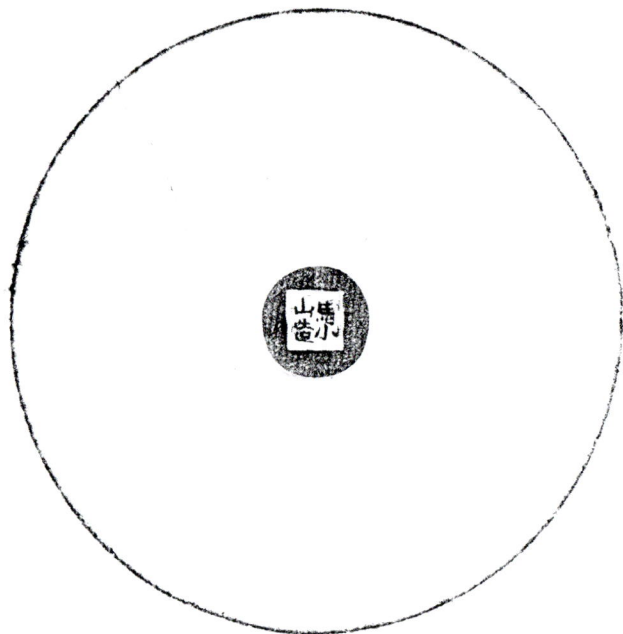

# 114. 素面镜

## 114. Mirror without design

元

旧藏

直径 8.4 厘米，缘厚 0.3 厘米

Yuan Dynasty

Old collection

Diameter: 8.4cm. Edge thickness: 0.3cm

　　圆形，圆钮，钮顶平，钮顶饰交叉斜线组成菱形网格纹。镜背素面。

Round, round button, flat button top with rhombus patterns composed of intersecting diagonal lines. Plain mirror back.

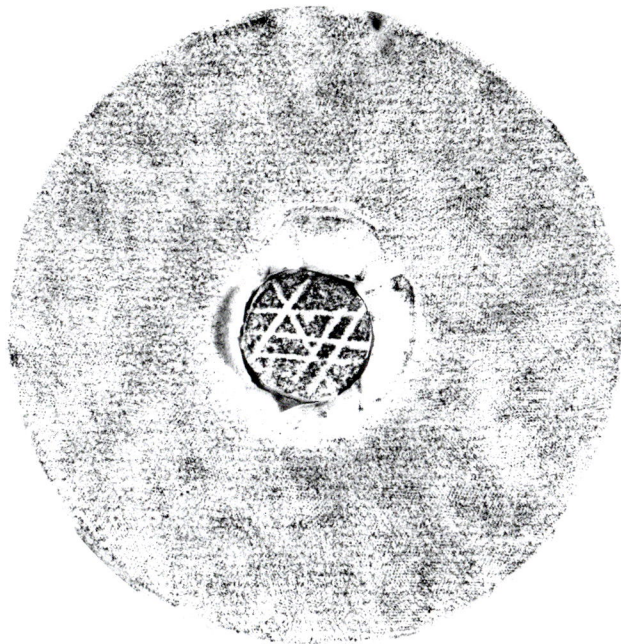

## 115. 重圈纹镜

明

1989 年征集

直径 12.2 厘米，厚 1.25 厘米

　　镜为圆形，半球钮，镜面微凸，背面饰两周凸起弦纹，素卷缘。镜体厚重。

## 115. Mirror with double strings design

Ming Dynasty

It was collected in 1989

Diameter: 12.2cm. Thickness: 1.25cm

The mirror is circular, with a hemispherical knob and a slightly convex surface. The back is decorated with two raised string patterns, with a plain rolled-up edge. The mirror body is thick and heavy.

# 116. 弦纹镜

## 116. Mirror with string design

明

1979 年征集

直径 15.4 厘米，厚 0.65 厘米

Ming Dynasty

It was collected in 1979

Diameter: 15.4cm. Thickness: 0.65cm

　　镜为圆形，平顶圆钮，钮上有四字铭文，铭文模糊，难以辨识。素镜背，近缘处环一周凸起弦纹，卷缘。

The mirror is circular, with a flat top and round knob. There are four indistinct inscriptions on the knob.There is no decoration on the back of the mirror.The edge of the mirror has a raised string. Rolled-up edge.

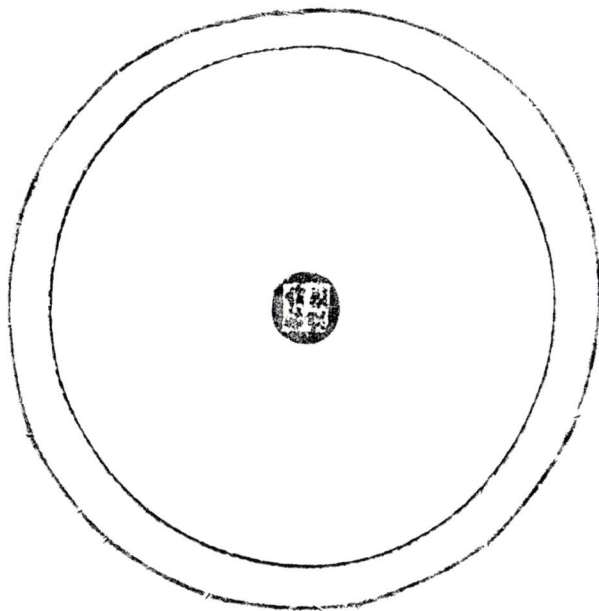

# 117. 弦纹镜

明

旧藏

直径 14.1 厘米，厚 0.4 厘米

　　镜为圆形，平顶圆钮，镜背近缘处环饰一周弦纹，卷缘。

# 117. Mirror with string design

Ming Dynasty

Old collection

Diameter: 14.1cm. Thickness: 0.4cm

The mirror is circular, with a flat top and round button. The back of the mirror is adorned with a circular string pattern near the edge, with rolled-up edge.

# 118. 弦纹镜

明

1985 年在苗庵王集尹陈村征集

直径 8 厘米，缘厚 0.7 厘米

镜为圆形，圆钮，钮顶平。钮外主纹区饰两周凸弦纹，卷缘。

# 118. Mirror with string design

Ming Dynasty

It was collected from Yinchen Village, Wangji Miaoan Village in 1985

Diameter: 8cm. Edge thickness: 0.7cm

The mirror is circular, with round button and a flat top. The main pattern area outside the button is decorated with two convex string patterns, with rolled-up edge.

## 119. "福寿双全"镜

## 119. Mirror with string design and inscription of "Good fortune and longevity"

明

1979 年征集

直径 13 厘米，厚 0.6 厘米

Ming Dynasty

It was collected in 1979

Diameter: 13cm. Thickness: 0.6cm

镜为圆形，拱形钮。钮上下左右各置一方框，框内各置一字铭，字体为楷书。按上下右左的顺序，依次为"福寿双全"。近缘处环一周凸起弦纹。卷缘。

The mirror is circular with arched button. There are boxes on the top, bottom, left, and right sides of the mirror, with a character inscription placed inside each box. The font is regular script. In the order of top, bottom, right, and left, it is the inscription of "Good fortune and longevity". Near the edge, there is a raised string pattern. Rolled-up edge.

## 120. "福寿双全"镜

## 120. Mirror with string design and inscription of "Good fortune and longevity"

明

1984 年从祁县王楼村征集

直径 13.3 厘米, 缘厚 0.6 厘米

Ming Dynasty

It was collected from Wanglou Village, Qixian Town in 1984

Diameter: 13.3cm. Edge thickness: 0.6cm

　　圆形, 圆钮。钮外等间距饰四个宽弦纹方框, 方框内各饰一楷书铭文, 按照上下右左的顺序, 依次为福寿双全, 外围一周凸起弦纹圈。卷缘。

Round, round button. Four wide string patterned boxes are evenly spaced outside the button, and each box is adorned with a regular script inscription. In the order of top, bottom, right, and left, it is the inscription of "Good fortune and longevity", with a raised string patterned circle around the periphery. Rolled-up edge.

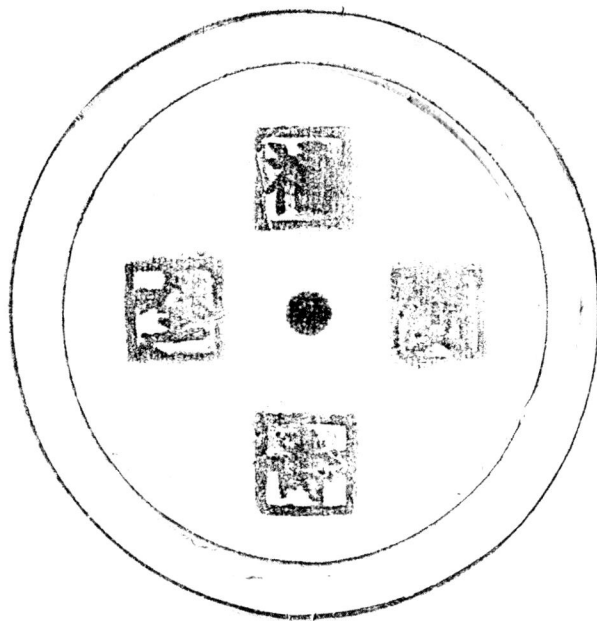

## 121. "五子登科" 弦纹镜

## 121. Mirror with string design and inscription of "Five sons passing the imperial examination"

———————

明

1979 年征集

直径 18.2 厘米，缘厚 0.8 厘米

Ming Dynasty

It was collected in 1979

Diameter: 18.2cm. Edge thickness: 0.8cm

　　镜为圆形，圆钮。钮外等间距饰四个凸弦纹方框，方框内各饰一铭文，字体为楷书。按照上下右左的顺序依次为"五子登科"。近缘处饰一周凸起弦纹。卷缘。

The mirror is circular with round button. Four convex string pattern boxes are evenly spaced outside the button, and each box is adorned with an inscription in regular script. According to the order of top, bottom, right, and left, is the inscription of "Five sons passing the imperial examination". Decorate a raised string pattern around the edge. Rolled-up edge.

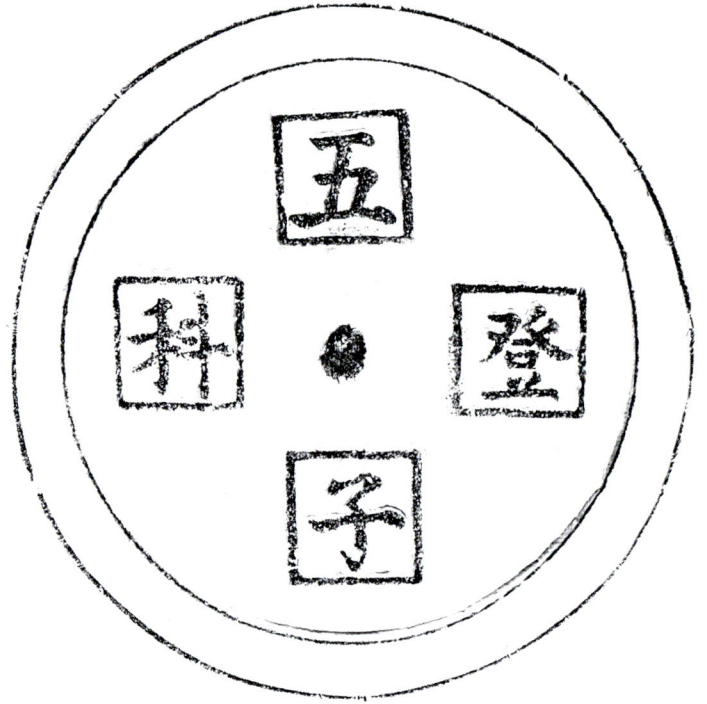

## 122. "五子登科" 弦纹镜

## 122. Mirror with string design and inscription of "Five sons passing the imperial examination"

明

1979 年征集

直径 9.7 厘米，缘厚 0.4 厘米

Ming Dynasty

It was collected in 1979

Diameter: 9.7cm. Edge thickness: 0.4cm

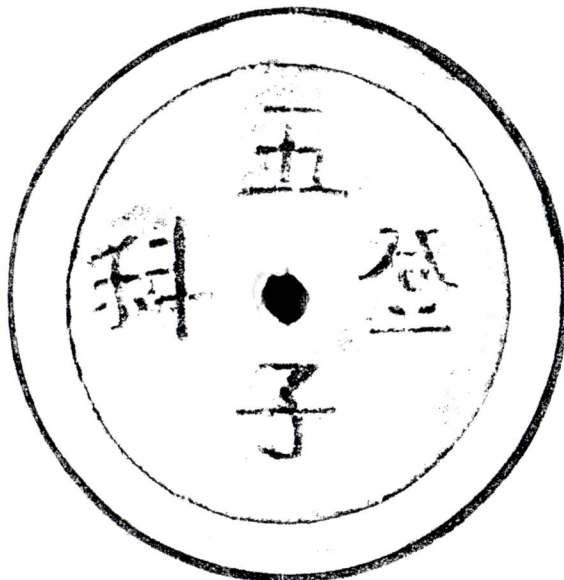

镜身圆形，圆钮，钮顶平。钮外等距分布"五子登科"四字楷书铭文。铭文外饰一周凸起弦纹。卷缘。

The mirror body is circular, with round button and a flat top. On the back of the mirror with equidistant distribution outside the button, there are four regular script characters which can be translated as "Five sons passing the imperial examination". The outer decoration of the inscription features a raised string pattern around it. Rolled-up edge.

## 123. "长命富贵" 镜

## 123. Mirror with inscription of "A long life of abundance and respectability"

明

灵璧出土

直径 18 厘米，缘厚 0.6 厘米

Ming Dynasty

It was unearthed in Ling Bi

Diameter: 18cm. Thickness: 0.6cm

圆形，圆钮，兽纹钮座。钮座外 "长命富贵" 四字铭文与四人物相间均匀分布，外饰一周弦纹。卷缘。

The mirror is round in shape, it has a round button with beast button seat.The inscription of "A long life of abundance and respectability" and four characters are evenly distributed outside the button seat. There is a raised string pattern near the edge. Rolled-up edge.

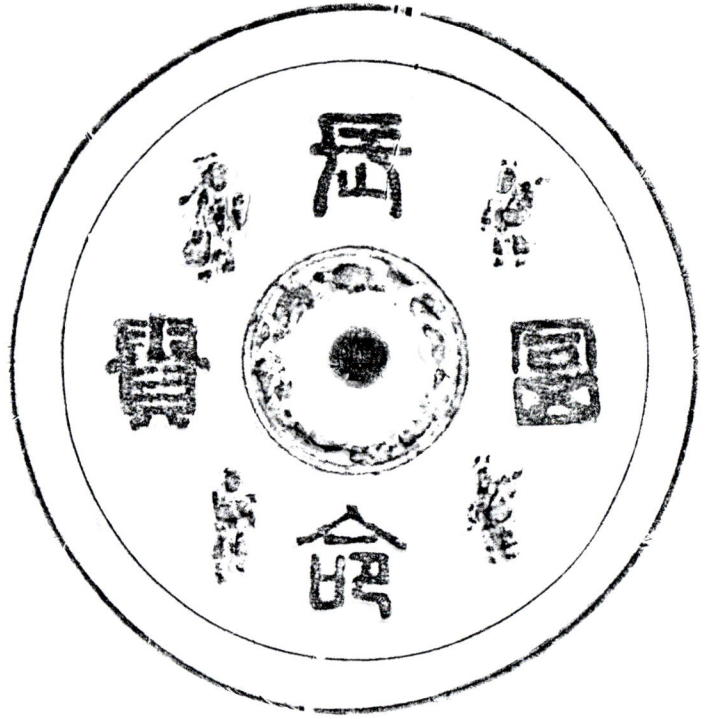

## 124. 双龙八卦镜

## 124. Mirror with design of double dragons and eight diagrams

明

灵璧出土

直径 5.4 厘米，厚 0.2 厘米

Ming Dynasty

It was unearthed in Ling Bi

Diameter: 5.4cm. Thickness: 0.2cm

　　圆形，平顶桥形钮，八卦纹钮座。镜钮两侧
各有一龙纹，首尾相接，间饰火球。卷缘。

The mirror is round in shape, it has a flat bridge button
with base in Eight Trigrams shaped. Both sides of the
mirror button has a dragon pattern connected from head
to the end, decorated with fireballs. Rolled-up edge.

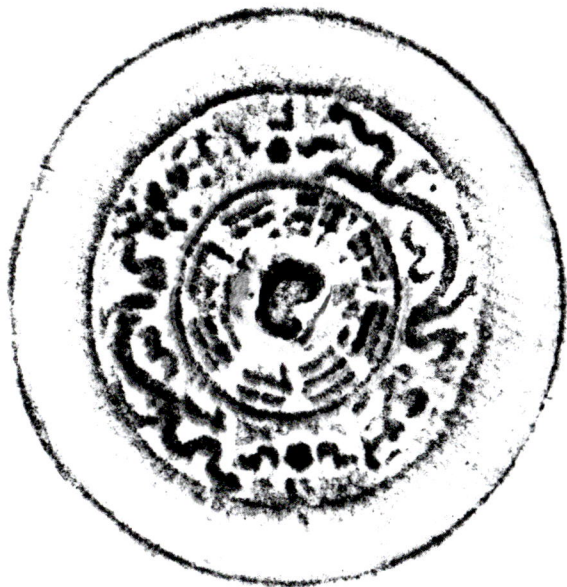

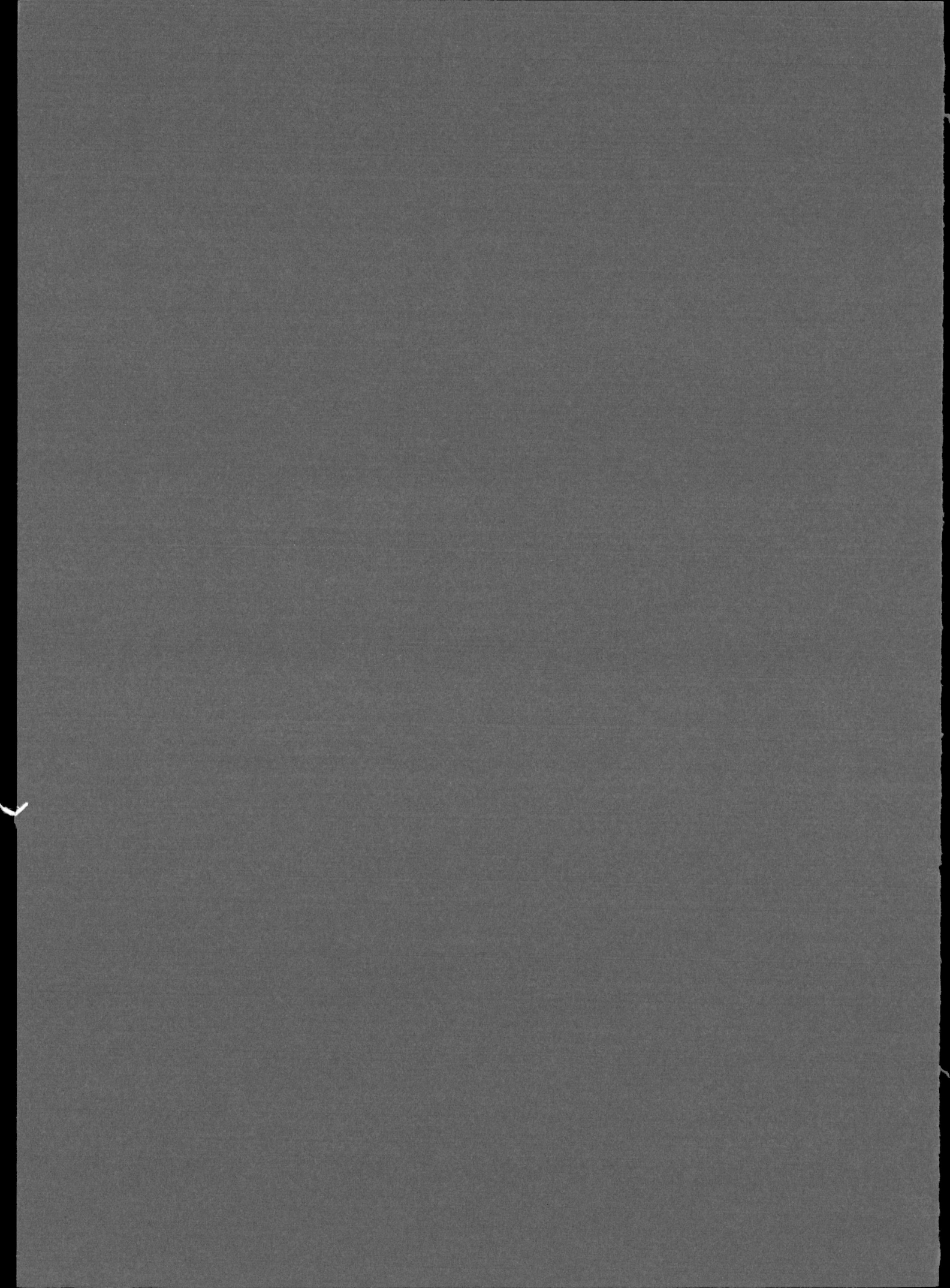